Teaching Indigenous Students

Teaching Indigenous Students

Honoring Place, Community, and Culture

Edited by
JON REYHNER

UNIVERSITY OF OKLAHOMA PRESS : NORMAN

Parts of chapter 3 are adapted, with permission, from Reyhner's contribution to Jon Reyhner and Denny S. Hurtado (2008), "Reading First, Literacy, and American Indian/Alaska Native Students," *Journal of American Indian Education* 7, no. 1: 82–95. Chapter 10 is partly adapted, with permission, from Jon Reyhner (2010), "Indigenous Language Immersion Schools for Strong Indigenous Identities," *Heritage Language Journal* 7, no. 2: 138–52.

Library of Congress Cataloging-in-Publication Data
Teaching indigenous students : honoring place, community, and culture / edited by Jon Reyhner.
    pages cm
  Includes bibliographical references and index.
  ISBN 978-0-8061-4699-7 (pbk. : alk. paper)
1. Indigenous peoples—Education. 2. Indians of North America—Education.
3. Indigenous peoples—Education—Social aspects. 4. Indians of North America—Education—Social aspects. I. Reyhner, Jon Allan
  LC3715.T48 2015
  371.829'97073—dc23
                              2014046331

The paper in this book meets the guidelines for permanence and durability of the Committee on Production Guidelines for Book Longevity of the Council on Library Resources, Inc. ∞

1 2 3 4 5 6 7 8 9 10

Contents

Appendixes

Illustrations

Teaching Indigenous Students

Introduction

JON REYHNER

The contributors to *Teaching Indigenous Students* recognize the importance of teachers' valuing and utilizing the languages and cultures of Indigenous families as they seek to prepare their students to be successful in our modern world. This belief is enshrined in the 2007 United Nations Declaration on the Rights of Indigenous Peoples. Article 13, paragraph 1, of this declaration states: "Indigenous peoples have the right to revitalize, use, develop and transmit to future generations their histories, languages, oral traditions, philosophies, writing systems and literatures, and to designate and retain their own names for communities, places and persons." And Article 14, paragraph 1, proclaims: "Indigenous peoples have the right to establish and control their educational systems and institutions providing education in their own languages, in a manner appropriate to their cultural methods of teaching and learning." Thus, culturally appropriate education for Indigenous children is reconfirmed by the United Nations as a basic human right, a right that, as chapter 1 of this book shows, has far too often been ignored with disastrous results.

In the United States, for example, the 2011 National Assessment of Educational Progress (NAEP) reports that reading scores for American Indian and Alaska Native (AI/AN) fourth- and eighth-graders are "not significantly different from the scores in 2009 or 2005" and that the gap between Native and non-Native students' mathematics scores was greater in 2011 than it was in 2005 (NCES 2012, 2–3). This differential persists despite the passage of the No Child Left Behind (NCLB) Act of 2001, which was designed to close that gap. The cultural bias of NCLB toward English language learning is shown by the name change it instituted for the U.S. Department of Education's Office of Bilingual Education and Minority Language Affairs, which became the Office of English Language Acquisition—with the resultant loss of support for bilingual education programs. After the passage of the original Bilingual Education Act in 1968, many U.S. school districts serving Indigenous students took advantage of its funding to make culturally sensitive education available to their students. With the 2001 passage of NCLB, funding largely ceased to be available for teaching Indigenous languages.

An Australian parallel of ongoing efforts to promote assimilationist education is Bruce Wilson's draft report, *Indigenous Education in the Northern Territory*. Early in the document he states his position clearly:

> This review has made a decision to focus on the English language skills and knowledge that underpin success in the western education system. Some people will find this a challenging position. The recommendation is based on the view that Indigenous children learn English in the way that other children learn English: through rigorous and relentless attention to the foundations of the language and the skills that support participation in a modern democracy and economy. The review does not support continued efforts to use biliteracy approaches, or to teach the content of the curriculum through first languages other than English. This report recommends the explicit teaching and assessment of foundational elements of English literacy, including phonemic awareness, phonics and vocabulary. (2014a, 7)

Thankfully, in response to comments on his draft report Wilson backtracked somewhat from this English-only recommendation in his final report, supporting "the teaching of literacy in the first language where feasible." But he continued to insist that the "priority in the primary years should be ensuring that all Indigenous children gain English literacy" with the curriculum to be delivered in English (Wilson 2014b, 20).

Hearings held across the United States by the National Indian Education Association (NIEA 2005) documented the pressures educators face under NCLB to provide English-only instruction geared toward scoring well on high-stakes standardized tests. Findings claimed that NCLB had narrowed "the broad public purposes of schools" with its emphasis on teaching and testing reading and math at the expense of also teaching music, literature, art, history, and Native studies (NIEA 2005, 6). Emphasis on high-stakes testing in a few academic areas had drawn attention away from improving the social, mental, and physical well-being of Native children. Testimony indicated that NCLB promoted a "one size fits all" curriculum that made it difficult for teachers to "connect education to the lives of students in their communities," with the result that schooling became "increasingly boring and disconnected from student lives" (6). An Arizona State University study similarly documented NCLB-related pressures on new Native teachers to use "rigid prescribed" teaching methods and "canned" commercial curricula because school administrators worried about their school being labeled "underperforming" (Reyhner 2006a, 69). In the years since these hearings, NCLB has done little to increase Native American students' test scores, to reduce their achievement gap, or to lower their dropout rates (see Figure 1), a stasis that has driven teachers from the profession ("Native Americans" 2013; NIEA 2005).

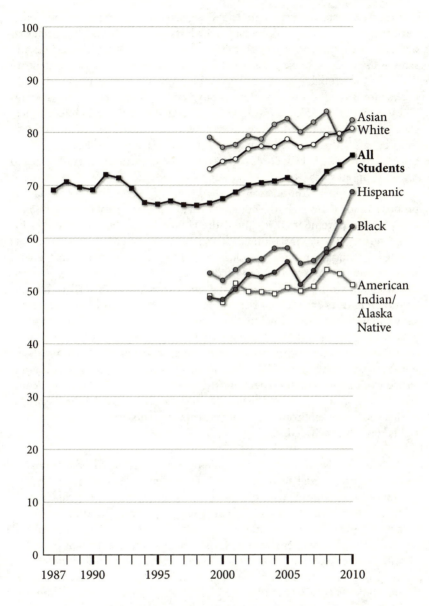

Figure 1. Native American high school graduation rates, 1987–2010 (percentages).
Source: Education Week Resource Center.

Despite the stated aim of the NCLB legislation to improve the academic performance of all U.S. children, a particularly troubling result has been that one of the easiest ways for schools to raise their test scores, which teachers and schools are under intense pressure to do, is for the lowest-scoring students to drop out (or, probably more accurately, be pushed out) of school or be kept back from promotion to grade levels targeted by a high-stakes test (Nichols and Berliner 2007). NCLB testing provisions mandate that all children meet state requirements in order to be promoted to the next grade. But, as found in a review of dropout research for the U.S. Department of Education's Indian Nations at Risk Task Force early in the 1990s, retention in grade leads to higher dropout rates (Reyhner 1992a; 1992b).

In 2003 the U.S. Commission on Civil Rights (USCCR) observed that the proposed 2004 national budget did not provide the necessary funding to meet the NCLB requirements throughout the United States, but especially in Indian Country. The commission found that only 66 percent of Native students were graduating from high school, as compared to 75 percent of the general student population. It further reported: "Dropout rates among Native American students are high because, among other reasons, their civil rights and cultural identities are often at risk in the educational environment. Research shows that Native American students experience difficulty maintaining rapport with teachers and establishing relationships with other students; feelings of isolation; racist threats; and frequent suspension" (USCCR 2003, 84). For example, in the state of Washington, dropout rates for individual schools varied from 25 percent to 90 percent. The commission pointed out that "community responsibility for and ownership of schools are crucial for creating a positive learning environment that respects students' civil and educational rights" (85). It concluded,

> As a group, Native American students are not afforded educational opportunities equal to other American students. They routinely face deteriorating school facilities, underpaid teachers, weak curricula, discriminatory treatment, and outdated learning tools. In addition, the cultural histories and practices of Native students are rarely incorporated in the learning environment. As a result, achievement gaps persist with Native American students scoring lower than any other racial/ethnic group in basic levels of reading, math, and history. Native American students are also less likely to graduate from high school and more likely to drop out in earlier grades. (111–12)

Using more recent data from the seven U.S. states with the highest percentage of American Indian and Alaska Native students, as well as from five states in the Pacific and Northwestern region, Faircloth and Tippeconnic (2010) found that on average, less than 50 percent of Native students were graduating each year.

Efforts that have involved teaching Indigenous students English and academic subjects in *addition* to rather than as a *replacement* for their Native language and culture have shown success in improving the academic performance of Indigenous students in the United States and in other countries. Hawaii developed a pre-K through university-level immersion program starting in 1984, patterned after a similar effort by the Māori in New Zealand. Hawaiian language–immersion schools do not introduce English into the classroom until the fifth grade, even though the students come to school speaking English and use it outside of school. Students learn mathematics and other academic subjects and the use of computers in the Hawaiian language (McCarty 2013). Another notable culturally sensitive and academically successful program is the Rough Rock English-Navajo Language Arts Program in Arizona (McCarty and Dick 2003).

Using research-based educational approaches and disaggregating test scores by ethnic group, as mandated by NCLB, makes a lot of sense. However, the research being applied involves Indigenous children only minimally, at most, and thus has limited application to them. A national colloquium held in 2005 on improving academic performance among American Indian, Alaska Native, and Native Hawaiian students emphasized the need for culturally and linguistically appropriate education for Indigenous students (McCardle and Demmert 2006). Promising programs include the K–12 curriculum described in *Creating Sacred Places for Children* (Fox 2000, 2001a, 2001b, 2001c, 2003) and Indigenous language programs that immerse English-speaking Native students in their heritage language at the preschool and primary grade level (Reyhner 2010; see also, Reyhner and Johnson, chapter 10 in this volume). Innovative Indigenous language and culture programs need longitudinal research to track the academic and social gains made by students at least into college, as a means of supporting or rejecting anecdotal findings of lower dropout rates, more positive identities, and greater academic success for Native students in culturally appropriate educational programs.

Teaching Indigenous Students seeks to improve the quality of education for Indigenous students through the promotion of culturally and linguistically appropriate schooling. In chapter 1 Jon Reyhner and Navin Kumar Singh chronicle past, often failed, efforts to help Native American students by replacing their Indigenous languages and cultures with the languages and cultures of colonizing European nations. Past efforts at cultural assimilation are now seen as violations of basic human rights as described in the 2007 Declaration on the Rights of Indigenous Peoples and in other United Nations documents. These assimilation practices failed to erase the social, economic, and educational gaps between Indigenous and colonizing peoples, and teachers who are unaware of these past failures are only too likely to continue harming Indigenous youth by devaluing Native cultures as they promote colonial languages and cultures.

In chapter 2, Sheilah E. Nicholas (Hopi) and Teresa L. McCarty report research about the unique oral and literacy knowledge that Indigenous students bring from their homes—knowledge that teachers too often ignore, or even denigrate, rather than build upon. They describe Navajo, Mohawk, and Hawaiian programs that recognize and build on the important relationships between language, culture, and identity and show how modern technology can enhance culturally sensitive efforts to improve Indigenous education.

Drawing on evidence that students who read well tend to do well generally in school, Jon Reyhner and Ward Cockrum describe in chapter 3 the dangers of ethnocentrism and how dominant groups can devalue the cultures of minority groups. The authors supply examples of how teachers have adapted their instruction to make it compatible with these students' experiential backgrounds. They emphasize the importance of encouraging students to read a lot by providing books of high-interest to students. They also demonstrate how "back to basics" and other reform efforts in the United States and elsewhere can direct efforts away from culturally appropriate reading instruction for Indigenous youth.

In chapter 4 David Sanders (Oglala Sioux) reflects on his own experiences learning and teaching mathematics and the influence of behaviorist and constructivist theories on how we teach students. He argues for social constructivism and relates it to teaching mathematics using culturally relevant curriculum and teaching practices and aspects of Indigenous responsibility, relationship, and place, offering examples from experience with Alaskan Yup'ik students. Sanders emphasizes the importance of place and local context and comments on the importance of students "doing" math rather than simply being passively taught how to do math.

In chapter 5 Willard Sakiestewa Gilbert (Hopi) reports on research he did on inquiry-based versus direct instruction in elementary science, and he explains how developing culturally appropriate science lesson plans improved the academic performance of Indigenous students. Christine K. Lemley, Jeremy D. Stoddard, and Loren Hudson (Navajo) describe in chapter 6 how pedagogy incorporating community, culture, and place-based inquiry, using oral history, can enhance the education of Indigenous students.

Too often with the current educational emphasis on science, technology, engineering, and mathematics (STEM) training, we forget the whole child and sideline crucial learning in fields such as music, physical education, and art. In chapter 7 Chad Hamill (Spokane tribe) addresses the important role of music in Indigenous cultures, emphasizing that both traditional and modern Indigenous music are appropriate educational subjects that "solidify students' sense of themselves and open cognitive pathways that will give them every opportunity to succeed academically." In chapter 8, Willard Sakiestewa Gilbert describes the importance of American Indian games as a factor in students' health and their cultural identity.

Washington State University professor Michael Holloman (Confederated Tribes, Colville Reservation) describes, in chapter 9, how Indigenous art is too often trivialized in classrooms, for example, when U.S. students decorate paper teepees or make headdresses with paper feathers. Holloman highlights the need for a more respectful attitude toward traditional art and the need for Native American students to study and create contemporary Indian art that helps them establish their identity as modern Indigenous peoples and also helps non-Indigenous students and teachers better understand Indigenous peoples today.

In the final chapter, Jon Reyhner and Florian Johnson (Navajo/Diné) discuss the effects of the loss of Indigenous cultures and how the Māori, Navajos, Hawaiians, Blackfeet, and other Indigenous peoples are successfully using Indigenous language–immersion schools to revitalize their traditional cultural values and improve the academic success of their children.

Overall, the contributors to this volume advocate culturally responsive schooling (Castagno and Brayboy 2008) with an experiential and interactive instructional approach (Cummins 1992). This approach includes providing place-, community-, and culture-based education that gives students hands-on experiences interacting with their local community and environment, along with their texts, teachers, and each other. In regard to literacy this means having students read, write, and talk about things they find meaningful. In mathematics, experiential interactive pedagogy supports the use of manipulatives and giving students a chance to write and solve their own word problems and other math exercises. The goal is that students not only learn a series of steps to get the right answers to math problems, but that they also understand the reasons *why* those steps lead to the correct answers and how math is used beyond the classroom. In science, this means using an inquiry approach in which students use the scientific method to find the solution to questions that they themselves wish answered. This includes making hypotheses and observing and experimenting to test them. Overall, the suggestions for teachers presented in this book are in line with the constructivist learning theory recommended in the United States by research reviews featured in the National Research Council's *How People Learn* (NRC 2000) and *How Students Learn* (2005), as well as the assisted performance approach advocated by Roland Tharp and Ronald Gallimore in *Rousing Minds to Life* (1988).

Taken as a whole, Indigenous students' school experiences should lead them to better understand what it means to be a human being. Science and physical education can lead to a better understanding of what it takes to live a healthy life, especially the importance of diet and exercise. Social studies can help students understand how the world they live in developed over time and what it means to be responsible citizens of their Indigenous nations and of the world. Music and art extend these students' understanding and appreciation of beauty and of Native cultures, as well as enhancing their mental development. In sum, it is long past time to remember what Sioux author and teacher Luther Standing Bear wrote in *Land of the Spotted Eagle* (1933): Indigenous youth need to be "doubly educated" so they may learn "to appreciate both their traditional life and modern life" (252).

1

Overcoming the Legacy
of Assimilationist Schooling

JON REYHNER AND NAVIN KUMAR SINGH

For today's educators to understand the need to find new and better ways to teach Indigenous students, it is important to briefly chronicle the destruction and transformation of Indigenous cultures through a history of culturally assimilationist schooling in Australia, Canada, New Zealand, and the United States and to examine which aspects of this history can be considered cultural genocide and which can be considered voluntary cultural change. We will then discuss current efforts to reverse assimilation and revitalize Indigenous cultures through language-immersion programs and conclude this chapter with examples of human rights rhetoric on the treatment of Indigenous peoples.

Too often, schooling for Indigenous children has amounted to cultural genocide. Polish scholar and attorney Raphaël Lemkin coined the word "genocide" in his 1944 book *Axis Rule in Occupied Europe* and defined it as:

> a coordinated plan of different actions aiming at the destruction of essential foundations of the life of national groups, with the aim of annihilating the groups themselves. . . . The objectives of such a plan would be disintegration of the political and social institutions, of culture, language, national feelings, religion, and the economic existence of national groups, and the destruction of the personal security, liberty, health, dignity, and even the lives of the individuals belonging to such groups. . . .
>
> Genocide has two phases: one, destruction of the national pattern of the oppressed group; the other, the imposition of the national pattern of the oppressor. (79)

This definition includes cultural genocide (also termed ethnocide), the destruction of a people's culture (see Nersessian 2005). Cultural genocide is much more widespread and ongoing than the murder of ethnic minorities.

In the four countries discussed here, government policies promoted English-only schooling and conversion to Christianity, making schools instruments of cultural genocide. If Indigenous students resisted, they were further marginalized, and if they attempted assimilation, they often found that their skin color still excluded them from full equality.

Some people think that democracies are immune to genocide, but through pervasive ethnocentrism and the "tyranny of the majority," laws can be passed that suppress minority languages and cultures, as do the various "English-only" and "Official English" laws in effect in some U.S. states today (see, e.g., Crawford 2000). In his original discussion of genocide, Lemkin included the "prohibition of the use of their own language by the population of an occupied country" (1944, x). Instances of this policy are by no means a present-day phenomenon. For example, the 1868 Report of the U.S. Indian Peace Commission stated, "Schools should be established, which [American Indian] children should be required to attend; their barbarous dialect should be blotted out and the English language substituted." Besides suppressing Indigenous languages, colonial governments have suppressed Indigenous cultural practices, including potlatches, Sun Dances, and other religious activities.

Since the formation of the United Nations (UN) at the end of World War II, and informed by Lemkin's definition of the crime of genocide during that war, the UN has issued a series of declarations promoting human rights, condemning various forms of genocide, and affirming the rights of ethnic minorities and Indigenous peoples to self-governance. This stand is exemplified by the UN's 2007 Declaration on the Rights of Indigenous Peoples, which only Australia, Canada, New Zealand, and the United States initially voted against. Since then, all four countries have reversed their position. These four predominantly English-speaking countries have a history of English-only assimilationist education dating back to the nineteenth century and before.[1] In most colonized countries in Africa and Asia, colonized populations have largely taken control of their countries back from their colonizers. However, in these four English-speaking democracies, immigrants from Europe rapidly outpopulated the Indigenous inhabitants, and by the time colonized peoples finally got the right to vote in the twentieth century, they could easily be outvoted in anything other than very small, local elections.

With more efficient agricultural practices that could support larger populations, European immigrants tended to displace smaller Indigenous populations. Such displacement is not new. Ranchers with cattle and other animals tended to displace Indigenous hunter-gatherers, because herding allowed for denser populations, and farmers displace herders because farming can support even larger populations if the land is arable. That larger population, constantly increased by immigration from Europe in the case of the United States, Australia, Canada, and New Zealand, usually overran the Indigenous populations within decades, killing or pushing them aside to marginal lands. The experiences of Indigenous peoples in Asia and Africa, as well as the continued existence of New Mexico pueblos, shows that it was harder to displace settled Indigenous farming populations than more mobile groups. Adding to the population imbalance caused by the flood of immigrants to Australia, New Zealand, and the Americas was the depopulation that occurred due to virgin-ground epidemics, which killed many Indigenous people.[2]

However, to describe the European settlers as merely greedy, power-hungry people interested in overrunning Indigenous nations is to ignore that many were the "huddled masses" and "wretched refuse" portrayed by American poet Emma Lazarus in "The New Colossus" (1883). Many were displaced from Europe, including Indigenous refugees from Ireland who were escaping the 1840s potato famine, which was exacerbated by the inhumane policies of their English colonial rulers. Struggling to survive themselves, these impoverished and often desperate newcomers threatened the survival of Indigenous peoples in the Americas and elsewhere.

The perception of the American West as empty land to be taken and settled lured European and other immigrants to the United States, while the many attractive things European technology had to offer Indigenous peoples often promoted voluntary cultural change. When they got the chance, Indigenous people tended to quickly adopt guns, horses, and metal utensils that made hunting and other aspects of their lives easier. Today, automobiles to drive and homes with electricity and running water are the technological boons that make life easier for Indigenous people and give them entry to the modern cash economy. These cultural adoptions could change Indigenous life radically, as was the case when Plains Indians in the Americas rapidly acquired horses to make hunting buffalo easier. Militarily defeated tribes sometimes voluntarily adopted Christianity, because its god appeared to be stronger than theirs, since their own prayers for victory had gone unanswered. Sequoyah, a Cherokee, invented a syllabary that allowed Cherokee to become a written language, because he saw the advantages that literacy gave the colonists.

For Indigenous peoples to take full advantage of all the labor-saving technology brought by colonists, some education was indispensable. Education offered to Indigenous peoples by nation states in the name of progress and "civilization" could be genuinely welcomed. As human rights activist Gay J. McDougall noted:

As the UN Independent Expert on Minority Issues, over the past three years I have travelled to countries in practically every region of the world. I have talked extensively to people who belong to disadvantaged minorities on every continent. When I ask them to tell me their greatest problem, their most deeply felt concern, the answer is always the same.

> They are concerned that their children are not getting a quality educa-
> tion because they are minorities. They see educating their children as
> the only way out of their poverty; their under-dog status, their isolation.
> (McDougall 2009, 7)

Such education helps Indigenous children survive in the modern world and brings about cultural change because of necessity. But warnings about the loss of Indigenous cultures, often focused on language loss, are increasing exponentially as present-day globalization breaks down the isolation that protected Indigenous populations in the past. The National Geographic Society's Disappearing Languages web site (2014) notes, "By 2100, more than half of the more than 7,000 languages spoken on Earth—many of them not yet recorded—may disappear, taking with them a wealth of knowledge about history, culture, the natural environment, and the human brain."

Automobiles, airplanes, radio, television, and now the Internet, all things that Indigenous people can embrace voluntarily, are rapidly breaking down the protective isolation that, even in the Amazon basin and the far north, allowed many Indigenous cultures to survive well into the twentieth century. However, globalization has also allowed Indigenous peoples across the planet to learn from each other's experiences and to lobby for support from the United Nations and other supranational bodies, support which they often do not get locally because they represent only a small minority of their country's population.

Cultural change is inevitable for all people, but when does that change become cultural genocide? A key question is whether the change is forced, especially upon children in schools. What say do Indigenous students' families and communities have in determining the kind of education their children will receive? Especially important today is whether a national language and culture is taught as a replacement for, or in addition to, the students' Indigenous language and culture. In the words of the U.S. National Association for Bilingual Education and similar organizations, is it "English Plus" or "English Only" schooling that is being offered?

Many UN declarations support the rights of ethnic minority communities and parents. For example, the UN's 1948 Universal Declaration of Human Rights states in Article 26 that "Parents have a prior right to choose the kind of education that shall be given to their children." The 1992 Declaration on the Rights of Persons Belonging to National or Ethnic, Religious and Linguistic Minorities declares in Article 1: "States shall protect the existence and the national or ethnic, cultural, religious and linguistic identity of minorities within their respective territories and shall encourage conditions for the promotion of that identity." Article 2 affirms that "Persons belonging to national or ethnic, religious and linguistic minorities . . . have the right to enjoy their own culture, to profess and practice their own religion, and to use their own language, in private and in public, freely and without interference or any form of discrimination." The 2007 UN Declaration on the Rights of Indigenous Peoples reasserts and extends these rights.

Yet despite the 2007 declaration, schooling is often still a matter of cultural genocide because it is presented as, and is often accepted by students and their families as, an either/or proposition, as indicated in the title of Karen Stocker's book *I Won't Stay Indian, I'll Keep Studying* (2005). Stocker examined a problem in Costa Rica that is shared by Indigenous peoples worldwide: "the label *Indian* had connotations of backwardness and even inferior intellect. . . . Being Indian automatically set students up for being treated as inferior, and "for most students from the reservation, projecting an Indian identity seemed incompatible with school success" (2). From this explanation one could argue that assimilation is a matter of cultural suicide rather than cultural genocide, but that is because Indigenous peoples are presented with a false dichotomy: they must choose between the modern world and some "world language," often English, or remain seen as "savage" or at least "backward" second-class citizens.

While not universal, the ethnocentric attitude of the colonizers was nearly so. There have always been a few isolated examples of culturally sensitive recognition of Indigenous cultural strengths. For example, the explorer and first director of the U.S. Bureau of Ethnology, John Wesley Powell acknowledged, more than a century ago, "so few Americans yet realize that of all the people on this continent, including even ourselves, the most profoundly religious, if by religion is meant fidelity to teachings and observations that are regarded as sacred, are the American Indians, especially wherever still unchanged from their early condition, and this deeply religious feeling of theirs might, if properly appreciated, be made use of, not weakened or destroyed by opposition" (1896, 112–13).

A nineteenth-century example among the Cherokee Indians of what that cultural appreciation could accomplish can be seen in the way that Moravian missionaries, who never learned to speak Cherokee or see any value in Cherokee traditional beliefs, had little success in converting the Cherokees to Christianity. Whereas, Baptist missionaries, who learned the Cherokee language and utilized a syncretic approach that included traditional Cherokee practices in their services, were able to convert many Cherokees (McClinton 2007). Far too often, the pervasive colonial approach to education was to contrast Euro-American "civilization" with Indigenous "savagery," rather than recognizing and building on Indigenous cultural strengths. As teacher and Indian agent Albert H. Kneale noted, the U.S. government's Indian Bureau "went on the assumption that any Indian custom was, *per se*, objectionable, whereas the customs of whites were the ways of civilization" (1950, 4). In the late nineteenth century Darwin's theory of biological evolution was corrupted into a theory of "Social Darwinism," which posited that societies evolved in a way similar to living things, with the ethnocentric addition that "white" western/European societies were at the top of this evolutionary heap and Indigenous cultures were doomed to extinction through "natural selection."

BLAME THE VICTIM *VERSUS* BLAME THE OPPRESSOR

Historically the dominant theme in colonial education for Indigenous populations has been to blame the victims for their inability as a group to prosper given the schooling they were offered. Originally this blame was often based on racist ideas of non-white genetic inferiority. More recently it has been attributed to cultural deficit, whereby Indigenous cultures do not promote the type of behavior needed for success in the modern world, which tends to stress individualism. This latter notion promotes educational efforts that see assimilation into the dominant culture as the solution to the economic and social challenges faced by Indigenous peoples. Recent examples of this in the United States are state-level "Official English" and "English Only" laws in California, Arizona, and Massachusetts that discourage or even ban bilingual education in public schools (Reyhner 2001a). Thus even in the twenty-first century the United States, at least, has taken a step backward from efforts after World War II by the Civil Rights Movement and the UN that shifted the blame of culture loss from the victims to the oppressors.

The open discussion of the causes of Indigenous students' academic difficulties can be hampered, at times, by fits of "political correctness" that stifle the free exchange of ideas about equality and education to the point that "only males can be described as sexist and only whites can be described as racist" (Felson 1991). Māori author Alan Duff notes, "Racism, where many Māori, the Indigenous people of Aotearoa/New Zealand are concerned, cannot possibly cut both ways. And the reason for this is the classic noble oppressed concept that the 'victim is never very wrong'" (1993, 80). Duff declares that white people are fed "a message of one-sided guilt, one-sided culpability, a message that was hammered and hammered from every angle, everywhere you went" (x). From the colonizers' extreme of "blame the victim," Duff argues that the Māori had gone to the other extreme of blame the "Pākehā" (non-Māoris). Duff and others point out the failures of their Indigenous cultures, and they tend to be labeled as cultural traitors who are selling out to the beliefs of the oppressors. Duff's caveats, such as, "Admirable though many aspects of Māori culture are, equally there are aspects which are not," are seen as inadequate support for his people (47). Some of the negative aspects Duff finds in traditional Māori culture are its historical class structure with hereditary chiefs and its second-class status for women. He has also criticized contemporary Māori culture for its lack of a work ethic and poor health habits, including smoking and drinking. His antidote for Māori social problems is education and self-help, which mirrors individualistic Eurocentric cultural teachings and Horatio Algers's "rags to riches" myth.[3] A central problem of blaming the "oppressor," if you are a victim of oppression and a member of a dominated minority, is that you will be powerless in the face of the white/European power structure and will not be able to do much to change things. As Duff writes, "The great majority of Māori . . . do not accept for a moment that the bulk of their woes, if any, have a cause, let alone a solution in themselves" (1993, 26). Duff criticizes the contemporary Māori lifestyle, but for Indigenous peoples assimilating into the modern world too often means picking up a hedonistic and materialistic lifestyle that can lead to obesity, diabetes, and other negative effects. He concludes, "New Zealand white people do have a lot to answer for on most of the matters aggrieving Māori. But equally Māori have a lot to answer to themselves on what afflicts them right now" (60). This seeming middle ground did not insulate Duff from criticism.

Objecting to Duff's ideas, Māori author Andrew Eruera Vercoe contrasts the Māori sense of community and values of "stewardship, trustworthiness, integrity and humility" to the Eurocentric mindset of individualism, power, and domination (1998, 18). While Duff extols the possibilities of schooling that he claims many Māori fail to appreciate, Vercoe counters, "Given the education system that we've been lumped with, I can honestly say that unless Māori have a greater input into how structural mechanisms are organized, it may be a waste of time sending their children to school. If anything, generally 'the school' remains the ideological and cultural enemy of the Māori" (24).

Vercoe also asserts, "We need the healer's balm and, like all good medicine, it's going to taste a little foul. For Māori, education needs to go back to the marae, to the home, back to where the generation are hewn and moulded into shape" (33–34). The negative role of schools, especially in regard to the loss of Indigenous languages and cultures is well documented (see, e. g., Reyhner and Eder 2004). A study of data from 150 First Nations communities in British Columbia found that communities with less conversational knowledge of their native language had suicide rates six times greater than those with more knowledge (Hallett, Chandler, and LaLonde 2007).

Radical educational theorists following the lead of Ivan Illich (1971) have recommended that Indigenous people reject schooling because it destroys their cultures and communities (e.g., Prakash and Esteva 1998). But others see education, especially through community-controlled schools, as the *only* way that Indigenous people can learn how to protect their lands and communities in courts and legislatures and elsewhere from the onslaught of mainstream society (Enos 2002). Examples of Indigenous and mixed-ancestry peoples who have used their education to help their people include Douglas Nichols in Australia, Peter Jones (Kahkewaquonaby) in Canada, Apiraa Ngata in New Zealand, Samson Occum (Mohegan) and Charles Eastman (Sioux) in the United States, and countless others. Today Indigenous organizations, such as the National Congress of American Indians and National Indian Education Association in the United States and the Assembly of First Nations in Canada, lobby their governments for fair treatment.

Supporters of Indigenous self-determination see locally controlled schools as a way of protecting Indigenous students from culturally insensitive textbooks, curricula, and tests and of promoting place-, community-, and culture-based teaching methods and curricula that value Indigenous knowledge (see, e.g., Deloria and Wildcat 2001; May 1999). However, localizing education goes against the global modern tide of one-size-fits-all "common core" curricula. As education became more democratized in the nineteenth century and schools were staffed with less-educated teachers, both for reasons of cost and availability, mass-produced textbooks became increasingly popular as a tool to help less knowledgeable teachers. Indigenous peoples were often absent from these textbooks or, when included, were portrayed as savages. Writer George Wharton James reported:

> Again and again when I have visited Indian schools the thoughtful youths and maidens have come to me with complaints about the American history they were compelled to study. "When we read in the United States history of white men fighting to defend their females, their homes, their corn-fields, their towns, and their hunting-grounds, they are always called 'patriots,' and the children are urged to follow the example of these brave, noble, and gallant men. But when Indians—our ancestors, even our own parents—have fought to defend us and our homes, corn-fields, and hunting-grounds they are called vindictive and merciless savages, bloody murderers, and everything else that is vile." (1908, 25)

In the late twentieth century more Indigenous culture, history, and languages were incorporated into schools for Native students, but curriculum, especially textbook content even in many Indigenous-controlled schools, still overwhelmingly reflects the dominant, colonial cultures.

Extensive studies done in the USA, including the 1928 Meriam and 1969 Kennedy Reports describe the damage that ethnocentric and assimilationist schools can do to Indigenous students (Reyhner and Eder 2004). Dillon Platero, the first director of the Navajo Nation's Division of Education, described the experience of "Kee," an all too typical Navajo student in the United States:

> Kee was sent to boarding school as a child where—as was the practice —he was punished for speaking Navajo. Since he was only allowed to return home during Christmas and summer, he lost contact with his family. Kee withdrew from both the White and Navajo worlds as he

grew older because he could not comfortably communicate in either language. He became one of the many thousand Navajos who were non-lingual—a man without a language. By the time he was 16, Kee was an alcoholic, uneducated, and despondent—without identity. (1975, 58)

Dr. Lori Arviso Alvord, the first Navajo woman surgeon, wrote in her 1999 autobiography *The Scalpel and the Silver Bear,* which called for a fusion of traditional Navajo healing and modern medicine,

> In their childhoods both my father and my grandmother had been punished for speaking Navajo in school. Navajos were told by white educators that, in order to be successful, they would have to forget their language and culture and adopt American ways.
>
> They were warned that if they taught their children to speak Navajo, the children would have a harder time learning in school, and would therefore be at a disadvantage. A racist attitude existed. Navajo children were told that their culture and lifeways were inferior, and they were made to feel they could never be as good as white people. . . . My father suffered terribly from these events and conditions. (Alvord and Van Pelt 1999, 86)

Alvord concluded, "two or three generations of our tribe had been taught to feel shame about our culture, and parents had often not taught their children traditional Navajo beliefs—the very thing that would have shown them how to live, the very thing that could keep them strong" (88).

As Joy Harjo (Muscogee Creek) notes, "Colonization teaches us to hate ourselves. We are told that we are nothing until we adopt the ways of the colonizer, till we become the colonizer" (Mankiller 2004, 62). However, despite this "selling out" of Indigenous lifeways to become "civilized," because of racial prejudice, often based on skin color, assimilation of Indigenous peoples often did not end discrimination.

SUSTAINING INDIGENOUS LANGUAGES

In spite of decades of educational research proving the contrary, there still remains a popular belief that bilingualism is a disadvantage and that bilingual education harms children—a belief that Indigenous people and immigrants can sometimes buy into (Baker 2011). Some think that when an additional language is introduced into a curriculum the child can become confused and that academic concepts will need to be relearned in the new language, thus children should be introduced to the national language in their homes. The work of Stanford University Professor Kenji Hakuta and his colleagues (Hakuta 1986) as well as the experience at Rock Point Community School (Rosier and Holm 1980) and other bilingual schools provide clear evidence that an Indigenous child who acquires basic literacy or numeracy concepts in their home language can successfully learn to express this knowledge in English.

The literature is replete with examples confirming the importance of nurturing a child's mother tongue (Cenoz and Genessee 1998). For example, the authors of the 1953 United Nations Educational Scientific and Cultural Organization (UNESCO) monograph, *The Use of Vernacular Languages in Education,* state: "On educational grounds we recommend that the use of the mother tongue be extended as late a state in education as possible. In particular, pupils should begin their schooling through the medium of the mother tongue, because they understand it best and because to begin their school life in the mother tongue will make the break between home and school as small as possible (47–48).

In addition, the benefits of linguistically and culturally responsive education that reverse the assimilationist history of colonial education are well documented (Brayboy and Castagno 2009). In the last two decades researchers have shown that students who maintain a traditional cultural orientation, including speaking their Indigenous language, can be successful in school, even more successful than assimilated students (Deyhle 1992; Willeto 1999). In addition, traditional Indigenous values, such as respect, generosity, and humility, are as important to success as academic knowledge. In the 1970s, the all-Navajo Rock Point Community School Board concluded "that it was the breakdown of a working knowledge of Navajo kinship that caused much of what they perceived as inappropriate, un-Navajo, behavior; the way back, they felt was to teach students that system," which they did by establishing a bilingual education program that taught students through both Navajo and English (Holm and Holm, 1990, 178).

To reduce the extent of language and culture loss, parents can establish a strong policy to use their Indigenous language at home and provide ample opportunities for their children to expand the functions for which they use their mother tongue, including reading and writing, and the contexts in which they can use it, such as community mother-tongue day care or play groups. However, the very act of expanding language domains from orality to literacy leads to cultural change. Duff (1993) repeatedly stresses the need to emphasize literacy in the home if family members want their children to value it and be academically successful in school. Nonetheless, there is a danger in using Indigenous languages in schools because they can be transformed, for example, by teachers modifying the meanings of words to represent the values and thinking of the colonizing society (Benton 2007, 163–81).

School curricula and teachers can also help Indigenous children build strong positive identities and retain and develop their mother cultures and tongues by communicating strong affirmative messages to them about the value of knowing additional languages and the fact that bilingualism is an important linguistic and intellectual accomplishment (Reyhner 2010). Efforts at place-, community-, and culture-based education can overcome the ambivalent and even oppositional Indigenous attitude toward schools. As David N. Plank notes in his foreword to Maenette K. P. Benham and Ronald H. Heck's *Culture and Educational Policy in Hawai'i: The Silencing of Native Voices,* there is a "fundamental ambivalence of subaltern peoples toward schooling" (Plank 1998, x). In their preface Benham and Heck write, "School learning tends to be associated with learning the culture and language of the oppressors" (1998, xi). When national governments do offer education to their Indigenous populations, the assimilationist nature of the education projects often presents ideology that represents Indigenous cultures as inferior.

John Ogbu (1995) researched the effects of this "fundamental ambivalence" on the educational achievement of what he termed "involuntary" ethnic minorities, which in the United States included the descendants of slaves, Mexican immigrants, and American Indians. He describes how minority students can form "oppositional identities" toward schooling, resulting in an achievement gap. While Ogbu did not specifically study Indigenous students, sociologist Alan Peshkin has studied a group of Pueblo students in an Indian-controlled school in New Mexico. He found that students participated with sustained effort and enthusiasm in basketball, but added, "regrettably, I saw no academic counterpart to this stellar athletic performance" (Peshkin 1997, 5). Interestingly, Duff (1993) notes that in New Zealand rugby has a similar draw on Māori youths' attention.

Peshkin witnessed a "student malaise" originating from an ambivalent attitude of the Pueblo Indians toward schooling. After more than four hundred years of contact with Europeans, the Pueblos were suspicious of anything "white," and schools, even Indian-controlled schools with Indian administrators and Indian teachers, remain basically alien "white" institutions to many Indian people. He notes, "Schooling is necessary to become competent in the very world that Pueblo [Indian] people perceive as rejecting them"; school is a place of "becoming white" (Peshkin 1997, 107, 117).

A counterexample to the situation Peshkin studied can be found in the Navajo Nation's Rock Point Community School, which became community controlled in the United States. At Rock Point in the 1970s, a bilingual education program that taught speaking, reading, and writing in the Navajo language, as well as English, was started because even the most advanced English as a Second Language (ESL) teaching methodologies were not bringing the students' achievement up to national averages. Under bilingual instruction, which was implemented at both the elementary and secondary levels, student test scores increased and were higher than comparable Navajo students in surrounding schools receiving only ESL instruction (Reyhner 1990).

ASSIMILATIONIST INDIGENOUS
SCHOOLING IN THE USA

Assimilationist schooling, which is still ongoing, can devastate Indigenous communities, because it devalues and replaces Indigenous cultures, especially their religions and languages. For example, non-Native educators of Indigenous students tend to hold up patriarchal nuclear families as the norm, in opposition to the extended families, often matriarchal, found in Indigenous cultures. And they often promote individualism in contrast to the communitarianism valued by many Indigenous societies.

In their history of American Indian education in the United States and Canada, Jon Reyhner and Jeanne Eder summed up the impact of boarding schools on American Indian students, who were sometimes forcibly removed from their homes to attend them:

> Upon enrolling, boarding and day school Indian students in the USA in the late nineteenth and early twentieth centuries were reclothed, regroomed, and renamed. They found it difficult to adjust to schools that devalued their family's way of life and taught in an alien tongue. Some were eager to learn and, despite hardships, adjusted well to their new settings. Others resisted by running away or by refusing to cooperate. Some, like the Stockholm hostages and kidnap victim and heiress Patty Hearst, began to identify with their captors and to despise their own upbringing. (2004, 168)

In the late nineteenth and early twentieth century in the United States, boarding schools for American Indians were usually run as military schools where students were marched around and enjoyed little freedom. Students in these schools were often punished for speaking the language of their parents or practicing any Indian cultural activities. The U.S. commissioner of Indian affairs wrote in his 1866 annual report, "Indians should be taught the English language only. . . . There is not an Indian pupil whose tuition and maintenance is paid for by the United States Government who is permitted to study any other language than our own vernacular—the language of the greatest, most powerful, and enterprising nationalities beneath the sun (Atkins 1866, xxiii).

This ethnocentric attitude was nearly universal, but even in the nineteenth century Indians were not blamed for everything. In 1868 a congressionally appointed peace commission, which included the U.S. commissioner of Indian affairs and four army generals, was sent to deal with hostile Indigenous tribes, and reported to President Andrew Johnson: "The history of the Government connections with the Indians is a shameful record of broken treaties and unfulfilled promises. The history of the border white man's connection with the Indians is a sickening record of murder, outrage, robbery, and wrongs committed by the former as the rule, and occasional savage outbreaks and unspeakable barbarous deeds of retaliation by the latter as the exception" (quoted in ARBIC 1869, 7). However, massacres and other atrocities continued for another several decades in the United States despite this rhetoric (Lindsay 2012).

Not all Indigenous students were forced to attend schools and some went voluntarily, however, much too often education for Indigenous peoples in the settler states was clearly a matter of cultural genocide, starting with the forced removal of children from their parents. Some of the worst examples include the 1886 report of the Mescalero Apache Indian Agent:

> Everything in the way of persuasion and argument having failed [to get parents to send their children to school], it became necessary to visit the camps unexpectedly with a detachment of police, and seize such children as were proper and take them way to school, willing or unwilling. Some hurried their children off to the mountains or hid them away in camp, and the police had to chase and capture them like so many wild rabbits. This unusual proceeding created quite an outcry. The men were sullen and muttering, the women loud in their lamentations and the children almost out of their wits with fright. (Quoted in Adams 1995, 211)

Willard Beatty, director of the federal government's Indian education program from 1936 to 1952, related a story told to him by the first director of Navajo education programs about how he had "recruited" Navajo students on "orders from Congress":

> He and a Navajo policeman had started out in a buckboard drawn by two horses and went from hogan [a Navajo home] to hogan looking for children. As they got in sight of a hogan and the Indians recognized who they were and guessed at their purpose, the children could be seen darting out of the hogan and running into the brush. Whereupon the Navajo policeman stood up in the buckboard and fired a shotgun into the air to scare the children and make them stop running—if possible. Then he jumped out of the wagon and ran after the children. If he caught them (and many times he didn't), he wrestled them to the ground, tied their legs and arms, and with the help of Mr. Blair put them in the back part of the wagon, where they lay until Blair had gathered in the quota for the day. Then they returned to the Albuquerque school and enrolled the children they had captured. (1961, 12)

Because they spoke no English, these children did not understand what was happening to them and no one at the school where they were sent spoke Navajo. Beatty reported, "The average Navajo parents felt a school education was a relatively useless thing, so far as they could see" (Beatty 1961, 14). Testimony in a 1929 hearing by the U.S. Senate Subcommittee of the Committee on Indian Affairs affirmed the accuracy of the activities Beatty described (DeJong 1993, 117–18).

Overrun and outpopulated by settlers, Indigenous peoples were, and still are, caught between the devil and the deep blue sea. If they do not come to terms with the literate, technologically advanced culture that surrounds them, they will only be further marginalized. In 1947 when some progressive reforms were made in the United States, a Navajo tribal council delegate spoke in favor of compulsory education, "When I ran away [from school] they sent a policeman after me to bring me back and gave me whipping like that. That knocked some sense into me and I did not have the desire to run away. The Government says it [now] cannot whip children, cannot punish them. How can we get somewhere? I blame the Government. . . . I sent my boy to school at Bacone College. I realize that education is the only salvation for the Navajo tribe" (quoted in Iverson 2002, 102).

Another tribal council delegate declared in 1952 that he was glad a policeman had been sent to return him to school after he ran away (Iverson 2002, 107). The Navajo Nation's population was rapidly increasing at the time and it still is, making it more and more difficult to survive by sheepherding and dry land farming, the traditional pattern of Navajo life.

However, cultural change can be a two-way street. In 1917, the Ponca Agency Superintendent in Oklahoma reported the story, "An old Ponca Indian, now dead, once said that it takes Chilocco [boarding school] three years to make a White man out of an Indian boy, but that when the boy comes home and the tribe has a feast, it takes but three days for the tribe to make the boy an Indian again" (*Returned Student Survey* 1917, p. 88).

Fred Kabotie, a Hopi Indian, recalled, "I've found the more outside education I receive, the more I appreciate the true Hopi way. When the missionaries would come into the village and try to convert us, I used to wonder why anyone would want to be a Christian if it meant becoming like those people" (1977, 12). Carl Gorman (1907–1998) recalled going to school at the Christian Dutch Reform movement's Rehoboth Mission: "The students got up every morning at 6:00 A.M. After cleaning up, they sat at attention while the matron read from the Bible and prayed. At breakfast, they prayed before they ate, then someone read from the Bible, and they prayed again. In every class, the teacher prayed first before they began their studies in grammar, figures, inspirational readings. At the end of each class the teacher read the Bible and prayed again. It was stifling and overwhelming" (Greenberg and Greenberg, 1996, 34). This harsh treatment turned him against Christianity. Missionaries were known to tell Indigenous peoples that the language they spoke was the language of the Devil and all traditional activities were "devil worship" (Bowden 1981, 122).

Based on testimony from hearings across the United States, in 1969 the U.S. Senate's Committee on Labor and Public Welfare's Special Subcommittee on Indian Education issued a report titled *Indian Education: A National Tragedy—A National Challenge*. It declared Indian education in the United States to be "a national disgrace" (Special Subcommittee 1969, x). A simultaneous U.S. government–funded National Study of Indian Education led to the conclusion:

> With minor exceptions the history of Indian education had been primarily the transmission of white American education, little altered, to the Indian child as a one-way process. The institution of the school is one that was imposed by and controlled by the non-Indian society, its pedagogy and curriculum little changed for the Indian children, its goals primarily aimed at removing the child from his aboriginal culture and assimilating him into the dominant white culture. Whether coercive or persuasive, this assimilationist goal of schooling has been minimally effective with Indian children, as indicated by their record of absenteeism, retardation, and high dropout rates. (Fuchs and Havighurst 1972, 19)

In a special message to Congress in 1970, U.S. president Richard Nixon declared:

> The story of the Indian in America is something more than the record of the white man's frequent aggression, broken agreements, intermittent remorse and prolonged failure. It is a record also of endurance, of survival, of adaptation and creativity in the face of overwhelming obstacles.
>
> It is a record of enormous contributions to this country—to its art and culture, to its strength and spirit, to its sense of history and its sense of purpose.
>
> It is long past time that the Indian policies of the Federal government began to recognize and build upon the capacities and insights of the Indian people. Both as a matter of justice and as a matter of enlightened social policy, we must begin to act on the basis of what the Indians themselves have long been telling us. The time has come to break decisively with the past and to create the conditions for a new era in which the Indian future is determined by Indian acts and Indian decisions. (Nixon 1971, 575)

Nixon's declaration helped usher in a policy of Indian self-determination that continues in the United States to this day. The damning national study and Senate Subcommittee report led to the passage in 1972 of the Indian

Education Act, which provides funding for supplemental programs to help Indian students in public schools. In 1975 an Indian Self-Determination and Education Assistance Act made it possible, among other things, for Indian Nations to take over federal Indian schools if they so desired. Today, local school boards run over half of these schools and the rest have advisory school boards.

Along with assimilationist English-only educational policies, the U.S. government has also suppressed Indian religious beliefs, banning Sun Dances, potlatches and other ceremonies in the late nineteenth century. It was not until 1978 that two laws were enacted to recognize the right of American Indians to religious freedom and family solidarity. The American Indian Religious Freedom Act and the Indian Child Welfare Act were both passed in 1978. In sharp contrast to the individualism rooted in most American law, the latter recognized Indian children as collective tribal resources, essential to Indigenous survival, and made it very difficult for non-Indians to adopt Indian children.

Using some of their newfound power under the self-determination policy, Indian nations started taking over control of their lands. In 1984 the Navajo Tribal Council adopted new education policies. In their preface the tribal chairman wrote, "We believe that an excellent education can produce achievement in the basic academic skills and skills required by modern technology and still educate young Navajo citizens in their language, history, government and culture" (Zah 1985, vii). However, these policies have never been fully enforced because funding for public and federal schools does not flow through the Navajo Nation's government.

In 1990 the U.S. Congress passed a Native American Languages Act, making it the policy of the government to protect, promote, and preserve Indigenous languages, and two years later a couple of million dollars was authorized to fund language programs, but even today there are only token efforts. In 1991, the Indian Nations at Risk Task Force appointed by the U.S. secretary of education identified four important reasons why Indian nations were at risk. The second reason listed was, "the language and culture base of the American Native are rapidly eroding" (Indian Nations At Risk Task Force 1991, iv). The most recent reauthorization of the Indian Education Act of 1972 is Title VII of the No Child Left Behind Act (NCLB) of 2001. The rhetoric about the need for culturally appropriate education remains in NCLB's Title VII's Statement of Policy: "It is the policy of the USA to fulfill the Federal Government's unique and continuing trust relationship with and responsibility to the Indian people for the education of Indian children. The Federal Government will continue to work with local educational agencies, ensuring that programs that serve Indian children are of the highest quality and provide for not only the basic elementary and secondary educational needs, but also the unique educational and culturally related academic needs of these children."

However, the overall thrust of NCLB was for a one-size-fits-all education that emphasizes academic accountability through the use of high-stakes tests (Reyhner and Hurtado 2008). Researcher James Crawford (2007) saw NCLB as a shift in focus from equal opportunity for America's minorities to closing the achievement gap by bringing up scores on tests that currently focus only on English literacy and mathematics—tests that pressure schools to narrow their curriculum and to exclude "extras," such as instruction in Indigenous languages. In 2010, the U.S. Senate Subcommittee on Indian Affairs held an Oversight Hearing on Indian education titled, "Did the No Child Left Behind Act Leave Indian Students Behind?" At the hearing a former president of the National Indian Education Association testified, "There is policy incongruence between federal Native language policy and the implementation of NCLB. The federal policy focused on revitalizing and maintaining Native languages needs to find a viable functional reference within NCLB so that federal education policy enables rather than stunts existing school based efforts such as immersion schools and programs, language nests and other such efforts in state and BIE schools" (Beaulieau 2010).

CANADA'S RESIDENTIAL SCHOOLS

Under British rule, the Proclamation of 1763 gave limited recognition to Indian territorial possessions, which continued into the nineteenth century. An 1857 Gradual Civilization Act promoted assimilation, including allotment of Indian lands. According to historian John S. Milloy, this law redefined civilizing Indians from developing community self-sufficiency to assimilating them individually. The passage of the British North America Act of 1867 defined the federal government's "responsibility" for Indians, but that responsibility was only assumed under pressure in 1939 (Milloy 1999).

Canada's First Nations educational policies in many ways paralleled those of the United States. U.S. schools were unrelentingly assimilationist and designed to separate parents from their children so that the children could join modern society. Students were taught English and punished for speaking their Native languages. However, Canada's residential (boarding) schools inadequately prepared students to live in white society or to return to their reserves. Milloy (1999) documents with government records the unhealthy and brutal conditions in Canada's government funded but church-run residential schools, which served about a third of Native children. He found that Canada's residential schools were "marked by the persistent neglect and abuse of children and through them of Aboriginal communities in general" and were characterized by widespread physical and sexual abuse until the last residential school closed in 1986 (Milloy 1999, xiii). In the "mini-monarchies" that were residential schools, "discipline was curriculum and punishment was pedagogy" (Milloy 1999, 34, 134). Even worse, from the 1879 beginning of these efforts, the Canadian government chronically underfunded the schools, which were operated by Catholics, Methodists, Presbyterians, and Anglicans.

The 1924 *Memorandum* of the Convention of Catholic Principals declared, "All true civilization must be based on moral law, which christian religion alone can give. Pagan superstition could not . . . suffice to make the Indians practice the virtues of our civilization and avoid its attendant vices. Several people have desired us to countenance the dances of the Indians and to observe their festivals; but their habits, being the result of free and easy mode of life, cannot conform to the intense struggle for life which our social conditions require (quoted in Milloy 1999, 36–37).

In 1938 a joint delegation of all the churches called on the government to provide school uniforms, declaring them essential: "There would be no true cohesion without a uniform. Further if modern Dictators [Hitler and Mussolini] find that a coloured shirt assists in implanting political doctrines and even racial and theological ideas, it would be obvious that the adoption of a bright and attractive uniform would assist in implanting all that we desire in the children under our care" (quoted in Milloy 1999, 125).

In 1939 there were nine thousand students in seventy-nine residential schools. After World War II, Canada worked to close Indian schools and integrate Indians into the provincial school systems. In opposition to the desires of the Catholic Church, some residential schools were closed and day schools received more government support. In the 1950s the Canadian Parliament dropped sanctions against some Indian traditional practices and an effort was made to start parent advisory committees for schools, but initially these local committees had little real power.

While the United States phased out direct federal funding of mission schools for Indians in the 1890s, it was not until 1969 that Canada's Department of Indian Affairs took complete control of its schools for Indigenous children. As in the United States, orphans and children from dysfunctional Canadian families who were seen as having nowhere else to go increasingly filled the remaining residential schools.

Many First Nations students lacked adequate preparation for provincial schools, which often did little to accommodate their special needs, leading to an increased dropout rate. By 1969 only twelve residential schools remained. In 1970 local Indians took over the Blue Quills School in Alberta nonviolently when the government tried to close it.

As in the United States, a reevaluation of Indian policy occurred in Canada in the 1970s. The minister of Indian and northern affairs declared in 1972 that Indian education was "a whitewash . . . a process to equip him with white values, goals, language, skills needed to succeed in the dominant society" that served "no purpose in the child's world. . . . Rather it alienates him from his own people" (quoted in Milloy 1999, 199). In 1973 a Cree Way Project was started at Waskaganish on the eastern shore of James Bay, seven hundred miles north of Quebec, to "bridge the seemingly unbridgeable gulf between two alien nations: the native peoples nomadic hunters and the European Canadians—once agricultural, now post-industrial city dwellers" (Feurer 1990, 7). The project's goals "were to use Cree language in the schools to validate Cree culture and create a Cree tribal identity, to make reading and writing more important within their previously oral culture, to create a curriculum reflecting Cree culture and the Cree conceptual framework, and to implement that curriculum in the public schools" (Stiles 1997, 249).

In 1975 the James Bay and Northern Quebec Agreement provided for Inuit and Cree self-governance, including running the schools serving their children. In 1978 the Kativik School Board serving schools in fourteen villages became the first Inuit-controlled school board in Canada. In 1989 the Nunavik Educational Task Force was set up to look at the languages of education, curriculum, teacher training, post-secondary education, adult education, and the role of family and community in education in Northern Quebec. However, as in the United States, self-governance in Canada did not automatically lead to more culturally relevant education or greater student academic achievement. In her 2002 study of Inuit-controlled education in northern Canada Ann Vick-Westgate found that the "village school was, and still too often is, a Westernized formal institution that has excluded the knowledge and values of the community it serves and done a poor job of preparing young people for future roles" (Vick-Westgate 2002, 13).

The Royal Commission on Aboriginal Peoples reported in 1996 on the "grievous harms suffered by countless Aboriginal children, families, and communities as a result of the residential school system," and in 1998 the Canadian Minister of Indian Affairs declared:

> One aspect of our relationship with Aboriginal people over this period that requires particular attention is the Residential School system. The system separated many children from their families and communities and prevented them from speaking their own languages and from learning about their heritage and cultures. In the worst cases, it left legacies of personal pain and distress that continue to reverberate in Aboriginal communities to this day. Tragically, some children were the victims of physical and sexual abuse. (Quoted in Milloy 1999, 303–304)

AUSTRALIA'S "STOLEN GENERATIONS"

Australia was founded as a penal colony, a dumping ground, for English prisoners. Its harsh treatment of its Aboriginal population paralleled the English treatment of prisoners, but even the descendants of those prisoners fared better than the Aboriginals. As in the United States frontier warfare ensued in Australia as settlers moved in on Aboriginal lands, leading to a "violent mindset" among settlers and genocidal activity that, even in western news-paper editorials in the United States was expressed as "the only good Indian is a dead Indian" (see, e.g., Decker 2004, Lindsay 2012). In 1865 a Queensland legal clause allowed the forcible removal of Aboriginal children from their families on racial grounds. These removals, designed to assimilate Aborigi-nal children, continued into the 1970s, creating what is known today as the "stolen generations." As in the United States the removed children usually re-ceived a largely "industrial," rather than academic, education and their child labor was used both in schools and out of schools to teach them a work ethic (Robinson and Patten 2008). But unlike the United States, where the mixing of races was largely taboo and often made illegal by anti-miscegenation laws that existed until the 1950s in twenty-eight states, in Australia miscegenation was seen by some as a way to eventually incorporate its Aboriginal population genetically into the mainstream population.

In 1997 the National Inquiry into the "Separation of Aboriginal and Torres Strait Islander Children from Their Families" issued its report *Bringing Them Home,* which documented the suffering of Aboriginal children removed with-out parental consent from their homes, a practice that continued into the early 1970s. An Australian example of the complexity of the cultural transformation of Indigenous peoples that resulted from contact with European immigrants can be seen Graham McKay's report *The Land Still Speaks.* McKay writes,

> While most people . . . tended to see the term 'language maintenance activities' as including only formally organized language programs and activities, Saibai Island Council, in its response, made explicit what other communities assume: that traditional ceremonies and other tra-ditional activities (they mention dancing, singing and story-telling—others would include hunting) are an important means of keeping the traditional language strong. At the same time, the people of Saibai in-clude church services and tombstone unveiling in this arena, showing that Christianity and other post-contact developments have been firmly adopted by members of the community in the ongoing development of their Indigenous culture and life. The church has become part of their heritage . . . but not the school. (McKay 1996, 110)

AOTEAROA/NEW ZEALAND AND MĀORI IMMERSION SCHOOLS

The Māori of Aotearoa (New Zealand) seem to have escaped some of the worst experiences of the Indigenous peoples of the United States, Canada, and Australia. Making up about 15 percent of Aotearoa's population of four mil-lion, the Māori's have been able, at least recently, to steer government policies considerably in regard to extending the use of their language and culture in schools. The 1840 Treaty of Waitangi between the Māori and the British colonial government, New Zealand's founding document, gave some protection to Māori rights. And as with nineteenth-century Canadian and U.S. Indian treaties, post–World War II Indigenous activism has reasserted Māori treaty rights, some of which had long been ignored. Unlike the Treaty of Waitangi, many U.S. and Canadian treaties contained educational provisions, sometimes added at the request of the Indigenous parties.

A separate Native system of day schools was set up for the Māori in 1867 that continued to operate until 1947. While these schools were English-only, they were set up originally only when a Māori community asked for them and they were partially locally funded. They were small day schools over which the local community had some influence (Barrington 2008). Older students could transfer to a residential school, but it was not forced on them or their families. From the 1940s on there was some Māori language and culture at teacher training colleges. The Māori community treated teachers with respect and there is evidence that respect was returned (Simon and Smith 2001). According to James Belich, "It was not the Native school system, but mass urbanization after 1945, that brought the Māori language to its knees in the 1970s" (Belich 2001, x).

In the 1960s a Play Centre preschool movement encouraged Māori mothers to use English with their children, and the spread of English-language radio and television accelerated Māori language loss to the point that only a very few children could speak Māori. To counter the accelerating Indigenous language loss, Māori leaders looked for ways to use still fluent elders to keep their language alive. In 1982 Māori grandparents volunteered to run day-care centers, Te Kōhanga Reo, which featured an immersion program in their language. The success of the centers led to their rapid expansion. In 1988 there were 521 centers with 8,000 children, including 15 percent of the Māoris under five years old. In 1998 there were more than 600. In an informal, extended-family, childcare setting, Māori preschoolers are saturated with Māori language and culture (Belich 2001, x). Part of the Ministry of Education, the Te Kōhanga Reo o Ngaio web site (2014) states that language nests have been established in every district and that "Kōhanga Reo centres provide a location and a purpose for people of all ages to meet and work together. The Kōhanga Reo kaupapa [program] is powerful in drawing people together to support each other and work toward the ultimate goal of a bilingual and bicultural nation. The programme reaches young families who would not otherwise have taken part in early childhood services."

Language nests provide strong support to families in the effort to preserve native languages and cultures, provide a valuable service to working parents, and strengthen the values associated with the traditional Māori extended family (Fleras 1989). Based on the success of the language nests and popular demand, Māori-based education has been extended into the elementary, then the secondary, and now the university level.

In 1986 the Waitangi Tribunal acknowledged Māori language as a "taonga" (treasure) under Article II of the 1840 Treaty of Waitangi and that the national government therefore has a responsibility for its preservation. The 1987 Māori Language Act declared "the Māori language to be an official language of New Zealand, to confer the right to speak Māori in certain legal proceedings, and to establish Te Komihana Mo Te Reo Māori" (Māori Language Commission).

REVERSING ASSIMILATION

Facing the same drastic language loss and hearing of the success of the Māori, Native Hawaiians started their own Pūnano Leo language nests in 1984 (Wilson 1991). The English translation of their mission statement reads, "The Pūnana Leo Movement grew out of a dream that there be reestablished throughout Hawaiʻi the mana of a living Hawaiian language from the depth of our origins. The Pūnana Leo initiates, provides for and nurtures various Hawaiian Language environments, and we find our strength in our spirituality, love of our language, love of our people, love of our land, and love of knowledge." (ʻAha Pūnana Leo 2010)

To extend Hawaiian language–based education into the public schools of Hawaiʻi it was necessary to repeal the 1896 law, passed after the Hawaiian monarchy was overthrown, that prohibited the use of Hawaiian in both public and private schools. That repeal was accomplished in 1987. In 2003 there were twelve preschools and twenty-three public schools with Hawaiian immersion classes. In 1982 the University of Hawaiʻi at Hilo started a Hawaiian Studies degree program taught in Hawaiian and focusing on traditional Hawaiian language and culture. In 2004 the University of Hawaiʻi Board of Regents approved a doctoral program in Indigenous language and cultural revitalization, and some doctoral dissertations are now being written in the Hawaiian language.

In the mainland United States efforts to promote immersion schools for Indigenous students have been fewer and farther between. In the Window Rock Public Schools in the Navajo Nation most of today's kindergarten students enter school speaking only English. Students in the immersion school, which only includes students voluntarily enrolled by their parents, are immersed the entire school day in Navajo during kindergarten and first grade. English is gradually added starting in second grade, so that half the school day is taught in English by the sixth grade. The curriculum is determined by the Navajo Nation's 2000 *Diné Cultural Content Standards* and the Arizona state academic standards. Fifth grade English language achievement test scores for the immersion students show that they substantially outperform other district students in reading, writing, and math (Johnson and Wilson 2005; Johnson and Legatz 2006).

By and large, there are only token efforts to reverse assimilationist schooling in the former British colonies. However, especially in New Zealand and Hawai'i these efforts show much promise, and recent United Nations declarations point toward a positive future for these and other revitalization attempts. Australian Prime Minister Kevin Rudd stated:

> That today we honour the Indigenous peoples of this land, the oldest continuing cultures in human history. We reflect on their past mistreatment. We reflect in particular on the mistreatment of those who were Stolen Generations—this blemished chapter in our nation's history. The time has now come for the nation to turn a new page in Australia's history by righting the wrongs of the past and so moving forward with confidence to the future. We apologise for the laws and policies of successive Parliaments and governments that have inflicted profound grief, suffering and loss on these our fellow Australians. We apologise especially for the removal of Aboriginal and Torres Strait Islander children from their families, their communities and their country. For the pain, suffering and hurt of these Stolen Generations, their descendants and for their families left behind, we say sorry. To the mothers and the fathers, the brothers and the sisters, for the breaking up of families and communities, we say sorry. (2009)

Rudd called for "a new beginning . . . to right a great wrong" that had continued into the 1970s. He quoted Nanna Fejo, a member of the stolen generations, who said: "Families—keeping them together is very important. It's a good thing that you are surrounded by love and that love is passed down the generations. That's what gives you happiness."

In June 2008, pressured partly by Rudd's apology, Canada's Prime Minister Stephen Harper acknowledged in a speech to the House of Commons the ongoing, generational impacts of Canada's residential schools for Indians: "We now recognize that, in separating children from their families, we undermined the ability of many to adequately parent their own children and sowed the seeds for generations to follow. . . . Not only did you suffer these abuses as children, but as you became parents, you were powerless to protect your own children from suffering the same experience, and for this we are sorry." He concluded. "The government of Canada sincerely apologizes and asks the forgiveness of aboriginal peoples for failing them so badly" (Harper 2009). However, unlike the Australian Prime Minister, Harper did not promise to improve Canadian First Nations (aboriginal) social conditions.

High-minded rhetoric can count, even though sometimes it takes a very long time to see its promise realized. The phrase "all men are created equal" in the thirteen colonies' 1776 Declaration of Independence helped lead to the end of slavery, but only after more than eight decades, and it took well over two centuries for a black president to be elected to lead the United States.

CONCLUSION

Education is not neutral. What children hear, read, learn, and do in school can help them build a strong positive identity or it may, through insensitivity and ethnocentric assimilationist curriculum and instruction, destroy Indigenous cultural and family values and leave students susceptible to the allure of today's negative peer and popular media–dominated consumer culture. Most of the history of colonialism in Australia, Canada, New Zealand, and the United States is a record of cultural genocide, in which Indigenous peoples were forced become assimilated into Euro-American society through English-only education in order to be successful and join the modern world (Reyhner and Eder 2004). However, in today's society students of any race or culture who are not embedded in their traditional values are only too likely to pick up unhealthy lifestyles in our increasingly materialistic and hedonistic modern culture. They can also reject schooling in an effort to hang on to their traditional cultures. This oppositional identity hinders their success in the modern global economy and lack of education can relegate them to living in poverty with all its stresses.

Ethnic groups rightly tend to focus on their traditional moral and spiritual strengths, but it is important as Daniel Wildcat writes not to "romanticize the past" (Deloria and Wildcat 2001, 8). There is, in fact, a danger that Indigenous and other minority groups can define themselves as the "white man's shadow," as opposite to everything that the materialistic and individualistic "white man" is perceived as being (House 2002; Simard 1990). This topsy-turvy version of "blame the victim" can become an unthinking "blame the oppressor" for everything that is going wrong in one's life and community. This victimization can also lead to self-destructive anger, "red rage," and hinder positive efforts toward decolonization.

More and more Indigenous peoples are working to reclaim basic human rights and heal the wounds resulting from the long history of cultural genocide and to reverse the negative effects of assimilation while giving their students an education that prepares them to live in our modern technology-dominated world. These efforts include language and cultural revitalization and are not anti-educational efforts that will hold back Indigenous students from academic success. Just the opposite, today's revitalization efforts hold the promise of closing the centuries-old academic achievement gap that, aggravated by assimilationist education, is too often found between Indigenous and non-Indigenous students.

NOTES

Parts of this chapter appeared in, and other parts were adapted from, the authors' 2010 article "Cultural Genocide in Australia, Canada, New Zealand, and the United States: The Destruction and Transformation of Indigenous Cultures" published in the *Indigenous Policy Journal* 21(4): 1–26.

1. For information on the situation in Australia see the lengthy government report *Bringing Them Home: National Inquiry into the Separation of Aboriginal and Torres Strait Islander Children from Their Families* (Wilson and Dodson 1997); for Canada, see Milloy 1999 and Miller 1996; for New Zealand, Judith Simon and Linda Tuhiwai Smith's 2001 edited volume; and for the United States, see Adams 1995 and Reyhner and Eder 2004. For the special case of Hawai'i see Benham and Heck 1998.

2. The Indigenous populations did not have centuries to build up immunity to smallpox, measles, and other European diseases, as had the colonists, leading to high death rates among Indigenous people in the early phases of contact with European explorers and settlers. In addition, forced removal to boarding schools, reservations, and reserves, and other physical and cultural shocks, such as changes in climate and diet, that colonization brought to Indigenous peoples weakened their resistance to disease.

3. Horatio Algers (1832–1899) was a prolific American novelist who wrote about poor boys who only needed to work hard (and have good luck) to become successful.

2

The Continuum of Literacy in Native American Classrooms

SHEILAH E. NICHOLAS AND TERESA L. MCCARTY

We begin this discussion of Native American literacy with an observation from a recent lunch period at a tribal preschool:

> Kevin, the four-year-old son of Anglo professionals in the community, asked Melanie, a child of the community, "What's your cat's name?"
> "I don't have a cat," Melanie responded.
> Kevin made a second attempt to keep the interaction alive by providing a communicative routine he was familiar with using at home, and that mirrored many school-based scripts. "You ask me," he explained, "'what's your cat's name?'"
> This time Melanie responded according to the routine that Kevin had initiated: "What's your cat's name?"
> Kevin then stated the name of his cat. The anticipated conversation that Kevin initiated proceeded no further.

This interaction between two culturally different children in the teaching-learning environment of a tribal program calls our attention to the learned interactive and communication styles that each child brings to the classroom from home and community. For Kevin, the English-language pattern of interaction in which he was socialized at home mirrored the direct question-response routine he was learning in school. For Melanie, that routine seemed awkward, even intrusive, and made little sense within the framework of her home- and community-based language socialization. Given her socialization, she appropriately responded to Kevin's initial question, signifying that the interaction was complete.

As an abundant body of research attests, these culturally patterned ways of speaking, knowing, and being are often tacit and invisible, yet their recognition or misrecognition by educators can have profound impacts on children's learning trajectories. In illustration of this, we offer a second vignette from a family gathering:

Amid the hustle and bustle of Hopi women cooking the fresh corn gifted to the people earlier that morning by the *katsinam,* spirit beings believed to have control over the rains, three-year-old Kara was busy on the floor playing with the discarded corn husks and an aluminum pan she had turned upside down so that the bottom offered a flat surface upon which to lay the husks. When she finished, Kara picked up the pan with its carefully arranged rows of corn husks and announced, "I made *piiki,*" a reference to the traditional paper-thin blue corn flour bread she had observed her grandmother and mother making on numerous occasions. Kara's arranged rows of husks resembled the blue corn batter cooking on a hot stone griddle. She had been an active observer of such cultural traditions since infancy.

Two years later, Kara entered kindergarten. At the end of the school year she was required to attend summer school. "I have to go to summer school because I talk too much and don't listen," Kara matter-of-factly explained to everyone at the dinner table.

In contrast to Melanie in the first vignette, Kara entered the classroom environment with abundant sociolinguistic skills that paralleled many of those she encountered in school, and that would presumably enhance her school-based learning. In this case, misrecognition of those skills resulted in her assignment to a remedial track explicitly aimed at silencing her talk, which sent incalculably detrimental messages about her abilities and developing self-image, as her own explanation clearly reveals.

In this chapter we explore the relationships between language, culture, and the literacy development of Indigenous children and youth, focusing on the ways in which that development can be supported in school. The literature is replete with accounts of educational disparities for Indigenous learners, with the 2011 National Assessment of Educational Progress (NAEP) reading scores for American Indian and Alaska Native fourth and eighth graders in the United States "not significantly different from the scores in 2009 or 2005," and the gap between Native and non-Native students' mathematics scores greater in 2011 than it was in 2005 (NCES 2012, 2–3). Such a negative accounting of students' abilities begs explanation. With NAEP and other data showing little change from year to year, we must ask, following Ray McDermott, how the school system works "so that it conveniently winds up generation after generation producing the same problems and the same nasty results?" (2005, 121). Drawing on her work with the Hualapai Bilingual-Bicultural Program in Arizona, Lucille Watahomigie asks the question this way: "Why have the schools failed to educate our people?" (Watahomigie and McCarty 1996, 105).

A significant part of the answer to these questions and their transformation into positive terms lies in an appropriate *recognition* of the sociolinguistic and intellectual resources that make up students' communicative repertoires (Romero-Little 2010). We take as a starting point the notion of literacy as a social and cultural practice. This entails a pedagogy of multiliteracies, which acknowledges and values the multiplicity of children's meaning-making strategies, and explicitly links print literacies with oralcy and with visual, tactile, and spatial modes of communication (New London Group 1996, 64). Such an approach, says literacy scholar Brian Street, "offers a more culturally sensitive view of literacy practices as they vary from one context to another" (2008, 4).

We also recognize that within any classroom setting, Native American children, like Melanie and Kara in the examples above, enter school with diverse communicative repertoires. While some students may have exposure to the Native language at home and enter school as bi/multilinguals, others may have little or no such exposure. As research also shows, this does not lessen the latter students' desire or ability to activate their Native-language potentials (Wyman, McCarty, and Nicholas 2014). Regardless of their Native-language proficiency, Native students are likely to speak a variety of English reflecting the structure, sound system, and use patterns of their Indigenous heritage language. Sometimes called American Indian English or Village English, these linguistic abilities are expressions of fully developed linguistic systems—*not* partial or imperfect emulations of dominant English—and thus constitute immense learning resources. Describing this language variety for Navajo, Benally and Viri affirm that it "is a rich and effective form of expression that is shared throughout Navajo country," including among Navajo teachers and other school personnel (2005, 103).

Finally, we posit that we cannot understand any of these issues separate from an understanding of history and power. In the introductory vignette, for example, why is Kevin's prior knowledge privileged over Melanie's in school? As the NAEP data show, Native Americans have endured a long history of education policies and practices that have excluded Indigenous languages, cultures, and ways of speaking and knowing, with persistent negative effects (see, e.g., Reyhner and Eder 2004).

Our goal in this chapter is to offer fresh understandings of Indigenous students' language and literacy practices, with an eye toward supporting them in accessing a wide range of linguistic and communicative skills essential for their academic self-empowerment and full participation in their communities and the wider society. The National Indian Education Association (NIEA) has asserted that with the vast majority of the nation's 700,000 Native American students attending public schools more attention needs to be paid to meeting these students' "unique educational and culturally-related academic needs" (Dawn Mackety, in NIEA 2012, para. 5).

We begin with some foundational understandings of the relationships among language, culture, and identity. We then introduce the notion of the literacy continuum developed by Tohono O'odham linguist Ofelia Zepeda

(1992, 1995), and elaborated in our work together and with others (McCarty and Dick 2003; McCarty and Zepeda 2010). The literacy continuum helps us move beyond the binaries of oralcy versus literacy, Native languages versus English, and Indigenous versus Euro-American ways of knowing and speaking. We follow this with a discussion of promising programs that illuminate the pedagogical possibilities inherent within the literacy continuum, drawing on examples from throughout Native America. We conclude with a presentation of concrete classroom projects designed to enable educators to engage the literacy continuum in practice.

FOUNDATIONS:
LANGUAGE, CULTURE, AND IDENTITY

> I live Hopi, I just don't speak it [the Hopi language].
>
> Dorian (Hopi), age nineteen

Dorian's assertion, and the Hopi context, illuminates a foundational perspective on the relationships among language, culture, identity, and literacy development. Dorian, like many Indigenous youth, is not a speaker of her heritage language despite having been raised in her community among adult Hopi speakers and her active participation in Hopi cultural traditions (Nicholas 2008). Yet she asserts a strong personal, social, and cultural identity that is distinctly Hopi even without proficiency in the Hopi language.

According to Dorian, through her involvement in myriad Hopi traditions and institutions—religious and secular, and guided by significant kin—she learned the cultural expectations for her role in this extended kinship network, her community, and society. Much of this knowledge is tacit, such as the rules for communicative interaction evident in the interaction between Melanie and Kevin, above. In the process, Dorian also internalized important Hopi values and ways of knowing and being.

Language is fundamental to these socialization processes. Although Dorian is not a speaker of Hopi, Hopi ways of knowing and being are nonetheless part of the "total communicative framework" (E. T. Hall 1976) through which shared cultural knowledge is conveyed in her social environment. Language is thus inherent to identity formation. As Hopi research anthropologist Emory Sekaquaptewa has stated, "Words have a home in the context of culture, in the course of daily activities, in social institutions . . . they have meaning within these contexts" (cited in Nicholas 2005, 31).

The important point is that this total communicative framework is embedded in oral tradition and manifest in cultural institutions, religious ceremonies, symbolism, song words and phrases, prayer, teachings, and everyday expressions, all of which constitute the transmission mechanisms for a traditionally unwritten language. It is through such cultural forms of communication and expression in daily and specialized interactions with others that "concepts of a socioculturally structured universe" are transmitted and acquired (Ochs 1988, 14).

Hopi oral tradition illustrates the diversity of communicative genres that Indigenous communicative systems employ. In most Native American societies, oral tradition embodies the concepts and fundamental principles of a distinctive way of life. As Norbert Francis and Jon Reyhner note, "All indigenous peoples [have] created and preserved, through the oral tradition, an extensive body of narrative, poetry, and other kinds of formal genre" (2002, 134). Oral tradition is literally the literature of the people, defining for them how to be a people in heart, thought, and conduct as they pursue the fulfillment of life goals. In Dorian's case, she had become a *literate* member of the Hopi world through a culturally patterned language and literacy development model, despite her lack of fluency in the Hopi language.

Throughout Native America, these oral traditions persist and are resurging as socializing narratives for moral instruction, healing, community building, and communicative practices (Kroskrity 2012; Kroskrity and Field 2009). In contemporary contexts of rapid sociocultural and sociolinguistic change, revitalizing oral traditions is becoming an increasingly significant "strategy for cultural survival" (Montejo 1998). Natalie Diaz, a young adult Mojave language learner, teacher, and poet whose heritage language is spoken primarily by a small group of elders, recounts how this work began in her community: "We first asked ourselves how have we been Mojave for the last 80 years? . . . [Now], we're beating it [Mojave language and identity] back into our hearts" (Diaz 2013, n.p.). Identity becomes central as well because "people . . . organize their social meaning . . . on the basis of what (who) they are" (Warschauer 2001, para. 4, citing Castells 1996). Myaamia (Miami) language educator Daryl Baldwin (2013, n.p.) expresses the unifying power of language in asserting a collective identity: "We are Myaamia," he states, as the Myaamia Center and the Miami Tribe carry out their work in assisting community youth to (re)connect with their community, each other, and the culture. As we discuss in later sections, the oral traditions in which this work is anchored are central to activating the literacy continuum.

ENGLISH AND SECOND LANGUAGE
AND CULTURE LEARNING

What is the role of English regarding these community-based sociolinguistic resources? As Dorian's case exemplifies, many Native American students enter school as speakers of English and/or a variety recognized as Indian English (or Hopi, Navajo, Lakota, or Yup'ik English, etc.). It is these youths' first language and thus plays a central role in forging and expressing new identities as Native Americans engage with larger globalizing processes. As Dorian further stated, "A lot of our elders and our parents . . . are counting on us to keep the traditions going and that heritage, that culture . . . [but] I don't think it's fully complete without that missing piece of language—the tongue, the speaking" (Nicholas 2009, 333). While community language revitalization efforts are under way to assist youth such as Dorian in meeting their own and their communities' expectations for cultural continuity, the challenge is to successfully "work out that balance between [the Indigenous language] and English" that these young people's parents were unable to achieve (Nicholas 2008, 209).

Part of this balance includes what bilingual education scholar Jim Cummins (1989, 2000) has called "conversational" and "academic" English. While these notions have been critiqued as over simplified when used as either-or dichotomies (see Cummins 2000 for a discussion), properly understood as part of a complex and dynamic sociolinguistic continuum, the two notions cue us to the multiplicity of Englishes that Native students bring to school, as well as to the complicated language-learning task faced by students who enter school speaking an Indigenous language as a primary language. For example, Justin (age nineteen) described the shift not only in language but in culture when he entered kindergarten and his childhood language, Hopi, was abruptly "dropped" as a medium of instruction (Nicholas 2008). Jonathan (age sixteen) a ninth-grader and first-language speaker of Navajo, similarly described being "caught up in the confusion of learning English" on entering school (McCarty, Romero, and Zepeda 2006, 35). As Martha Crago points out in her study of second-language acquisition among Inuit students, "The acquisition of a second language implies the acquisition of a second culture for many learners" (1992, 488). Such student and teacher needs have not been sufficiently addressed in teacher preparation programs (Scarcella 2003; Wong Fillmore and Snow 2000). While we cannot address the full scope of these language and culture issues in a single chapter, we provide a brief discussion of conversational (often characterized as oral) and academic (often characterized as written) language development here.

Second-language learners like Justin and Jonathan must acquire oral proficiency in English alongside academic English proficiency essential for cognitively demanding tasks while keeping pace with their native English-speaking peers (Hakuta, Butler, and Witt 2000). Often, when students such as Justin or Jonathan master sufficient oral proficiency in their second language—what Cummins (1989, 2000) calls conversational proficiency—we assume they are ready to negotiate the English literacy demands they encounter in school, including English standardized tests. However, extensive research demonstrates that it takes four to seven years for second-language learners to develop high levels of academic proficiency in a second language, and up to ten years to develop fully competitive uses of academic English to achieve parity with their native English-speaking peers (Crawford 2004; Cummins 2000; García and

Baker 2007). A key factor in mastering oral/conversational and academic/ written language proficiency in a second language is the length of time and quality of exposure to the target language. Research also shows that this is accelerated by strong and consistent educational support for students' linguistic, cognitive, and social-affective development in the mother tongue (Cummins 2000; Francis and Reyhner 2002; García 2009; McCarty 2003; Skutnabb-Kangas and Dunbar, 2010).

From work in a Navajo school setting, Marie Arviso and Wayne Holm show that these principles apply equally to students whose first language is Navajo and to those whose first language is English but who are not yet proficient in school-based academic English (1990, 2001). Using Cummins's constructs, they point out that Navajo children enter school with many kinds of communicative repertoires: Some possess academic Navajo and academic English abilities, others possess academic Navajo and conversational English abilities, and still others have different levels of proficiency in one language but little exposure to the other. Arviso and Holm's point is that appropriate recognition of children's *specific* and *multiple* communicative repertoires makes their academic success more likely (McCarty 2013, 72). The literacy continuum provides a heuristic to guide the development of these multifaceted sociolinguistic resources.

THE LITERACY CONTINUUM AND THE "POWER OF WORDS"

"I saw about four deer running by a stream and a big waterfall," a young Tohono O'odham student wrote. "When I looked at their faces, they had my dad's, mom's, and sisters' faces."

"Some hunters came," the narrative continues. "I heard shots. The deer fell over. I woke up this morning and my heart was beating fast" (Clinton Antone, cited in Zepeda 1995, 11).

With this second-grade student's written narrative, Ofelia Zepeda illustrates the *continuum of literacy*—a blending of the oral and the written as "young writers 'urge things up' from the oral tradition" (1995, 12). In doing so, she adds, "these writers are inspired by the formulas of stories which lead them to create specific scenes and events also found in the oral tradition" (12). In the writing sample above, the writer "urges up" a common Indigenous storytelling theme in which the protagonist experiences a transcendental experience in the pursuit of an epic adventure or problem-solving journey (12). "These students' writings [give] the reader a small window into their world— the world of growing up in a special place," Zepeda maintains. "They may write about a specific topic as assigned, but at the same time they gather insights from their own experience, their community, home and family to write what they feel makes a good story. . . . As with the oral tradition, the writer is playing and . . . experimenting with the power of words. . . . [Young Native writers] tantalize the reader in the same way the storyteller holds the audience in an oral performance" (1995, 10).

Zepeda's point is that regardless of whether students are speakers of their ancestral language, an Indigenous variety of English, other language varieties (and, we add, "academic" and/or "conversational" proficiencies in one or all of these varieties), they bring with them to the classroom unique oral literacy knowledge from their communities. This includes the patterning and rhythm of storytelling and its culturally specific content, and, as we saw for Dorian in the previous section, the cultural identifications associated with those traditions. "Here the students [mesh] the oral and written tradition into one," Zepeda states, demonstrating "the movement from oral to written [and] making the seamless continuum" (1995, 10). Their ability to engage "the power of words" across the oral-written continuum is a strength "that can and should be tapped in promoting American Indian and Alaska Native children's . . . literacy" (14).

The continuum metaphor privileges family and community knowledge and ways of speaking as foundations for learning. Within the continuum, Indigenous oral tradition is valued equally with alphabetic or school-based literacy, spotlighting often unrecognized or overlooked possibilities for language and literacy development. "Often the continuum manifests itself in . . . repetition of text, the text structure itself, and formulaic beginnings and endings," Zepeda explains (1995, 13). "It is critical for educators and promoters of literacy among young [Native Americans] to be aware of the cultural and linguistic resources these [students] employ" (13).

Across Native America there are many education programs that illuminate the possibilities of the literacy continuum in practice. Next, we will highlight a few exemplars of this approach.

THE LITERACY CONTINUUM IN PRACTICE: THREE PROGRAM EXAMPLES

Nestled against the foothills of mountains sacred to Native peoples, and in a town of moderate size, is a K–5 school called Puente de Hózhǫ́. Named for Spanish *puente de,* "bridge of," and Navajo *hózhǫ́,* "beauty" or "harmony," this is the Bridge of Beauty School. The name mirrors the school's vision to "create an educational environment where students from diverse language and cultural backgrounds"—Native American, Latino/a, and Anglo—"can harmoniously learn together" while pursing the goals of Academic excellence, Bilingualism, and Cultural enrichment: ABC (Fillerup 2011, 149–50). In a school district in which 25 percent of students are American Indian (mostly Navajo), and 20 percent are Latino, "local educators were searching for innovative ways to bridge the seemingly unbridgeable gap between the academic achievement of language-minority and language-majority children," explains school founder Michael Fillerup (2005, 15).

Puente de Hózhǫ offers two parallel bilingual programs: a Spanish-English dual language track for native Spanish-speaking and native English-speaking children, and a Navajo immersion program for English-dominant Native American students learning their heritage language as a second language. In the latter program, everything takes place in Navajo for a significant portion of the day. Not surprisingly, this requires a great deal of teacher innovation—"remaking" English-language materials by overlaying them with Navajo text, for example, as well as creating new Navajo literacy materials and involving students in bookmaking.

As one second-grade teacher described these activities:

> We make . . . at least one or two little books a week, . . . and we work on comprehension throughout the week on those books, so this . . . reinforces the skills that they are going to learn in reading and writing. . . . And I read the lunch menu in Navajo. . . . They are learning different types of foods every day. . . . Every week they are learning new words. . . . And we keep the words in journals and we use the journal throughout the whole week. . . . So they have a word bank that they can refer to. (Cited in McCarty 2012, 105)

The content of these materials is organized around four culture-based themes: earth and sky, health, living things, and family and community. "We have monthly themes," a teacher explains. "We incorporate science, we incorporate social studies, we incorporate math. So our first month will be about the self. . . . Self-esteem—your clanship, your kinship, who you are, where you come from: 'You are of the Diné [Navajo] people, you should be proud of who you are.' . . . That's all intertwined with [Navajo oral] stories as well" (teacher interview, cited in McCarty 2012, 106).

In addition to its formal curriculum, Puente de Hózhǫ exemplifies the literacy continuum in a multitude of nonformal practices: On entering the school, students, teachers, parents, and visitors are greeted by student-created wall murals depicting the Navajo girls' puberty ceremony, *Kinaaldá,* and the canyon lands of nearby *Diné Bikeyah,* Navajoland. Bulletin boards display Navajo, Spanish, and English print. Indigenous song, dance, and visual arts are all part of the literacies the school cultivates. This positions the Indigenous language and culture on an equal footing with English and Euro-American ways of knowing. As one teacher describes the school's strengths-based pedagogy: "I think once we can instill [in students] that they can be *proud* of who they are, they're going to feel honored to share their Native language and culture and to . . . be motivated to learn" (cited in McCarty 2012, 107).

On the other side of the North American continent, the Akwesasne Mohawk reserve straddles 41 square miles over the U.S.-Canadian border. Here, in 1979, Mohawk parents founded the Akwesasne Freedom School as a way to "maintain their culture and save their language" (Stairs, Peters, and Perkins 1999, 45). Situated in a facility built by parents and other volunteers to resemble a traditional Haudenosaunee (Iroquois) longhouse, the Akwesasne Freedom School has twelve teachers and enrolls sixty to sixty-five students in a year-round, pre-K through grade 8 program. Kanienkeha (the Mohawk language) is the sole language of instruction until the end of grade 7.

Mohawk oral tradition, reflected in the *Ohonten Kariwahtekwa* (Thanksgiving Address), which teaches gratitude to the earth and living things, and the *Kaianere:kowa* (Great Law of Peace, the charter of the Iroquois Confederacy) anchor the school curriculum. Each day begins and ends with a student delivering the *Ohonten Kariwahtekwa* from memory. According to Mohawk scholar Louellyn White, the cultural knowledge and values embedded in this oral narrative are "to be understood and lived [internalized], not merely recited," with the Thanksgiving Address providing "structure to the curriculum and allow[ing] students to explore . . . botany, fisheries, astronomy, and planting" (2009, 116). The Indigenous language "is heard almost everywhere," she adds (2009, 175–76). These efforts are designed to develop students' full language and literacy potentials, including helping young Mohawk learners to "find [their] talk" (177). Like Puente de Hózhǫ́, the Akwesasne example illuminates the ways in which the literacy continuum can be deployed to support students' academic growth alongside their emerging identities and self-esteem. "These youth have an interest in learning their language," White maintains; "they take pride in the language, and they value the language" as "critical in Mohawk identity formation and continuance of Mohawk culture" (2009, 201, 202).

Our third program example is the Nāwahīokalani'ōpu'u (Nāwahī) Laboratory School, a full-immersion, early childhood through high school program affiliated with the University of Hawai'i at Hilo's College of Hawaiian Language and the 'Aha Pūnana Leo (Hawaiian Language Nest), a nonprofit organization. Nāwahī offers a college preparatory curriculum and teaches all subjects in the Hawaiian language. Of special interest is Nāwahī's role within a larger set of structures called *honua,* an integrated system designed to "develop, protect, nurture and enrich young adult and child fluency in Hawaiian" language and culture (Wilson and Kawai'ae'a 2007, 38). For example, in school gardens, students tend the crops and the animals that connect them "to traditional Hawaiian practices and the natural environment that has nurtured their culture for generations" (Wilson and Kamanā 2008, para. 2). In these activities, all communication among students and between students and their teachers is carried out in the Hawaiian language.

In each of these three cases, students are able to acquire multiple literacies across a range of proficiencies ("conversational" and "academic") in the Native language and English. In addition to learning oral language and literacy skills in Navajo, for example, Puente de Hózhǫ students outperform their peers in English-only classrooms in English reading, writing, and mathematics (Fillerup 2011). Nāwahī students surpass their non-Hawaiian immersion peers on English standardized tests and have outperformed the state average for all ethnic groups on high school graduation, college attendance, and academic honors (Wilson and Kamanā 2011). Programs such as these demonstrate that "programming that is highly focused on the [Indigenous language] and its heritage can produce exceptional [Indigenous language] results, without negatively affecting academic outcomes or English proficiency" (Wilson and Kamanā 2011, 53).

CLASSROOM TEACHERS "AT THE HEART" OF THE LITERACY CONTINUUM

While the previous section offered programmatic examples of the literacy continuum in practice, in this section we explore more closely how and through what instructional processes, tools, and content educators can provide critical support to Native American students in the classroom that will ensure they are learning to become full and active participants in their community and mainstream worlds.

The sociocultural dimensions of language and literacy learning for Native American students challenge universal notions of language socialization. Crago's (1992) study among the Inuit, for instance, shows that Inuit children are socialized to be attentive listeners in the presence of adults, and that children's talk has a place primarily among peers and in their role as sibling caregivers. Susan Philips (1993) reached similar conclusions about Warm Springs Indian students in Oregon, who are socialized in culturally distinctive ways that emphasize listening and observing over talking and speaking up, sharing control versus hierarchical structures, and voluntary versus involuntary participation in group activities. These "invisible" cultural differences in the regulation of talk, as well as dialect differences, caused teachers to misunderstand their Indian pupils, or to define what they heard as being unacceptable (127).

It is important that teachers concerned about their Native American students' literacy development be aware that through their instructional approach, communicative style, and structuring of social activities, they play a highly influential role in organizing the ways students perceive themselves and the world. Understanding culturally patterned language socialization processes is one crucial step in this process, enabling teachers to structure cooperative peer-interactive activities that maximize language learning while minimizing cognitive dissonance and language and culture loss. We turn now to several key studies that afford a more detailed look into the ways in which this can be achieved.

"Developing a Self"

Cleary's (2008) study of the schooling experiences of 120 First Nations, American Indian, and Alaska Native high school students is one of the few that has sought the perspectives of students themselves on their language and literacy development. Importantly, the study highlights the connection between "choice," effective instructional tasks and activities, and student motivation in literacy acquisition.

Students advocated for instructional tasks that motivated them to engage in the selection and interpretation of literature, individual and collaborative writing, creative writing, essay writing, and poetry writing—all with family support. Given a choice in selecting reading materials, these Native students revealed a wide variety of reading interests, from nonfiction and historical fiction to science fiction, classics to romances, Shakespeare and Poe to Stephen King, to biographies of deceased rock stars, country music stars, and rappers. Their reading choices included texts about Native peoples that "diminished the distance" from their culture, community, and history, particularly for students in mainstream schools (Cleary 2008, 102). Teachers, in turn, expanded students' reading genres by introducing them to literature such as *Romeo and Juliet* or *A Tale of Two Cities*. However, students sought teachers' assistance in finding the relevancy and benefit of this literature to their lives, or help in finding the "hidden meanings" embedded in these stories. Students noted that some teachers effectively cultivated such connections to literature by becoming positive role models themselves, reading with students, reading books suggested by students, and providing opportunities for independent reading in the classroom.

Students' ability to choose reading-related writing topics provided an opportunity to ground connections to the readings in their lived realities. This helped students to continue developing their competencies—writing more to "get better," seeking out new vocabulary, and trying out new ideas through new writing genres. Teacher support entailed introducing the writing process in manageable tasks aimed at more complex competencies, and providing consistent encouragement of students' developing competencies and confidence as writers.

Students conveyed that stories and poetry were their preferred writing genres and suggested that these genres were compatible with the traditional oral narrative style more familiar to them. Their comments on their struggles with expository writing, however, indicate that this is an area in which they may need further assistance. Moreover, one student reminds us to be cognizant that students differ in the form of self-expression they feel most comfortable using; some may express themselves best through other forms such as art, music, or performance. Flexibility on the teacher's part also contributed to student motivation. One "talkative" student, for example, was allowed to "talk his journals" rather than receiving detention for his behavior.

Reading and writing for the benefit of family, community, and tribe—a "real" purpose and audience—supported student motivation. Cleary highlights examples of student literacy projects that, in addition to affirming cultural identity, created "strong intrinsic motivation" or "feelings of self-determination" to explore and speak up about important issues and rights (2008, 112). One student wrote a poem that was read aloud in a nationally broadcast documentary, while another garnered a first-place award in a poetry contest with her Hoopa-language poem. A Dakota student compelled to "explain what [*really*] happened" at Wounded Knee for his history paper (Cleary 2008, 113) thoroughly researched that history. This was followed by a powerful telling of his own historical account. As part of his presentation, he used visuals of the Gatling gun used to kill women and children. Even more powerfully, he turned off the classroom lights and asked everyone to close their eyes as he narrated this history. This presentation, Cleary tells us, brought the student's class members to tears, even as they were empowered by the transformative impact of the project.

Another student's development of a personal web site provided a venue to express her personal and cultural identity to a receptive audience—other members of her community. As a medium for literacy development, the web site allowed her to peel away her "student persona"—reserved and quiet—and, as she asserted, "speak of who I am on it" (113). As Cleary points out, such student literacy projects demonstrate the importance of "recognizing, acknowledging and acting on the advice" of students (115). To this we would add that the projects exemplify perceptions of self-determination that both motivate and compel Native youth to address the concerns of their communities.

"We Can Be Alive in Cyberspace":
Expressing the Hawaiian Mana on the World Wide Web

Mark Warschauer's study on the use of online technology for Hawaiian language and literacy development found that "interacting in cyberspace" provides students with "an opportunity to explore and strengthen their sense of individual and collective Hawaiian identity" in highly personal ways (2001. para. 33). Students in a university-level Hawaiian language class were required to conduct research on a self-selected aspect of Hawaiian life and culture and create a web page as the final project, later linked to a class web site. The Hawaiian language was the medium of knowledge-sharing. Onaona, a young woman in her early twenties, created one web page on the life of one of Hawai'i's last princesses and a second on the history and nature of Hawaiian

Creole English, commonly spoken in Hawai'i. Malina, a Hawaiian Studies major in her forties, produced a web page on Hawaiian wetlands through the language of poetry, texts, drawings, and photos. Kamahele, a talented hula dancer and chanter, focused on Hawaiian chants for his web page; his final product provided a history and description of the meaning of chants, including an audio file of recorded chants.

Warschauer identified several factors that support the use of technology as an effective tool for advancing heritage language and literacy development among learners. First, it offered students of multiracial Hawaiian heritage a safe space to project a Native Hawaiian identity and to fully explore and express aspects of their heritage and ethnic identity denied in real life because they don't "look the part" (2001, para. 39). Second, students conveyed that technology-based communication and learning were consistent with Hawaiian ways of interacting and learning—through extensive informal communicative interaction, also known as *talk story* (K. Au 2001). Third, technology is viewed as one other medium to add to the wide variety within Hawaiian oral tradition, which includes chant and hula as well as the integration of modern ways of expression that are part of the Hawaiian *mana,* or spirit force. Technology is a modern vehicle to "bring the language forward" into new domains with contemporary meaning, and to maintain intergenerational transmission (Hornberger and King 1996). Finally, says Warschauer, technology foregrounds the flexibility of language as a medium for the assertion of identity and cultural survival and continuance.

On the International Front:
Opening up "Ideological and Implementational Space"

Our final examples are international ones in which teachers, motivated by a commitment to fostering the language and literacy potentials of their learners, are transforming the language policies of their classrooms and schools. This is achieved as teachers open up what educational linguist Nancy Hornberger calls "ideological and implementational space" where Indigenous languages and literacies can "evolve and flourish" (2002, 30). This places education practitioners "at the heart" of language and literacy planning and policy within their classrooms and schools (Ricento and Hornberger 1996, 417). Hornberger uses the example of South African Zulu and South American Andean teachers employing a multicultural and collaborative group discourse in their respective observations that use of the Indigenous language in the classroom benefits student growth, as does more group work, peer mentoring, and culturally appropriate participant structuring. Andean teachers, for example, opened up a Mother's Day celebration with a child's recitation of a poem and a dramatization of a local story, using local materials and local music.

Multilingual language policies open up space where minority . . . identities can be introduced and a range of media—including dissimilar, divergent, nonstandard [language] varieties as well as visual and other communicative modes—can be employed simultaneously in instruction. What is needed is to find as many ways as possible to open ideological spaces for multiple languages and literacies in classroom, community, and society. (Hornberger 2002, 43, 45)

LANGUAGE AND LITERACY BEYOND THE NAEP RESULTS

In this chapter we have used Zepeda's (1995) metaphor of the literacy continuum to suggest the ways in which educators can fruitfully bring Native students' home- and community-based linguistic and cultural resources into their literacy development in school. The essence of the literacy continuum is its emphasis on harmonizing oral and written language practices and forms, and its valorization of multiple ways of speaking, listening, reading, and writing as pathways to knowledge and student self-empowerment.

We realize that activating the literacy continuum is not a simple task; as the examples provided here have demonstrated, this work takes time, commitment, and focus, often in the face of pressure from education policies that promote a single language variety—dominant English—and a high-stakes, "one size fits all" approach. The persistent educational disparities reflected in the NAEP data presented earlier offer compelling evidence that this approach has failed Native American learners and communities.

We offer instead the notion of the literacy continuum as a more inclusive, holistic approach that moves beyond the binaries of oral versus written language and mother tongue versus "other" tongue. In addition to its potential to ameliorate academic disparities, this multiliteracy pedagogy enables learners to access their heritage language, regardless of their proficiency levels, as a means of identity affirmation and cultural continuance. With these goals in mind, we close with the statement of April, a young Cochiti Pueblo learner:

I am a Pueblo child and I love to listen to my grandparents tell stories. From their example I learn to take what I need from the earth to live, but also how to leave something behind for future generations. Every day, I am learning to live in harmony with the world and every day I am collecting memories of my life to share one day with my own children and grandchildren. (Cited in Hoyt-Goldschmidt, 1993)

3
Promoting Indigenous Literacy

JON REYHNER AND WARD COCKRUM

Too often Indigenous students are taught from textbooks designed for use by middle-class white children. These textbooks are not particularly appropriate for Indigenous students, and teachers responsive to their Indigenous students' needs will seek out culturally appropriate curricula, especially reading material. Luckily, teachers who wish to supplement or replace reading textbooks have a wide variety of materials by and about Indigenous peoples they can use. There are thousands of children's books with Indigenous characters, but many contain highly objectionable stereotypes, including some classics. For example, in Mark Twain's *The Adventures of Tom Sawyer,* the villain is "Injun Joe"—a "murderin half-breed" who tortures women (Twain [1876] 1958, 87, 148). In Laura Ingalls Wilder's *Little House on the Prairie,* first published in 1935, "two naked, wild [Indian] men" who visit the Ingalls' homestead are described as "tall, thin, fierce-looking" with eyes that are "black and still and glittering, like snake's eyes" (1971, 134–39). The fact that these men just visit and do no harm does not take away from the negative description of them.

Textbooks used to teach reading and other subjects are frequently updated and receive editorial screening that eliminates the more objectionable minority-group stereotypes. However, stereotyped characters are difficult to avoid in stories, because they represent a highly visible portion of reality. The danger to students is not the stereotypes themselves, but the possibility that students will come to believe that the stereotypes accurately portray every member of a group. Teachers can avoid this danger by making students aware of stereotyping and giving students a variety of literature to read.

Students reading books with stereotyped characters, such as those described above, need teachers to provide an explanation of Indigenous cultures and of frontier settlers' unwarranted negative attitudes toward them (Lindsay 2012). They also need to understand how the Indigenous peoples felt toward settlers who moved in on their lands—lands that were often taken by force without any attempt to purchase them. For example, in the Caldecott Medal–winning book *They Were Strong and Good,* the young narrator explains that his pioneer mother did not like Indians because "they would stalk into the kitchen without knocking and sit on the floor. Then they would rub their stomachs and point to their mouths to show that they were hungry. They would not leave until my mother's mother gave them something to eat" (Lawson 1940).

An explanation of Indigenous customs would help students put such descriptions in perspective. For example, teaching students about American Indian expectations of mutual hospitality would explain the reason the Indians wanted food from strangers. A lesson on sign language, as a method of communication with people who speak another language, could also help students understand the Indians' behavior. Teachers could explain that American tourists in Europe can be seen every day using "primitive" sign language. Reading assignments that include books by authors who lived on the frontier and had extensive contacts with Indians, such as Mari Sandoz's *These Were the Sioux* (1961) or, better yet, books written by Indigenous authors, such as Charles Eastman's *Indian Boyhood* (1902), Francis LaFlesche's *The Middle Five* (1911), and Luther Standing Bear's *My People the Sioux* (1928), can do much to correct impressions left by negative descriptions by authors who had little or no contact with Indigenous peoples.

ETHNOCENTRISM IN STORIES

Negative stereotypes are a symptom of a larger problem of ethnocentrism. There is a natural tendency for each culture to perceive itself as superior to all other cultures. This tendency to see other cultures as inferior, called ethnocentrism, has led to repeated violations of the human rights of ethnic minorities, including Indigenous peoples, by dominant groups. Ethnocentrism comes naturally to children who are brought up to believe that the way of life of their family's culture is the only way to live, as many children are raised (LeVine and Campbell 1972). Villains and fools in the stories the children hear and read are often portrayed as coming from other cultures, and sometimes even from other planets. When these children grow up and interact with people from other cultures, they may think the behavior of those "other" persons is not only different, but wrong. And since the children think they know the proper way to live and that the other person's behavior and actions are wrong, they naturally feel superior to the "ignorant" outsiders.

Ethnocentrism lies at the heart of the problem of Indigenous education. Rather than being communication between equals, attempts at communication between colonial settlers and Indigenous cultures tended to be on matters of the dominant society seeking to replace the Indigenous peoples by taking their lands, or, at best, trying to assimilate them. The original ideal of Indigenous education in the United States and much of the world was to "civilize" and assimilate the Native peoples into the culture European emigrants brought to America. Behind these efforts was military, political, and economic power exercised by the dominant groups.

Indigenous children are no different from children from the dominant culture. They have a right, like all children, to be educated in schools that reinforce the culture of their homes in keeping with the United Nations' Declaration on the Rights of Indigenous Peoples. School curricula should include local Indigenous stories and history to teach reading, language arts, and social studies. As Indigenous students get older they need to be introduced to the wider non-Indigenous world in a way that it does not make their own culture and worldview seem automatically inferior or superior, but just different.

Ethnocentrism can become resurgent in countries when immigration increases or in times of economic recession. In the United States, this is especially true with increased immigration from Latin America and Asia. If current demographic trends continue, white non-Hispanic Americans will soon be a minority of the U.S. population, and the fear of becoming a minority has led to the formation of groups that wish to stop immigration, especially from Latin America, and enforce assimilation on all U.S. minorities. "English only" organizations, which advocate adopting English as the official language of the United States, jeopardize the use of Indigenous languages and culturally appropriate curriculum for minority group children and the early education of non-English-speaking children.

WHAT EXEMPLARY TEACHERS OF INDIGENOUS STUDENTS HAVE FOUND

Many teachers, Indigenous and non-Native, have found success teaching Indigenous students. Sylvia Ashton-Warner learned in New Zealand to teach reading using material drawn from her Māori students' experiential background, rather than from commercially available reading programs, helping ensure that her students would have the prior knowledge necessary for reading comprehension. She emphasized the power of words, an idea that is familiar to many Indigenous cultures, and wrote about her experiences in her book *Teacher:* "First words must have intense meaning for a child. They must be a part of his being. How much hangs on the love of reading, the instinctive inclination to hold a book! . . . Pleasant words won't do. Respectable words won't do. They must be words organically tied up, organically born from the dynamic life itself. They must be words that are already part of the child's being" (1963/1971, 30).

Ashton-Warner's teaching experience led her to believe that in order for her to get students' maximum attention, they needed to already have a deep emotional tie with the first words they were learning to read, not the often unfamiliar words found in reading textbooks. Using words written on the chalkboard that were suggested by her students, Ashton-Warner built up a "key vocabulary" for her students, and these words were put on cards for the children to identify and were reviewed daily. The words were then combined to form sentence-length captions for drawings done by the students. Children then wrote their own simple storybooks, which were used to teach reading. She also encouraged autobiographical (journal) writing. Daily journal writing is well worth encouraging throughout the school years and as a lifelong activity, which leads students to practice writing and to examine their own lives. It was important to Ashton-Warner that the students' words and writing were not criticized. As she notes, getting to know your students' key words is getting to know your students—their hopes, fears, and the challenges they face growing up. She believed in *using*, rather than suppressing, students' energy, letting them work together, and having them read to each other. It is important that students learn that reading it not just something one has to do in school; it can be an enjoyable recreational activity.

In her autobiography, *Journey to the People,* Ann Nolan Clark (1969), another exemplary teacher and award-winning author, writes that Willard Beatty, chief of the U.S. Indian Office's Branch of Education from 1936 to 1952 and a former president of the Progressive Education Association, encouraged experimentation in teaching approaches and methods. She found that all the Indian-school teachers were using "Experience Reading Charts," in which students described their experiences and the teacher wrote them down on chart paper. But rather than learning to read from them, her students were memorizing what she wrote and singsonging it back to her. "But these were charts, and to the children charts were charts and had no connection with books" (56). She even folded paper and bound it with yarn to make booklets, but still her Tesuque Pueblo students in New Mexico did not see these as books, and the students were still against books because they believed books were some sort of white-man's magic that was closed to them. To counteract that attitude, she involved her students in publishing. Her students printed thirty copies of *A Courier in New Mexico* and then printed *A Third Grade Home Geography,* a book about everyday life in Tesuque, written by Clark. This book made its way to New York City, where it was published in 1941 by Viking Press as *In My Mother's House* and named a Caldecott Honor Book. Clark's initially reluctant readers went on to Haskell and Sherman Indian Schools, and one student went on to college while another became an artist.

Clark writes,

What a book "says" must be interesting to the child who reads it or listens to it read to him. The story must be vital to him. He must be able to "live it" as the pages turn. It must enrich the world he knows and lead him into a wider, larger unfamiliar world. The experience of having known it must have been an adventure and a delight. . . . A good book has an inner quality that may have a deep, personal, special meaning for some child, somewhere. It is an unfortunate adult who does not remember certain books of his childhood that he will hold forever dear. (1969, 101)

She asserts that children need "to have books written for them that will help them develop an understanding of themselves, their potentialities and resources, and the pressures and problems of their immediate world," and they also need "books to be written that will help give them an insight into, and an acceptance of, the larger world outside their own" (1969, 88). She concludes, "Books for children should help develop an appreciation of life and all that life means and holds and promises" (1993, 97). The reality is that stories in the anthologies used to teach reading in elementary schools seldom live up to Clark's definition of a good book.

Working with and building on students' background knowledge does not just apply to reading. T. D. Allen's 1982 book, *Writing to Create Ourselves,* describes what she learned from five years of teaching American Indian students at the Institute of American Indian Arts in Santa Fe, New Mexico, where she started teaching in 1963, as well as her subsequent years spent working with Indian school teachers across the country. Allen started with her students using their "five doors" (the five senses) to describe something, then had them do short "here and now" exercises that capture the look, feel, smell, sound, and/or taste of a moment in time, and then went on to have them write life stories. As the book jacket states, "Allen shows that, by helping a student discover what it is he has to say that is uniquely his own, the student motivates himself to gain language skills and define himself as a person." One of her students, Emerson Blackhorse "Barney" Mitchell, got so carried away writing his life story that it was published as *Miracle Hill* by the University of Oklahoma Press in 1967. Her students also had their writing commercially published in the *Arrow* series of anthologies.

Allen's ideas to develop young writers parallel those of Mick Fedullo who wrote *Light of the Feather* about his experiences across the western United States getting American Indian students to write poetry. He echoes Allen's advice about students using their five senses to paint a picture in words of a scene or event and letting the readers draw their own conclusions. Fedullo tells students not to use adjectives like "beautiful," "bad," "cute," "good," "nice," "pretty" and "ugly" that don't really describe anything—"show, don't tell" is his advice. Some of the students he worked with had their poetry commercially published in *Rising Voices* (Hirschfelder and Singer 1992).

Famous writers like Louisa Mae Alcott, who wrote *Little Women,* and Lucy Maud Montgomery, who wrote *Anne of Green Gables,* got nowhere with their writing until they took advice to write about what they knew, about the people and places they grew up around. Well-known Indian writers such as N. Scott

Momaday, Virginia Driving Hawk Sneve, Luci Tapahonso, Laura Tohe, and Sherman Alexie have built much of their success on this same principle. However, short essays, poems, and life stories are just one type of writing that students should learn in school. Also useful to master are five paragraph (or more) essays and various forms of process writing, in which students brainstorm ideas, write drafts, discuss drafts with fellow students and the teacher, edit, and finally publish their writing in some form.

In his book *Lives on the Boundary* (1989/2005), Mike Rose writes about students he met while working at the University of California at Los Angeles Tutorial Center who got high grades on their essays in high school and then low grades for writing the same way in college. They had learned to write good summaries of what they read, but not how to do critical analysis, which is what their university professors demanded. Daniel McLaughlin writes in his book *When Literacy Empowers* (1992) about a Navajo student who did well in a reservation school and then went to a Harvard University summer program where just writing papers from "the top of her head" was not enough. The student was disappointed to learn she would need to take a remedial writing class. She later wrote to students back at her high school, "Think what you're writing. What are you saying? What is your thesis? Thesis, thesis, thesis: everything has to relate to your main topic" (1988, 8). The Applied Literacy Program at her school got students to develop their writing skills in Navajo and English by writing in a variety of ways, including writing scripts for the school's low-power television station and award-winning newspaper. Much of their writing was based on interviewing elders, tribal officials, and other community members.

Rose, who was born into poverty and initially did poorly in school, emphasizes again and again that a few of his teachers made all the difference in his life with their encouragement and help. Part of the encouragement and help teachers can provide is to give students some choices about what they read and write about and to let them use their experiential and cultural background to inform that writing. Of course, teachers also need to provide guidance in how this and other types of writing can be improved.

Polingaysi Qöyawayma, an exemplary Hopi teacher, realized "she could not go amiss by teaching from the familiar to the unknown" (1964, 143). Responding to being told by her supervisors in the 1920s to teach only in English, she wrote, "What do these white-men stories mean to a Hopi child? What is a choo-choo to these little ones who have never seen a train? No! I will not begin with the outside world of which they have no knowledge. I shall begin with the familiar. The everyday things. The things of home and family" (165). For "Little Red Riding Hood" Qöyawayma substituted familiar Hopi legends, songs, and stories. Initially reprimanded by her school administrator for her audacity, her talents were recognized by Ho Chunk educator Henry

Roe Cloud, the first Indian graduate of Yale University, who became superintendent of Haskell Institute in 1933 and supervisor of Indian Education for the U.S. Indian Office in 1936. Commissioner of Indian Affairs John Collier also recognized her work and asked her to give workshops for other Indian Office teachers.

In this Indigenous literacy effort, it is important not to forget the role of library media centers, which are ideally the heart of a school. Students learn about different kinds of writing by reading different kinds of writing. They develop reading fluency by reading a lot and writing fluency by writing a lot. The availability of interesting reading material in school classrooms and libraries, as well as encouragement by teachers and librarians to make use of that material, is critical for the academic success of students. Encouraging literacy should include some time at school for students to read books and other reading material that they select from the library, without any pressure to write reports or do other related assignments. Students need a chance to *enjoy* reading, because only when they enjoy reading will they read enough to get the practice they need to become fluent readers.

Ironically, the insights gained by Ann Nolan Clark, Mike Rose, Polingaysi Qöyawayma, T. D. Allen, Mick Fedullo, and many other teachers who have actually worked with Indigenous and other students are being lost in the unsuccessful efforts under 2001's No Child Left Behind Act to attempt to close the achievement gap between Indigenous and other ethnic minority students and "white" students by using teaching methods based on "scientific" educational studies. These studies did not focus on Indigenous students and too often ignored the role of motivation in student success. Volumes edited by Richard J. Meyer and Kathryn F. Whitmore, *Reclaiming Reading* (2011) and *Reclaiming Writing* (2014), describe what is going on in the United States and elsewhere as "readicide" and "writicide" (2014, 246): the killing of the love and joy of reading and writing as a result of government curricular mandates and the promotion of scripted commercial programs and high stakes testing. They and their contributors find that the No Child Left Behind Act of 2001, the Obama administration's Race to the Top initiative, and new "Common Core" standards repress students' voice and choice. In contrast, they support a child-centered, progressive, humanistic view of education with many examples that showcase student uniqueness and creativity. Writing is seen as a social activity, and the authors discuss the tensions between top-down curricular demands and teachers helping children recognize and build on their talents and interests, balancing writing inventions and conventions. Meyer and Whitmore view learning to write as "an act of identity" (2014, 24) and conclude, "Reclaiming writing means understanding ourselves and honoring our relationships with our students by listening and making decisions about how to create spaces for the dynamic lives of writers" (249).

WHAT MAKES READERS AND WRITERS PROFICIENT AND ENGAGED?

Just as lots of practice helps produce good basketball players, children need to read a lot in order to become good readers. Basketball coaching and teaching students to read are important, but it is the practice of shooting hoops or reading books, magazines, and other materials that develops great players and proficient readers. Stephen Krashen (2004) documents how reading a lot helps develop fluency and a large vocabulary and how important it is for communities and schools to support libraries, especially in low-income communities where families do not have the money to buy many books. The U.S. Department of Education's 2000 *National Report Card on Reading* found that fourth graders who are better readers watched less television, read more for fun, talked more about reading with family and friends, and had more books, magazines, and newspapers in their homes. In research that surveyed twenty-seven countries, Evans, Kelley, Sikora and Treiman found that "children growing up in homes with many books get 3 years more schooling than children from bookless homes, independent of their parent's education, occupation, and [social] class" (2010, 171).

Book abundance, the easy access to many affordable culturally and linguistically appropriate books, can be compared to food abundance. One provides food for the body and the other food for the mind. The emphasis that families, communities, and cultures put on reading will influence how much effort children put into reading. Teachers, especially at the elementary level, need large classroom libraries with material on a variety of topics and at a variety of grade levels to give their students choices about what they will read, while schools need large libraries that often, in isolated rural areas, must also serve the whole community because of the lack of public libraries. Oglala Sioux educator and National Indian Education Association Lifetime Achievement Award winner Sandra Fox writes, "reading to children is the single most important activity that parents can provide to help their children succeed in school" (2000, 3) and recommends that teachers: (1) "Use reading materials that relate to children's lives, to help them understand that literature is experience written down and that it is interesting to read"; (2) "Strengthen and expand children's language abilities by providing them many opportunities to have new experiences, to learn new words, and to practice oral language in English and in their Native language" (2000, 7). Children who are encouraged to read and have more access to reading material they find interesting will develop larger vocabularies, comprehend what they read better, have better mastery of complex sentences, and have improved spelling and writing (Krashen 2004; Moss and Young 2010).

Dr. Lori Arviso Alvord, the first Navajo woman surgeon and an associate dean at the University of Arizona College of Medicine, noted the importance of becoming a good reader in her 1999 autobiography, *The Scalpel and the Silver Bear*. Alvord attended the public high school at Crownpoint in the Navajo Nation where, she recalls, "I made good grades . . . but . . . received a very marginal education. I had a few good teachers, but teachers were difficult to recruit to our schools and they often didn't stay long. Funding was inadequate. I spent many hours in classrooms where, I now see, very little was being taught" (1999, 25–26). What saved her later in college was her "strong reading background." She writes, "I read my way through the tiny local library and the vans that came to our community from the Books on Wheels program." Encouraged by her parents "to read and dream," she was even able to get out of chores by reading (1999, 9).

EXPERIENCE IGNORED BY NCLB AND THE NATIONAL READING PANEL

In the United States, the No Child Left Behind Act (NCLB) of 2001 has been an unsuccessful attempt to close the achievement gap between mainstream "white" students and black, Hispanic, and American Indian students through increased testing of students and by penalizing schools that did not bring up the test scores of ethnic minority students (see, e. g., Meier and Wood 2004). NCLB's "Reading First" provisions rightly recognize that students who read well tend to do well in school and in life and were largely based on a review of research published in 2000 by the National Reading Panel, which was authorized by the U.S. Congress. However, this panel's extensive review of research ignored many of the recommendations in the National Research Council's review of research published in *How People Learn* (2000) and did not look at the issue of student motivation and looked only at experimental studies, none of which focused on Indigenous students. The panel did not look at any ethnographic studies in which researchers had actually gone into classrooms and observed the interactions between teachers, Indigenous students, and reading curriculum. The Department of Education demanded that only instructional programs validated by "Scientifically Based Reading Research" could receive NCLB funding. Who could be against that? However, this faith in science does not take into account the difficulties encountered in doing research in classrooms and the fact that Indigenous students might not respond in the same way to an instructional program as non-Indigenous students (Reyhner 2014). In fact, under NCLB and Reading First, American Indian and Alaska Native 4th grade reading scores actually decreased between 2005 and 2011, while other students' reading scores increased (NCES 2012, 2).

The National Reading Panel (NRP) strongly emphasized the importance of phonemic awareness despite the fact that many words in the English language do not follow commonly taught phonetic rules. Many "English" words are borrowed from other languages and can retain some of their foreign pronunciation. Observing an overemphasis on phonics, Luther Standing Bear, who became a teacher at the end of the nineteenth century, wrote: "The Indian children should have been taught how to translate the Sioux tongue into English properly; but the English teachers only taught them the English language, like a bunch of parrots. While they could read [meaning pronounce] all the words placed before them, they did not know the proper use of them; their meaning was a puzzle" (1928, 239).

An example of current educational malpractice being enforced under NCLB is the use the Dynamic Indicators of Basic Early Literacy Skills (DIBELS). For all practical purposes, recipients of Department of Education NCLB Reading First Grants are being required to use DIBELS. Author and reading specialists Michael Pressley of Michigan State University noted that DIBELS grade 3 level oral reading test only predicts 20 percent of the variance on more comprehensive reading tests and thus, while being quick to administer, it is a very poor measure of students' reading comprehension. Even worse, its oral reading measure is one of "word-calling" (pronouncing nonsense words as fast as possible) rather than comprehension. By ignoring the importance of student motivation and overemphasizing phonics, the Reading First provisions of NCLB have, unfortunately, moved teachers back toward the "parroting," drill and kill type teaching that Hopi educator Polingaysi Qöyawayma warned against in her autobiography, *No Turning Back* (1964).

Another glaring omission in the NRP's research review was of the lack of attention to the influence of motivation on academic success. The importance of student interest and engagement is highlighted by Bridgeland, DiIulio and Morison (2006), who found that almost half of high school dropouts said they left because classes were boring and over two-thirds said they were not motivated to work hard in school. In contrast, studies of effective primary classrooms found them to be "massively motivating" with teachers who are "exceptionally skilled at matching their teaching to the needs of individual students" (Allington 2002, 78).

Research by Peshkin (1997) and Ogbu (2003) supports the importance of student motivation and engagement. Peshkin's study of an American Indian high school in New Mexico found ambivalence toward schooling among both students and their families, and Ogbu found a similar "academic disengagement" among black students and their families in an affluent Ohio suburb. Ethnic minorities with highly positive attitudes toward schooling, such as many Asian Americans, perform on average very well in school, while students with ambivalent or oppositional feelings [because school is viewed as a place for cultural assimilation and "acting white" (Fordham and Ogbu 1986)] perform poorly. Schools with strong bilingual and bicultural programs that serve Native students have had considerable success overcoming negative attitudes produced by assimilationist, English-only schooling (Research Agenda 2003; Reyhner 2001b).

The NRP "did not touch on early learning and home support for literacy, matters which many experts believe are the critical determinants of schools' success or failure" (Yatvin 2000, 2). The questions that the NRP chose to address in its research review had a phonics orientation to reading instruction. However, it concluded that "phonics instruction produces the biggest impact on growth in reading when it begins in kindergarten or 1st grade before children have learned to read independently" and it "failed to exert a significant impact on the reading performance of low-achieving readers in 2nd through 6th grades" (NRP 2000, 2-93–94). The NRP also noted that "it is important to emphasize that systematic phonics instruction should be integrated with other reading instruction to create a balanced reading program. Phonics instruction is never a total reading program. . . . Phonics should not become the dominant component in a reading program, neither in amount of time devoted to it nor in the significance attached" (2-97). The NRP found that researchers had not paid attention to motivational factors for both students and teachers and that there was "common agreement that fluency develops from reading practice" (3-1). This emphasis on a "balanced approach" to teaching reading in the full NRP report was lost in both the official published report summary and in implementation of NCLB's Reading First provisions (Garan 2002). Educational psychologist Gerald Coles made a point-by-point rebuttal to the NRP's emphasis on phonics, calling it "harmful because it falsely holds out the promise of a simple, 'magic bullet' solution to the literacy failure of millions of children, especially those who are poor, while at the same time discouraging social policy attention to forces both in and out of schools that influence literacy outcomes" (2000, xvii). Allington (2002) points out there is little scientific evidence to show that students who do well with phonics in the primary grades will transition in the upper elementary grades into fluent readers with good reading comprehension.

The popular Success for All and Reading Recovery programs show some research support, but with all their research backing, they have been tried and dropped by schools in Indian Country and elsewhere (Pogrow 2000). Ironically, when the U.S. Department of Education's What Works Clearinghouse released its report on beginning reading intervention programs in 2007, of 24 programs with some research backing, only Reading Recovery was found to have positive or potentially positive effects in all areas reviewed: alphabetics, fluency, comprehension, and general reading achievement (What Works Clearinghouse 2007) and "none of the most popular commercial reading programs on the market had sufficiently rigorous studies to be included in the review by the clearinghouse" (Manzo 2007). Again, however, the research that was reviewed did not focus on Indigenous students. The Clearinghouse listed 129 programs that lacked scientific evidence to support their efficacy, including Direct Instruction/DISTAR, Direct Instruction/SRA, Hooked on Phonics, Saxon Phonics, and other popular programs.

There are few long-term well-designed research studies of Indigenous education. One of the best was the Kamehameha Early Education Program (Project KEEP) that substantiated the importance of understanding and using minority cultures in schools. Project KEEP was set up to find ways to improve the educational attainment of native Hawaiian children. Even though native Hawaiian children come to school speaking only English, they have done poorly in school. Initially, a phonics-oriented program was tried, but it failed to bring students up to the level of the non-Hawaiian students. After an ethnographic study of the students' homes, a culturally compatible curriculum was designed that emphasized reading comprehension, with the result that the average student reading score rose from the twenty-seventh percentile to above the fiftieth (Jordan 1984).

With KEEP, classroom organization was changed from large group to small group instruction, which emphasized active student participation in learning, including peer tutoring and a monitoring of student progress through criterion-referenced tests. Teachers worked with small groups of students in reading lessons that began by relating the reading material to the students' prior experiences. The reading lessons then focused on comprehension of the material read, and they were followed up with activities that related the material back to the students' lives. Students who were not receiving direct instruction from the teacher worked in small groups at learning centers (Jordan 1984: Tharp 1982).

ADVICE FOR TEACHERS

Because it can be effective to treat a child's beginning reading vocabulary as "sight words" (words to be memorized rather than sounded out) does not mean that students don't need to learn the relationship between the sounds of a language and its writing system (except for idiographic writing systems such as the one used in China). But even for phonically regular words, local "rez" (reservation) dialects may well pronounce a word differently than the "correct" way given in the textbook.

For words that follow common phonic rules, the rules need to be taught, but teachers will have more success using vocabulary words that students will know the meaning of once they sound the word out, in contrast to using whatever "canned" vocabulary list a reading textbook happens to include. One can start with something like the beginning sounds of the names of the students in a class and play with changing those sounds so every student's name starts with a different sound each day (e.g., Olin becomes Polin on Monday, Molin on Tuesday, Golin on Wednesday, etc.). Or teachers can do an activity with students, have them talk about it, and then write down what they say—their own stories—and use that for the reading lesson, which is called the "language experience" approach. The final part of any reading lesson needs to go beyond phonic and other activities and focus on comprehension, because getting the meaning from text is what reading is all about.

As Reyhner's 1992 research review done for the U.S. Secretary of Education's Indian Nations at Risk Task Force found, dropouts view school as boring and unrelated to their lives and they perceive teachers as uncaring—more interested in the subject they teach than the lives of their students (1992a, 1992b). In *Education and Language Restoration* (2006), Reyhner writes about his son Tsosie's chemistry teacher, Mansel Nelson, at Tuba City High School in the Navajo Nation. Mansel began to rethink the way he taught soon after arriving in Tuba City after his best chemistry student asked him "Why are we learning chemistry?" He began thinking of ways to make chemistry relevant to the lives of his Navajo students. He started incorporating local community issues and challenges—issues surrounding water quality, diabetes, and uranium mining—and teaching chemistry concepts around them. Like Ashton-Warner with her key words, Nelson sought to connect the "foreign" content of the mainstream curriculum to actual concerns of his students and their community. His students talked, read, and wrote about these concerns in Navajo and English, and by studying these issues they prepared themselves for sovereignty—taking control over their own lives and the life of their community.

Students need to read well to do well in advanced mathematics and science classes, as well as in language and literature classes, and to read well students need more than instruction. Whether learning basketball or reading, practice is vital: children need to read a lot in order to become better readers. Series books like *The Lord of the Rings* trilogy and Harry Potter books can provide students the practice they need to become fluent readers. They will also learn how much more is in these books than in the movies that are made from them. Besides popular books like the Harry Potter series, there are many excellent books by and about Indigenous people that students can read, especially if they are available in school libraries. Appendix A gives sources of further information on Indigenous children's books and includes a short list of children's literature written by Indigenous authors that are recommended by Choctaw author Tim Tingle.

THE RESPONSIVE TEACHER

Teachers need to remember it is important to work *with* students rather than just making students work. Fidelity to students is at least as important as fidelity to a curriculum. The teachers' role includes becoming guides and facilitators, rather than just authoritative sources of knowledge or unreflective disseminators of textbook material. Responsive teachers seek to understand the challenges faced by their students out of school, as well as in school, and view their job as requiring that they go beyond the classroom to encourage literacy in the home and community. Family literacy supports school literacy. Programs such as Reading Is FUNdamental (www.rif.org/), which provides free books for children to take home, encourage reading in the home. On the Navajo Nation in Chinle, Arizona, parents have contracted with responsive teachers to listen to their children read at home. Interviewing over one hundred Indigenous and non-Native teachers of Indigenous students, Cleary and Peacock (1998) found that too much emphasis on book reports and accuracy in reading and writing can discourage and even create resistance in students. To become good writers students need to do more than fill in the blanks on often boring classroom worksheets. They need to write a lot, and their writing should help students learn to reason and process information better about things that are important to them and their communities.

Students who are extrinsically motivated to learn at school (usually by their families) and who know the language and culture of the teacher and the textbook can survive academically in the classroom of a nonresponsive teacher. Nonresponsive teachers assume that they know what children need to learn and are not troubled by their students' feelings or their prior knowledge about course content. Responsive teachers are concerned about their relationship with their students, and these teachers are especially important when working with students of a cultural or language minority, since they are willing to shape the curriculum to meet their students' backgrounds and needs (Bishop, Ladwig, and Berryman 2014). Responsive teachers are more likely to adapt curriculum based on discussions with students, to focus lessons on topics meaningful to the students, and to allow students to practice language and thinking skills in real interactive situations. By having group discussions and allowing students to talk during group work, these teachers promote students to use language and help them develop communicative competency.

Scripted curriculum materials such as Direct Instruction System for Teaching Arithmetic and Reading (DISTAR) and the teaching guides for many popular basal reading series tell the teacher what questions to ask and provide the "right" responses expected of the students, but students with widely different backgrounds from most Americans can respond very differently to questions. For example, Kindergarten students from the Navajo Reservation were asked to match an animal to a pond of water. Two of the animals were a cow and a duck. Most Navajo students matched the cow with the pond rather than picking the "right" answer, the duck, because they usually do not see ducks swimming in local ponds but they do see cows gathered around them. In another Navajo community, some students matched an umbrella with the sun rather than with rain because when grandmother is out herding sheep, she shields herself from the sun with an umbrella to keep from getting sunburned. These students were marked as getting the question wrong. In a small town north of Flagstaff, Arizona, Navajo students matched a boat to a road, rather than a lake, because looking out their classroom window they saw boats being pulled by cars to a lake many miles up the road. A teacher from Alaska gave a similar example. One test question asked, "Which of these would most likely take you to the hospital if you got hurt?" and listed as possible answers an ambulance, a boat, a bicycle, or an airplane (Platt 2004). The "right" answer for most students in the U.S. is of course an ambulance, but in Alaska Native villages there are no highways, and if you are injured, you are taken to the hospital in an airplane. Indigenous students in the Alaskan arctic face many challenges when trying to understand things in their textbooks, having never seen firsthand a lawn mower, a forest, or many of the other things we assume children have seen and experienced.

Scripted teaching guides inhibit real dialogue between teacher and student—the kind of dialogue that was extremely effective in the Kamehameha Early Education Program—that can alert teachers to why students may be having difficulties understanding what they read. Reliance on these scripted materials also implicitly limits the teacher's discussion of how a story's words, characters, and situations are similar to or different from those of the children's native language, culture, and experiences.

The not so subtle message to the student of nonresponsive teachers is that the school's curriculum is more important than the students and that the culture of the school is more important than that of the home. Students are being educated to live in the dominant culture even though, in reality, they often live as adults in an environment closer to their Indigenous culture than the dominant culture. Also, these students are ill prepared by nonresponsive teachers to participate in a democratic society, as they learn in school to listen to the directions of authority figures and to memorize information without expressing their personal opinions or reflecting on what they are learning.

WHAT NEEDS TO BE DONE

For students who do not come to school speaking English or who are dominant in their Indigenous language, schools need a bilingual program that develops their Native language proficiency and includes an ESL program that develops their English speaking and reading proficiency. For Native students who are not fluent speakers of their tribal language, Native language revitalization programs have helped students strengthen their traditional values and build a strong positive sense of identity (see chapter 10, this volume). Where possible, a reading program that teaches students to read in their Native language while they are learning English can lead to increased English language reading skills (Francis and Reyhner 2002).

Despite the stated aim of the NCLB, Race to the Top, and Common Core initiatives in the United States to improve the academic performance of all children, there are signs that the implementation of these efforts increase dropout rates (see Figure 1), and this needs to be closely monitored.

With regard to the Reading First program, there is evidence that educational approaches in the 1970s that claimed the backing of scientific research and focused on teaching isolated reading "skills" are gaining renewed popularity. Students are being asked to pronounce lists of words from commercial reading programs, including many words that have no meaning for them. In the United States, Bureau of Indian Education test scores show Indian students performing worst on subtests of comprehension and vocabulary but performing better in phonics. As Sweet points out, it is "estimated that for most children, about 100 hours of reading instruction that is solidly based on the findings of research, is sufficient" to teach students to read (2004, 36). The phonics instruction called for by Reading First needs to be contextualized in meaningful ways, utilizing language that students actually use, rather than word lists and decodable texts comprised of words chosen for their sounds rather than their meaning.

Reading First tends to promote whole-class instruction, which assumes that all students are at the same level, and a lot of time is being spent on teaching phonics to the detriment of students reading for meaning. It is a disconcerting irony that the same mistaken approach was used over a century ago with American Indian students who were required to sound out reading passages "perfectly" with no idea of the meaning of what they were reading (Reyhner and Eder 2004). A research review by August, Goldenberg, and Rueda notes, "studies suggest that American Indian and Native Hawaiian children benefit from explicit phonics instruction . . . when it occurs in the context of meaningful material" (2006, 34).

Efforts that have involved teaching students English and academic subjects *in addition* rather than as a *replacement to* their Native language and culture have had success in improving the academic performance of Indigenous students in the United States and other countries. In Hawai'i, a pre-K through university language immersion program has been developed in the past two decades that is patterned after a similar effort by the Māori in New Zealand. The Hawaiian immersion schools do not introduce English in the classroom until the fifth grade, but the students come to school speaking English and use it outside of school. Students learn mathematics and other academic subjects and the use of computers in the Hawaiian language (Reyhner 2006c). Another culturally sensitive program that provided success for Indian students was the Rough Rock English-Navajo Language Arts Program (McCarty and Dick 2003; McCarty 2002; Dick, Estell and McCarty 1994).

The report of a national colloquium on improving academic performance among American Indian, Alaska Native, and Native Hawaiian students published in 2006 in the *Journal of American Indian Education* indicates the need for culturally and linguistically appropriate education for Native students, including their reading instruction (McCardle and Demmert 2006). An example of a promising program is the "Northwest Native American Reading

Curriculum," a supplemental reading program developed with input from tribal experts that builds on the experiential and cultural backgrounds of Indian students and incorporates teaching strategies from both general research on reading and specific research focusing on Native students (Costantino and Hurtado 2006).

A HERITAGE READING PROGRAM FOR INDIGENOUS STUDENTS

Indigenous students need a "heritage reading program." Students from minority cultures should first be introduced to their own cultural heritage and then the Western European heritage on which many modern democratic governments are based. A global, multicultural curriculum should be built on the foundation of the students' family and national (dominant) cultural knowledge. Teachers at the classroom level are in a position to get to know their students' backgrounds and to encourage their school librarians, administrators, and boards to acquire supplemental literature appropriate to the students' backgrounds. Under the capitalist economic system such literature will only be produced in large quantities if a market is created through such requests.

Teachers can model learning to their students by becoming familiar, through ethnographic literature and home visits, with their students' home cultures. Then they can adapt their teaching methods through trial and error to see what kinds and forms of classroom activities motivate their students to become literate. Teachers need to learn as much as they can about the particular community in which they work. Taking an interest in their students' lives and building relationships can, in itself, make a difference in students' academic performance (Bishop, Ladwig, and Berryman 2014; Kleinfeld 1979). When reading material about the community is not available, students can produce their own reading material through the language experience approach to reading (Allen and Allen 1982).

Schools need to have a variety of reading material from which students, parents, and teachers can select so students can find out the variety of information and entertainment that is available through reading. As Colin Scott wrote over a century ago, "If the schools do no more for reading than to teach people to read, it may be said paradoxically that they are not even teaching them to read" (1908, 212–13). Students who find in school that reading is boring and uninteresting learn to avoid reading, and they never get the practice needed to become fluent readers.

Reading textbooks need to be supplemented through classroom libraries. These libraries should have books and other reading materials available at various skill levels and on different topics (fiction and nonfiction), so students can select books and magazines that interest them. Minority group students need stories that relate to their lives, as well as stories through which they can learn about the outside world. Stephen Krashen (2004) examined ten studies that compared students using sustained silent reading (SSR), as part or all of their reading programs, with students not receiving SSR. He found that students who practice and refine their reading skills using self-selected, free reading in SSR programs did as well or better on tests of reading comprehension than students receiving no SSR in their reading program in eight out of the ten studies, including one study in which SSR was the exclusive language arts program.

Responsive teachers work to produce a curriculum suited to the needs of their students. Arthur Gates indicated a half-century ago that basal reading textbooks should be only a "small fraction" of the total reading program (1962, 445). Peter Winograd has written, "basal readers are least effective when they are used as the total reading program and children spend all of their allocated instructional time in the basals program, reading selections and completing various exercises" (1989, 1). Goodman et al. (1988) thoroughly investigated the publisher's claims about basal readers and gave a brief overview of the promising alternatives to basal readers being practiced in the U.S. and elsewhere. In 2012 the U.S. Department of Education's What Works Clearinghouse substantiated the work of Goodman and his colleagues.

It is up to the teacher to introduce students to literature beyond the bits and pieces that appear in basal readers. Children from the dominant culture can often learn to read well in spite of the school, because their parents recognize the need for providing reading material in the home and encourage their children to utilize public and school libraries. For Indigenous students, whose parents may be less familiar with books and libraries, the teachers' role in providing interesting literature for their students is especially critical if the students are to learn to read fluently and succeed in school.

If Indigenous students are to become productive members of their communities, informed citizens, and problem solvers for the future, they need to start reading with meaningful, realistic literature that they can think about and discuss. Reading textbooks can, at best, only provide an appetizer to encourage students to explore classroom, school, and community libraries, as well as bookstores. If meaningful and interesting stories are too difficult for beginning readers to read, then teachers need to read them aloud to their students.

An approach to reading that emphasizes letting students choose from a variety of literature and integrating reading, writing, listening, and speaking along with the teaching of social studies, science, and other subjects—proved particularly effective with Indigenous students. King (1990) presents a Bureau of Indian Affairs (BIA) school's ten years of experience with Whole Language, noting that not buying basal reading textbooks frees up money for buying children's books. A special BIA report described how "whole language maximizes the learning experience of each student-participant by building upon the student's knowledge gained outside the classroom" at the Chuska and Dil-con Boarding Schools (Report 1988, 45).

Four things are needed to help Indigenous and other students learn to read better. First, there need to be efforts to involve family members in reading to preschool children and demonstrating by their actions that they embrace literacy as an important part of life (Anderson et al. 1985). Second, except for the few students who enter kindergarten already knowing how to read, schools need a strong program of beginning reading instruction that teaches the alphabet, promotes phonemic awareness, promotes the application of phonic rules that have broad utility and that fit students' home language (including Indigenous dialects of national languages like English), and teaches high-frequency sight words that do not follow common phonic rules. Teachers need to make sure through language experience or other instruction that the words students are asked to read/decode are in their oral vocabulary. Third, students need frequent opportunities, in and out of school, to read interesting books, magazines, and newspapers that reflect their own experiential/cultural background, as well as mainstream "classic" and contemporary works of children's literature in order to get the practice they need to become fluent readers (Krashen 2004). Fourth, teachers need ongoing professional development to help them tailor their teaching to individual student needs (Allington 2002). It is critical that the process of teaching reading does not take the joy out of reading by making reading instruction a matter of completing worksheets, decoding stories that students cannot relate to or find boring, and taking tests.

Educators need to realize that commercial reading programs commonly used in schools tend to be one-size-fits-all approaches targeted toward a "standard" dialect of English and a white, middle-class knowledge of the world that Indigenous students often do not share. This approach violates their human rights as outlined in repeated United Nations declarations, including its 2007 Declaration on the Rights of Indigenous Peoples. Without adaptation or supplementation by teachers, these programs can turn off American Indian and other students to reading because the vocabulary and stories do not relate to their lives (Cleary 2008).

4

Mathematics

DAVID W. SANDERS

My views regarding the teaching of mathematics are heavily influenced by my undergraduate mathematics education, my pre-service secondary mathematics teacher education, and my time as a high school mathematics teacher at Chinle High School in the Navajo Nation. My experience learning mathematics as an undergraduate mathematics student mirrored in large part my learning experience as a high school math student. It was centered on direct instruction and took a predictable format. Davis (1996) aptly describes this format: "One need only step inside a typical mathematics classroom and make note of the teacher's position at the head of the room, the program of studies' place in the center of his or her desk, and the standardized textbooks located in front of each learner. Student authority and self-image are not priorities in today's math class" (86).

My time as a student in a pre-service teacher education program was different. I was introduced to other ways of describing mathematics and taught to look at it from a learning theory perspective. This caused my orientation to mathematics to shift from content to students. Once I received my secondary mathematics teaching license and became *the* teacher in a mathematics classroom, my view of teaching mathematics continued to evolve. My pedagogy became an amalgamation of direct instruction and the constructivist-influenced teaching techniques I had learned in my teacher education program. As my time as a teacher progressed, I came to understand that the art of teaching in real classroom situations (which cannot be rehearsed), required that I continually change and adapt my teaching to the constantly changing dynamics of individual classrooms and classrooms of individual learners.

As I look back on the years I learned to teach math as a student, then a teacher, and now as an educational researcher, I see many factors I consider important to contemplate and understand in order to succeed in teaching mathematics to Indigenous students. This understanding begins with an exploration of learning theory, especially the constructivist view of learning, since it has had the largest impact on the teaching of mathematics since the 1990s. It is important to know the basis of constructivist learning theory, its view of knowledge, and the way it is integrated into Indigenous mathematics pedagogy. After looking at learning theory, familiarization with pedagogy and curriculum becomes important, since both are developed in response to a teacher's view of knowledge and how students learn. "Beliefs about knowledge, then, inform, justify, and sustain our practices of education" (Gergen 1995, 17).

Finally, in discussing teaching Indigenous students' mathematics, it is important to know which ideas for mathematics curriculum and pedagogy have actually been explored in Indigenous communities. Thus, a look at culturally based pedagogy and culturally based curriculum that has been influenced by research in Indigenous communities and classrooms is essential (Reyhner and Singh 2013). Knowledge of research that investigates teaching mathematics in Indigenous schools is especially important for future math teachers of Indigenous students, because this research provides suggestions and tested teaching practices that have proven to be effective.

It is important to understand that in order to successfully teach mathematics to Indigenous students, a teacher must be able to deftly weave together learning theory, pedagogical practices, mathematical content, Indigenous cultural knowledge, community influence, school structure, and an awareness of each individual student. This is more an art than a science, because it depends in large part upon creating trusting relationships between teachers and students. This approach also centers on the fact that teachers must lose themselves in the process and trust that their students have the ability to learn. Becoming a successful math teacher for Indigenous students takes time, dedication, experience, creativity, and a willingness to learn.

SOME INFLUENTIAL LEARNING THEORIES IN MATHEMATICS EDUCATION

At least three major learning theories are associated with the evolving field of mathematics education: behaviorism, constructivism, and social constructionism. Each theory has distinct viewpoints regarding the nature of knowledge and learning and each emphasizes different factors in the learning process. These factors, in turn, suggest and promote different methods for teaching mathematics. Teaching practices promoted by these theories have been adapted and integrated into Indigenous pedagogy, and some of these teaching practices, coupled with culturally based curriculum and local Indigenous guidance, have been shown to be effective in helping Indigenous students learn mathematics well.

Behaviorism

For the behaviorist, knowledge is fixed. It is something that can be grasped. It is a thing. Consequently, knowledge is something that can be transferred (given) from a knower to a learner. Behaviorist learning theory assumes an objective reality wherein correct knowledge is the conception that best matches reality. "In this tradition, knowledge should represent a real world that is thought of as existing, separate and independent of the knower; and this knowledge should be considered true only if it correctly reflects that independent world" (von Glasersfeld 1995, 6).

Because there is separation between the knower and the environment and because behaviorism believes that truth exists independent of the knower, for the behaviorist learning involves being able to acquire, through transmission, bits of knowledge, built in a sequential manner until all aspects of a subject have been received. The behaviorist view of learning holds that repetition and drill can lead to a full understanding and increased retention of the concept/material being presented. This theory also assumes that an authority, specifically the one who knows, can impart knowledge to others. Behaviorist learning theorists also believe that positive and negative reinforcements, if used appropriately, will lead to desired learning outcomes.

Behaviorism has had the most influence on the way mathematics is taught. At the beginning of this chapter I described how I learned mathematics as a high school and college student, and I labeled the process of teaching that was used during my years as a student as "direct instruction." Direct instruction includes taking mathematical concepts and breaking them down into digestible bits of information. These bits are presented in a sequential manner in such a way that by the end of the teaching sequence, the concept itself is fully explored ("covered"). It is a very linear presentation. The process of teaching in the behaviorist view is primarily one of telling: that is, lecturing to students. The assumption is that teachers and textbooks are the sole authority on the subject in the classroom; it is the teacher who decides what is to be taught and how it is to be taught, and the teacher who determines the learning outcomes. It is the responsibility of the students to memorize the problem solving processes learned and to repeat them back to the teacher, essentially showing the teacher what was shown to them as learners. Their knowledge, or what they have learned, is then judged accordingly. This judgment is based on the changes in beliefs that have occurred by the end of the learning process in relation to the learners' conceptions at the beginning. Fosnot and Dolk (2005) summarize the behaviorist approach:

> Traditionally mathematics has been perceived as a ready-made discipline to be handed down by a teacher skilled in the art of transmitting, or explaining, clearly, In the classrooms most of us have attended, teachers stood at the chalkboard and explained fractions as shaded parts of a whole. They taught rules for making common denominators. They demonstrated procedures for operations with fractions, like invert and multiply, and students practiced them over and over. . . .

But the premise was always the same. The teacher was the fountain of wisdom who understood that mathematics was a discipline thought to comprise facts, concepts, formulas, and algorithms and this discipline could be transmitted, explained, practiced, and learned if teachers were well versed in it and learners were diligent. Most students in mathematics classrooms did not see mathematics as creative but instead as something to be explained by their teacher, then practiced and applied. One might call this traditional approach "school mathematics." (180–81)

Constructivism

Constructivist learning theory shares the behaviorist view of the separation of a learner from the environment: there is an "I" and there is an "other." However, this is about all the theories have in common. Constructivists deny the existence of an objective reality. They believe that knowledge is culturally shaped and that each individual can only make sense of the world through the lens of their own subjectivity. Thus, there is no mapping of an objective world within the mind to match the world that surrounds the individual to help someone determine whether or not they "know" something. Knowledge is not viewed as a fixed entity, but as a process. "The process of constructing meaning is the process of learning. We create our knowledge; we did not discover it" (Fosnot and Dolk 2005, 181). There is no "knowledge," only ways of knowing. "Knowing is an adaptive activity. This means that one should think about knowledge as a kind of compendium of concepts and actions that one has found to be successful, given the purposes one has in mind" (von Glasersfeld 1995, 7). Since there is no objective truth, knowledge cannot be *correct,* it can only be *viable.* In order for knowledge to be viable, it has to be put forth, shared, examined, discussed and, most importantly, useful in a given context. Constructivists are not concerned about what a real world might be and how this is represented in the mind. Their concern is how individuals are able to function in a subjective existence through adaptation and changes that best fit them for different situations. As Davis (1996) puts it:

> Briefly, constructivist *knowing* (a term that is used in contrast to "knowledge," in part to emphasize the dynamic nature of one's conceptualizations) is recast as "a search for fitting ways of behaving and thinking" . . . constructivists consider knowledge to be a human construction that is to be evaluated according to its fit with the world of human experience. "Representation" is thus redefined by constructivists as "the process of transforming the content of consciousness into a public forum so that they [ideas] can be stabilized, inspected, edited, and shared by others. It is thus that the criterion of *truth* (in the

modern sense of matching with an objective reality) is abandoned in favor of a requirement of *viability*. (183, emphasis in original)

Thus, constructivists view knowledge as something that is individually constructed, through questioning and hypothesis making, and presented to others for discussion, for experimentation, and for determination of its usefulness and viability.

For the constructivist, learning is not a goal but a process of development: "Learning *is* development" (Fosnot and Perry 2005, 33). It is a "process of experiencing and making sense of that experience" (Davis 1996, 232). Constructivism posits that the independent learner builds knowledge by actively constructing it. Because knowledge is a "process," it is never "final," rather it is continually shaped and informed. Knowledge adapts to outside stimuli. These stimuli include conversations with others and interactions with the environment that force learners to deal with concepts that do not match their own. This process is important because it makes learners come to terms with their own thinking about those outside conceptions. "Reflective abstraction is the driving force of learning" (Fosnot and Perry 2005, 34). A key component of this theory of learning is the need for learners to reconcile concepts that do not fit their own views:

> Learning from this perspective is viewed as a self-regulatory process of struggling with the conflict between existing personal models of the world and discrepant new insights, constructing new representations and models of reality as a human meaning-making venture with culturally developed tools and symbols and further negotiating such meaning through cooperative social activity, discourse and debate in communities of practice. (Fosnot 2005, ix)

This process of learning includes a relationship between the learner and others who form a community of practice. Together they shape, build, and influence the process of learning. The learners are the authority on any given subject matter, since it is they who determine whether or not what they have learned and put into practice is viable.

For the constructivist, then, learning is an individual act of constructing meaning, dependent on abstract reflection, which, in turn, is informed by others when shared and discussed. With the learner and the teacher, a community of practice is formed. Learning adjusts and adapts as new ideas and understandings conflict with what was held to be viable. In this conception, the key aspect of a learner is one who is an active participant in the learning process, not one who sits passively, receiving information.

As a pre-service teacher I was struck by the many stark differences between constructivist and behaviorist views on teaching. First and foremost in these differences is the constructivists' belief that conceptual knowledge cannot be transferred from teacher to student, thus they see the need to shift teaching methods to accommodate the way students perceive and talk about mathematics. Second, authority in the classroom shifts from the teacher to the students. This shift causes classroom dynamics to change, impacting discourse and student-teacher interactions. The teacher becomes a facilitator and guides students with questions aimed to prompt them to further investigation and discussion. This shift also moves teacher-student interactions away from the mold cast by the traditional direct-instruction transmission models of learning. Constructivism holds that part of the teacher's role is to let students take learning in the direction that arises naturally from their efforts and conversations. They ask the questions, they explore, and they discuss. The teacher also discusses with them and can present them with ideas that will, in turn, lead them to areas they had not considered or force them to reconsider the results of their outcomes. "Challenging, open-ended investigations in realistic, meaningful content need to be offered which allow learners to explore and generate many possibilities. . . . Contradictions . . . need to be illuminated, explored and discussed" (Fosnot and Perry 2005, 34).

Third, because constructivist teachers are diminishing their own influence in the learning process and giving the power, so to speak, to the students, they constitute, with the students, the community of learners (practitioners). It is the community of learners who determine the viability of the knowledge being presented. "The mathematics classroom was to become a community of inquiry, a problem-posing and problem-solving environment in which developing an approach to thinking about mathematical issues would be valued more highly than memorizing algorithms and using them to get right answers" (Schifter 2005, 85). In the math classroom this means discussing conjectures, thoughts, and outcomes as they relate to mathematics. Students in this learning environment are encouraged to explore, hypothesize, and attempt to come to solutions with others, as they try to make sense of their own struggles with mathematical content. In essence, a community of learners in a mathematics classroom tries to model how mathematic problems are solved and how they are created in the real world of mathematicians.

Finally, constructivists promote alternate modes of assessment as well, for it is through assessing students that they learn outcomes that guide teachers' efforts. Thus, assignments such as journal writing can also be used in math classrooms to determine students' understanding of math concepts. Students' writings about math concepts allow teachers to see what and how students are thinking about math. Using manipulatives (hands-on materials) provides another means of assessment. Manipulatives not only help students show visually what they are thinking (and help them assess their own knowledge in the process), but also allow them to demonstrate to the teacher how they construct their mathematical knowledge. "One might thus characterize 'constructivist teaching' as a process of making sense of the sense students are making (as opposed to trying to foster student sense-making . . .) founded as it is on the epistemological premise that learning has to do with the active and independent construction of meaning" (Davis 1996, 232).

Social Constructionism

Social constructionism offers a somewhat different perspective on knowledge than constructivist learning theory, though it shares the same disdain for the notion that knowledge "can be built up within the mind through dispassionate observation" (Gergen 1995, 27). For the social constructionist, first and foremost, knowledge is communal. In order for knowledge to be communal, it must rely on language as a medium through which the process of gaining knowledge occurs. Thus, social constructionism's focus is primarily on language as the medium and on the way language interactions function when knowledge is shared and examined. "To oversimplify the argument, the radical constructivist focuses on the individual act of construction on the learner, and the social constructionist focuses on the group conversation" (Richards 1995, 58–59). Social constructionists also view knowledge as a process, and they share the constructionist viewpoint on building knowledge through abstract examination, though the emphasis of social constructionism is really on the way the learning process occurs in social interactions. "Constructivists suggest that the subjective construction of knowledge occurs before social mediation, whereas social constructionists suggest that social mediation occurs before the subject's construction of knowledge . . . both recognize that individual and collective evolution are inextricably intertwining processes" (Davis 1996, 188).

Social constructionism grew from the work of Belarusian psychologist Lev Vygotsky and is especially concerned with his concept of the Zone of Proximal Development, "essentially a mental space between actual and potential cognitive functioning" (Gergen 1995, 25). This concept focuses on the social situations in which learning occurs, looking to the impact of social interaction as the driving force in constructing knowledge. It "places the human relationship in the foreground. . . . Thus the [social] constructionist is centrally concerned with such matters as negotiation, cooperation, conflict, rhetoric, ritual roles, social scenarios, and the like, but avoids psychological explanations of microsocial process" (Gergen 1995, 24–25).

Social constructionism shares the foundational learning premises that are found in constructivist thinking. It suggests that learning is an active process for individuals, but places more emphasis on influences from outside cultural factors than on inner abstraction. It also places the learner on equal footing with the teacher, thereby providing direction and contexts for study, in such a way that authority in the classroom is shared. This stance is also evident in the way learning becomes dependent on conversation between all involved in the learning, and teaching, process. Social constructivism shares the view that a teacher's role is one of facilitator and that learning is also essentially student-led and dependent on conversation and dialogue, as in the constructionist paradigm. Since language and conversation are seen as key components in the learning process, it is the responsibility of teachers to allow opportunities for students to talk and discuss topical matters and subsequently decide on the topics to be explored.

To that end, Gergen (1995) suggests four pedagogical practices that foster dialogue within the classroom: (1) Diffusion of authority, whereby students are more involved in the direction of the content and are an integral part of classroom conversations. In this way the classroom moves in directions seen as important in the eyes of the student; (2) The "vitalization of relationship" between students and teachers, which allows students' voices, honors their dialogue, and plays a key role in the types of relationships fostered in the classroom. "For the constructionist educator, the primary challenge is to enable students to participate in a range of conversations. In this case, the student's role shifts from object to be operated on to subject within relationships" (33–34); (3) The inclusion of relevant cultural content allows for "the generation of meaning in practice." This means that students should be encouraged to work with teachers to contextualize course content in areas that are both practical and relevant to students' lives (36); and (4) Generating meaning in practice will allow the breaking of boundaries, both between academic subjects and with the students' daily lives. What this essentially means is that students should be able to integrate mathematics across content areas. In doing so, they are more able to translate what they are learning to use in outside contexts.

Summary of Learning Theories

Behaviorism, constructivism, and social constructionism theories each hold varying views on the nature of knowledge and how humans learn. Each view of knowledge promotes certain teaching practices aimed at maximizing learning within their respective paradigms. Behaviorism has been the de facto learning theory used in the development of mathematics curriculum, and it has dictated the way teachers and students have interacted in the classroom with each other and to the math content of courses. It is a process that depends on the practice of teachers telling students the desired mathematical outcomes and clearly explaining the steps needed to reach those solutions. Behaviorist theory has been so influential that the teaching methods associated with it have been called the "traditional" approach to teaching math.

However, constructivists and social constructionists argue that behaviorism, as a learning theory, is inadequate. They promote a very different view of knowledge and of the learning process and offer an alternate approach to the mathematics classroom. The constructionist approach depends on dialogue between students and teachers and asks teachers to allow students to provide direction as to what will be learned. Since this process is dependent on dialogue, it pays heed to the importance of relationships between students, teachers, and content within the mathematics classroom. In this view, students are active participants in the construction of their own knowledge.

As we begin to discuss teaching methods influenced by research conducted in Indigenous communities, we should keep in mind the main pedagogical practices suggested by previously discussed learning theories. These practices include not only approaches to teaching content, but also examining the roles teachers and students play in the learning process:

1. What is the role of the teacher? Is the teacher the "all-knowing" authority in the classroom or a facilitator and guide?
2. Dialogue and conversation are important in the construction of knowledge. Who speaks and who controls the conversation and topics of conversation in the classroom? Are there opportunities in the classroom for students to talk, conjecture, and question?
3. What does the classroom environment look like? Is it made up of a community of learners? Is the teacher part of this community?
4. What are students' roles in the learning process? Are they active, engaged learners, or are they passive recipients of knowledge?
5. Are students learning mathematics or are they "doing" math problems? For example, is the process of "doing" mathematics, as practiced by mathematicians, being modeled and practiced in the classroom? Do students hypothesize, conjecture, and share their thoughts regarding mathematical content?
6. How do teachers inform their own teaching practices? Do students play a part in this? Do students write about the mathematical concepts they are learning? Do students use manipulatives to help construct and conceptualize their mathematical knowledge?
7. And finally, what contexts are used for teaching mathematics? Are they meaningful and related to the everyday experiences of students?

TEACHING MATHEMATICS TO INDIGENOUS STUDENTS

The inclusion of Indigenous cultures in mathematics classes did not occur until the mid-1980s with the influence of the emerging field of ethnomathematics (Closs 1986; Pinxten, van Dooren, and Soberon 1987). Culturally relevant pedagogical practices and culturally relevant curriculum co-emerged in the late 1980s and early 1990s with the pioneering work of Jerry Lipka and the

Ciulistet, a Yup'ik Eskimo teaching group in Alaska (Lipka 1989; Lipka 1991; Lipka 1994a, 1994b; Lipka et al. 1998). During this same time period, Hankes (1998) explored the correspondence between cognitively guided instruction (CGI) and the teaching practices of American Indian teachers in Wisconsin among the Oneidas.

Demmert and Towner (2003) expressed the need to rigorously test the impact and effectiveness of culturally relevant curriculum (often called culturally based education programs, or CBEs) on student academic performance. They were concerned with the fact that CBE programs and materials were being produced and argued to be important in Indigenous education while very few had been held up to the scrutiny of quantitative analysis: "The availability of quantitative research literature on culturally based education programs for Native American children is severely limited. Possible experimental or quasi-experimental research models appropriate for a national quasi-experimental and/or experimental study of Indigenous education are also in short supply" (iii). They wanted to know, definitively, if there was a direct relationship between CBE programs and Indigenous student academic success.

In the area of Indigenous mathematics teaching and curriculum, this question was answered with quantitative studies centering on the effectiveness of culturally based curriculum and culturally relevant pedagogy (Lipka and Adams 2004; Lipka et al. 2005a, 2005b, 2005c; McREL 2005; Rickard 2005; Webster et al. 2005; Sternberg et al. 2006; Lipka et al. 2007; Kagle 2007, Kisker et al. 2012). With the lone exception of the McREL (2005) study, the studies mentioned above center on the implementation and teaching of Jerry Lipka's curriculum, "Math in a Cultural Context" (MCC) (Lipka et al, 2005c). These studies, along with the early efforts of Lipka and his colleagues to develop a pedagogy based in Yup'ik culture, have proven successful in helping Alaska Native students gain a greater understanding of mathematical content. The analysis of Indigenous mathematical pedagogical practices that follows focuses on the descriptions of pedagogy offered by Lipka and his colleagues, because their work dominates the literature on Indigenous pedagogy in the mathematics classroom.

The Roots of Yup'ik Eskimo Pedagogy: The Ciulistet

The impetus for the study of Yup'ik culturally based curriculum, which eventually became Math in a Cultural Context (MCC), and the development of pedagogy that pertains to Yup'ik culture began with the Cross-Cultural Teacher Education Development Program (X-CED) based at the University of Alaska–Fairbanks. The X-CED program was originally designed to increase the number of Alaska Native teachers. (Jerry Lipka's association with this group began when he served as a field coordinator in X-CED in 1981.) A subgroup of Alaska Native teachers from the X-CED program formed the

Ciulistet Research Association in 1987 (Ilutisk 1994). The purpose of the Ciulistet group was to advise and provide direction to the local education systems in Alaska Native communities and to show local educators that their teaching methods were valid. From the beginning, culturally based pedagogical practices were an important area of study for this research group.

The Ciulistet were and are an invaluable component in the research conducted by Lipka and his colleagues in curriculum and pedagogy, and they have been strong advocates for a proper way of educating Yup'ik youth. They knew intuitively to include Yup'ik culture and language in the classroom, but they also realized that they would need to influence the greater educational structure if their educational efforts were going to be successful. They described their role as multifunctional, essentially impacting Alaska Native teaching and the local educational system. They offered four ways in which they would impact these areas, by: (1) validating, supporting, and enhancing their own professional growth as Native educators; (2) engaging in research related to Native education; (3) serving as role models; (4) encouraging young people and students to become teachers and leaders; and (5) making statements on educational issues to the local school boards and organizations (Ilutisk 1994).

The early research by Lipka and his colleagues that relates to pedagogy shows that the genesis of MCC was formed from the teaching practices of the Ciulistet (Lipka 1991; Lipka et al. 1998). Coupled with later research, this work highlights three main factors that play crucial roles in a Yup'ik way of teaching. The first centers on the importance of creating and maintaining strong, positive, kin-like relationships with students. These relationships emphasize student autonomy and allow for student ownership in the learning process. Second, is the purposeful, sequenced use of "expert apprentice modeling" and "joint productive activity" in teaching the MCC curriculum materials. Expert apprentice modeling and joint productive activity are viewed as natural components of the traditional ways in which Yup'ik children are taught in the community. The third step emphasizes the use of discourse patterns in the classroom that mirror those found in Yup'ik communities. The development of these Ciulistet recommended pedagogical practices coincided with the development of MCC materials. It is difficult to separate one from the other when trying to explain the effectiveness of MCC, consequently I will also provide a short description of MCC curriculum at the close of this section.

Relationships

Before looking at the way teachers of Yup'ik Eskimo students described their relationships with students in the classroom and how those relationships impact their teaching practices, I'd like to offer an analysis of a relational framework described in the American Indian educational philosophy of Vine Deloria, Jr. and Daniel Wildcat (2001). Deloria and Wildcat explore three aspects of Indian education. First, they discuss the purpose of educating Indian children, which they assert is to produce mature human beings. Second, they explain the process of educating American Indian students within this context. They show that this process must not be devoid of an Indigenous metaphysical understanding of the world the students live in. This entails coming to an understanding of where knowledge is found, how it is conveyed, and what to do with it. This process of learning about learning ties into the third aspect of the authors' educational philosophy, power and place, which is the notion found in their description of the Indian personality. According to Deloria, "Here power and place are dominant concepts—power being the living energy that inhabits and/or composes the universe, and place being the relationship of things to each other. . . . Power and place produce personality. This equation simply means that the universe is alive, but it also contains within it the very important suggestion that the universe is personal" (22–23).

Place is a fundamental aspect of the Indigenous worldview. Place must be included in the education of Indigenous children, because it is really the foundational context on which they build their understanding of the world and, in the end, that knowledge allows them the possibility of becoming mature adults within Indigenous communities. Relationships within this context are meaningful in that they imply certain responsibilities inherent in the makeup and well-being of Indigenous communities. How one responds to those responsibilities with the knowledge they have gained determines one's level of maturity. Deloria suggests that place is not just the physical environment in which a person lives but is also an entity that lives in the metaphysical realm. Its placement in both the physical and the metaphysical spheres speaks to the importance of understanding the world as having both physical and metaphysical characteristics—consequently, it is a living entity. Accepting the world as such, our responsibility toward the world and to each other has to be personal if we are to live in harmony. Good relationships provide a conduit by which knowledge can be shared and responsibility to each other can be taken seriously (Deloria and Wildcat 2001).

Richardson (2007) describes the intertwining, almost spiraling effect of the interrelated aspects of responsibility, relationship, and place, which culminates in the maturation of an Indigenous person for whom knowledge becomes experience, and vice versa:

> These multiple movements of maturity are central to understanding Deloria's comment that "our task is to live in such a way that the information we receive through analysis [of the relationality of the organic world] becomes—over the passing of time and through grace and good fortune—our experience also." It suggests a process of maturation that dissolves the distinctions between knowing and being—expressing an orientation focused on the becoming of the experience of being in a

maturing relation to the organic world in concert with a recognition of the emotional experiencing of that experience individually and as part of a social group (226).

All information and knowledge lead to wisdom in the Indigenous context. Wisdom, in this explanation, assumes knowledge as a fluid process, harkening to the constructivist/constructionist view of knowledge: that is, knowledge is both a state of being and a process of becoming. But this wisdom means nothing if it is not attached to how an individual in the Indigenous community uses it in response to his or her responsibility in maintaining healthy relationships within that community. The ability to make information/knowledge/wisdom the foundation for intertwining relationships and responsibilities for the betterment of one's place marks an individual's maturity. Deloria and Wildcat's (2001) emphasis on relationships, responsibilities, and maturity within the context of place and with the goal of producing mature individuals is precisely the meaning invoked by the Yup'ik teachers and elders as they articulated what qualities they believe are important in order to be a good teacher of Indigenous students—and the reasons for the inclusion of Yup'ik language and culture: "Yanez (a teacher) emphasizes cooperation and helping one another throughout this lesson. However, she is connecting 'cooperation' both to the task at hand, tying smelt, and to the larger Yup'ik culture of helping one another and helping one's family" (Lipka et al. 1998, 132). These Yup'ik teachers explained to researchers that relationships between teachers and students must be cultivated, first and foremost, if a student is to learn: "She (a Yup'ik teacher) . . . viewed the ability to teach content as dependent on, and inseparable from the teacher's ability to establish a strong personal relationship with students. She felt that one cannot underestimate the centrality of what the Ciulistet has termed a 'kin relationship' . . . those who qualify as 'real' teachers . . . 'care' about their students and 'really get to know them'" (Lipka et al. 1998, 101).

By identifying with her students in traditional Yup'ik kinship relational terms, the teacher adds a special emphasis to her approach to the students. She has much more responsibility to the students if she is somehow related to them: "I wasn't a 'teacher.' . . . I was Vicki, who knew each and every one of them personally—more like a relative. It wasn't my classroom, it was OUR classroom" (Lipka et al. 1998, 96, speaker's emphasis). Yup'ik educators used these relationships in the classroom as a way to express what they knew to be true in Yup'ik culture regarding their students' abilities; that the students were capable of learning and should be given the freedom to do so. This is in stark contrast to the standard Euro-American view of classroom relationships, in which teachers see children as "little vessels" ready to be "filled with information" (Lipka et al. 1998, 95). The Ciulistet naturally abhorred this form of teaching, for they knew how their students were to be raised, and consequently how they should be taught: "Children in the village are raised to be self-reliant and have a great deal of responsibility. However, when they come to school, they learn to depend on the teacher. They learn to look upon the teacher as an authority figure who tells them what to do, when to do it, and how to do it. Very seldom have students in rural schools been allowed to think for themselves" (Lipka et al. 1998, 95).

The Ciulistet also spoke of a student's responsibilities in these relationships. Students must be willing learners and active participants. If learning is to occur, both teachers and students have a responsibility in the educational process. However, if the student is not ready to learn, the teacher must respect that choice. In this way the teacher honors the student's individual autonomy and offers students a chance to own the material on their terms. "We don't force people to do things. It's the same with teaching. You don't force kids to learn. If they want to learn they can learn. That's one of the number one rules in our Yup'ik culture. You don't force people to do things if they are not ready" (Lipka et al. 2005a, 6). Cultivating strong, positive, caring relationships in the classroom with students is viewed as another way to help students motivate themselves to learn. If Indigenous students see that a teacher sincerely cares about them, they seem to feel an inherent desire to respond in a way that honors the relationship. It is a form of reciprocating the care that is shown to them.

These relationships are present in student and teacher interactions, but they also become important in the way students relate to classroom activities centering on Yup'ik subsistence practices. All work—picking berries, hunting, or any subsistence activity—is done in groups, because it means survival for the whole community. It is important for the community that their youth understand this: "In my community, we have cultural values that are passed down, and we use these values in learning survival skills in our community. For example, we are taught how to work in groups. One of the skills that we do in groups is hunting. . . . The weather is very unpredictable, and a hunter can be stranded in an isolated place for weeks without any help or food. This is why it is important for the students to work together in the classroom, because outside the classroom we work in groups" (Lipka et al. 1998, 124).

Thus, group work, which is a fundamental part of normal Yup'ik cultural life, is also something held as an ideal in the MCC/Yup'ik mathematics classroom. Teachers model these situations in the classroom, exhibiting how activities should be done and also participating in group work with individual students and subgroups of students. Teachers allow students the freedom to create relationships with other students, which in turn aids the teacher in the teaching process. Later research on the effectiveness of MCC curriculum and pedagogy confirms that fostering good relationships continues to be a foundational cornerstone in the pedagogy of teachers working with MCC curriculum materials. Webster et al. (2005) describes and analyzes a non-Yup'ik teacher's approach to teaching MCC. This case study explores the factors that contribute to students' academic success and focuses on the key elements that underpin these variables, one of which is relationships: "This theme is the foundation for the first two themes. Without the trust and respect that pervaded both learning communities, Ms. Clark (a teacher) or the Mazahua school principal might not have recognized and honored the knowledge and experience that their students brought with them, and therefore, the students' autonomy and ownership of their learning would have been seriously threatened" (25).

Expert-Apprentice Modeling and Joint Productive Activity

A two-tiered pedagogical strategy has been developed to teach MCC curriculum. The first tier of this method is called "expert-apprentice modeling," whereby the teacher introduces students to topics or skills via guided practice. This form of pedagogy was described initially as "a combination of demonstrating and modeling while speaking and supporting group cohesiveness and student self-reliance" (Lipka 1991, 207). Here the teacher "expected the children to follow the demonstrations (instead of depending on verbal instruction)" (Lipka 1991, 213–14). This first method was recognized as a teaching practice that occurred naturally in most cultures. "In Indigenous cultures as well as many others, children traditionally learned through a process of observing skilled adults and then trying to accomplish small parts of what the adult demonstrated" (Kagle 2007, 34).

Once the introductory portion of the lesson was completed the second method, "joint productive activity," was employed. In this part of the lesson the teacher participates with students on the activity that was modeled during the introduction of the concepts and activities to be explored. Students work semi-independently as they attempt to copy (reproduce) what the teacher has shown them. The teacher works on the skill or project alongside students and is available to answer questions for them when they need assistance or direction. The students come to the teacher on their own volition. In the classroom, "Joint productive activity can be thought of as an extension of the modeling strategy because if students encounter difficulties working independently, they can return to observing the expert (teacher) working" (Kagle 2007, 176). The genesis of this two-part cultural pedagogical method was formed from "the ground up," that is, it grew directly from traditional Yup'ik cultural teaching practices. The Yup'ik belief is best expressed as, "you have to show it instead of just talking about (it) . . . verbally and kinesthetically, that is how I was raised. . . . My dad always says that a person could be verbally telling people how to do things but if he can't show them he may not know (how to do it)" (Webster et al. 2005, 49).

Integrating these two pedagogical practices, modeling and joint production, together in the classroom was intended to bring aspects of Yup'ik culture into the classroom, specifically Yup'ik teaching strategies, and also to take advantage of embedded values found in the use of these techniques. "However, the hidden curriculum in this lesson is about survival, patience, care, and doing things properly . . . the teacher . . . is conveying knowledge in a culturally appropriate manner through modeling and parallel work" (Lipka 1991, 218).

Yup'ik Discourse Patterns

There are some important consequences to using expert apprentice modeling and joint production activity techniques. The first highlights student autonomy: "Students were responsible for whom they worked with, where they sat, whom they spoke to, and whom they asked for help" (Webster et al. 2005, 49). The second takes advantage of Yup'ik discourse patterns, which includes talking less and the notion of the power of silence. Using this approach, teachers counter the usual over-reliance on "telling" typically seen in traditional math classes. The effective use of silence is highlighted by Kagle though the example of Sarah, a teacher participating in this study, who introduces a lesson from the MCC curriculum: "First Sarah's silence during the entire demonstration stands out. . . . By contrast, in most classrooms, a beginning of the lesson demonstration such as this one is usually done by the teacher alone who narrates what she is doing. . . . In Sarah's lesson, on the other hand, the student volunteered both information and assistance to the teacher despite having no formal invitation to do so, reflecting the practice of elders and teachers in the professional development" (2007, 81). This use of silence is viewed as critical in getting students to participate, again, on their own accord. The key to the use of silence and talking less is to get students to do the work of explaining, that is, to talk to each other about what it is they are doing, to question, and to make conjectures. In the process, they assist each other in the development of their own knowledge of the content and concepts found in the lesson at hand.

In addition to fostering student autonomy, silence, which in turn implies listening to student conversations, allows for a certain dynamic to occur in the classroom. This dynamic is described by Webster et al. (2005): "The time she spent listening to and observing her students as experts allowed her to establish a connection that was key to her goal of developing a learning community in her classroom" (26). Though teachers participate with the students in this framework, they become guides and facilitators. Adams et al. (2005) highlight another crucial aspect in this pedagogical strategy, that of maintaining "harmony" in the classroom. "Everyone was working towards a common goal, even if they seemed like they were arguing. This relates back to a phrase and idea that we have heard from many elders over the past decade: If we are of one mind then we can accomplish our goals" (76). Tharp and his associates describe harmony in the classroom as: "the achievement of some form of shared values and rules of relationships and process, some reconciled community of common understanding. The idea of harmony is also of primary importance in the function of Yup'ik society" (Kagle 2007, 35–36, see also Tharp and Gallimore 1988). In the MCC classroom students work together, along with the teacher, and discuss the skills they are developing. "So, even though participants may have differing views, they are all working toward the same goal—coming to a common understanding that is "good for everyone in the community as a whole" (Lipka et al. 2005a, 6).

The importance of identifying silence and integrating normal Yup'ik cultural discourse patterns into teaching practices in the classroom stems from earlier research, which spoke to the importance of including their Indigenous language in the schooling of Yup'ik children. One of the first important areas of concern for the Ciulistet was the role that Yup'ik language played in the education of Yup'ik children. "We see a different way, and when our way is used, the students will speak both languages well. They will know who they are as Yup'ik and speak English without shame or confusion" (Lipka et al. 1998, 56). Lipka and his colleagues pushed to integrate Yup'ik language into the classroom as part of their work as teachers and educators. Lipka (1994a, 1994b) and Lipka and McCarty (1994) tackled issues inherent in trying to accomplish this by specifically examining answers to the following questions: "What language should be used to teach Yup'ik children?" and "When should the Yup'ik language be used as the primary language of instruction?" These questions had a heightened sense of urgency given the fact that fewer and fewer children are able to speak the Yup'ik language as the years go by. The discussion of the inclusion of Yup'ik as a primary language of instruction evolved to mirror the discourse patterns seen in Yup'ik culture, especially in how elders and parents spoke with children about subsistence and survival activities.

Familiar Contexts—Math in a Cultural Context

Math in a Cultural Context (MCC) is the culmination of curricular work done by Lipka and his colleagues. MCC is a "series of modules that are intended to supplement a complete K–6 mathematics curriculum and explicitly connect important mathematics with the culture and knowledge of the Yup'ik people" (Rickard 2005, 81). This mathematics curriculum has found a way to bridge traditional Yup'ik cultural practices centering on survival and subsistence activities with mathematics. MCC consists of various units, each taking approximately six weeks to complete. Many units "have accompanying stories that connect cultural context and the specific cultural activity . . . such as berry picking, pattern making . . . to specific mathematics topics such as data collection and analysis, geometric patterns, and numeration" (Lipka et al. 2007, 101). The MCC curriculum is a combination of Euro-American mathematics, cultural knowledge, and pedagogy.

In its infancy, MCC arose from demonstrations of traditional lifeways offered up by Yup'ik elders. These demonstrations included the work done in fish camps, forecasting weather, making parkas, an analysis of the base-twenty Yup'ik number system, basket making, and story-knifing, in which elders drew pictures in the earth to illustrate stories they told. Researchers saw mathematics in all these activities. Parka designs and basket weaving provided a context for teaching geometrical concepts. The Yup'ik number system and its relation to the human body provided a natural coordinate system from which to measure. Elders guided Lipka and his associates into new areas of study, but they also made it explicitly clear that these new areas of study should inform Yup'ik children about how to survive, to be self-reliant, and to concern themselves with the "right behavior" in various cultural contexts.

Currently, there are ten supplemental MCC curriculum units consisting of the following titles, subjects, and grade levels: (1) "Picking Berries: Connections Between Data Collection, Graphing and Measuring," (2nd–3rd grades); (2) "Going to Egg Island: Adventures in Grouping and Place Values" (1st–2nd grades); (3) "Patterns and Parkas: Investigating Geometric Principles, Shapes, Patterns, and Measurement," (2nd grade); (4) "Designing Patterns: Exploring Shapes and Area" (3rd, 4th, and 5th grades); (5) "Building a Fish Rack: Investigations into Proofs, Properties, Perimeter, and Area (6th grade); (6) "Building a Smokehouse: The Geometry of Prisms" (6th–7th grades); (7) "Star Navigation: Explorations into Angles and Measurement" (5th, 6th, and 7th grades); (8) "Salmon Fishing: Investigations into Probability" (6th–7th grades); (9) "Drying Salmon: Journeys into Proportional and Pre-Algebraic Thinking" (6th–7th grades); and (10) "Kayak Design: Scientific Analysis and Statistical Analysis (6th–7th grades).

Social constructionists such as Gergen (1995) pointed to the need to situate mathematics in areas relevant and familiar to students and also to provide areas outside the classroom in which to direct conversations that will show the usefulness of mathematics in their daily lives. MCC provides Yup'ik educators and students an avenue to accomplish these goals.

INDIGENOUS PEDAGOGY: SOCIAL CONSTRUCTIONISM AND CONSTRUCTIVIST APPROACHES

Though local contexts and indigenous ways of teaching were sought as a basis for the development of culturally relevant pedagogical practices in Indigenous communities, the final pedagogical forms prescribed by researchers look very similar to pedagogies advocated in constructivist and social constructionist thought. Direct links to these ideas are sprinkled throughout the work of Lipka and his colleagues. These constructivist/constructionist tenants are evident in their description of teachers' implementation of MCC curriculum and the role they play as teacher. I have italicized portions in the text below, to illustrate the MCC connection to constructivist/constructionists views on teaching:

> She implemented the fish rack module in a way consistent with her belief in the importance of developing a culture of inquiry in the classroom. . . . [First, she] devoted a significant amount of class time *to open ended exploration.* The tasks were suitably complex so that *multiple solutions and strategies were possible.* . . . Second, she developed a learning environment in the classroom that was *largely student-centered.* She frequently made use of her students' *input to guide and direct her instruction,* which was consistent with her belief that the *students should take ownership* of the mathematics in which they are engaged. . . . She played a critical role in *guiding students* toward more sophisticated mathematical ideas by requiring them *to critically examine their statements and become more precise in the way that they talked about mathematics.* (Webster et al. 2005, 16, emphasis added)

Lipka and his colleagues also acknowledge that the work they did to develop MCC was influenced by reform mathematics and shares the same orientation to learning and teaching as that of constructivists and social constructionists:

> MCC is also a direct response to the top-down authoritarian ways of teaching mathematics in which there is one right answer and usually only one way to find it. Associated with the one right answer is a classroom discourse style of the teacher initiating questions about known facts, students responding, and the teacher evaluating students' responses. Through the development of MCC and work with elders and reform-oriented math educators and mathematicians, we have developed math as problem-solving. This is not open ended, but rather guided problem solving in which students are able to be semiautonomous. They "Discover" mathematical principles and properties. (Lipka et al. 2005a, 3)

Thus, my examination of pedagogical practices promoted by Lipka and his colleagues finds key constructivist/constructionist tenants as they relate to the teaching/learning process: (1) The classroom is seen as a community of learners. In Kagle (2007) and Lipka et al. (2005a) this is described as the process of maintaining "harmony" in the classroom. (2) The teacher is viewed as a guide and therefore authority shifts from the teacher to the students. This is evident in the use of joint-activity, whereby teachers work alongside students on skill development. (3) Because the classroom is a shared space, students tend to drive the direction in which learning takes place. "You don't force kids to learn. If they want to learn they can learn." (4) Teachers use multiple strategies to assess student thinking. As seen in our discussion of constructivist learning, it is important for teachers to periodically check students' understanding so teachers can offer students a contrasting or complementary model that will help them continue to learn the material. Webster and her colleagues describe one teacher telling her students to write down what they were thinking and to use their own dictionary of mathematical terms "even if they weren't the same as what would be in the textbook" (2005, 14). (5) A type of discourse is promoted in the classroom that allows students to discuss, conjecture, and "do" mathematics in the classroom. And finally, (6) Local context is important. The entire MCC curriculum was created directly from Yup'ik Eskimo culture. All these teaching activities occur in the community. Learning to use day-to-day activities in the mathematics classroom allows students to see connections between the mathematics they are learning and relevant, important aspects of their own culture. It is clear that a Yup'ik mathematical pedagogy shares the language and approaches to teaching mathematics offered by constructivist and reform-minded math educators.

CONCLUSION

How to teach Indigenous students mathematics has been an area of inquiry for more than twenty-five years. Recent scholarship on this topic shows that lesson plans that include mathematical activities grounded in local Indigenous contexts, coupled with teaching styles that use discourse patterns and ways of interacting that stem from local norms (practices also supported by constructivist/social constructionist learning theories) will lead to academic improvement in the math classroom. The research on Indigenous pedagogy suggests that teachers will experience success using many of the approaches that constructivist and social constructionist learning theories promote, generally, as good teaching. Mainly, students need to be active participants in the learning process. Teachers must allow for more student-centered classrooms, in which dialogue becomes both a means for teaching and a way to build relationships that foster learning. These relationships allow a heightened sense of student agency and ownership of the learning process. From the Indigenous pedagogical perspective, classroom discourse patterns should mirror the types of discourse found within the community. The contexts for mathematical content should also be drawn from activities in the community that should be familiar to students. Teachers should find ways to assess students to inform their own teaching. These assessments should allow students to share in the direction of learning practical applications for mathematics content. Finally, math classroom interactions should be more about "doing" mathematics rather than about *how* to do mathematics. Fosnot and Dolk (2005) call this mathematics versus "mathematizing": "Children, in learning to mathematize their world, will come to see mathematics as the living discipline it is, with themselves a part of a creative, constructive mathematical community, hard at work" (191). This means teachers should allow students opportunities to define mathematical terms, to develop mathematical thinking strategies, to be creative in their solutions, to allow for multiple ways of solving problems, and to conjecture, hypothesize, and test ideas. In this mathematizing process, students should also be given the opportunity to express their ideas in multiple ways and to defend them. This approach mirrors the way mathematics is normally done by mathematicians.

My criticism of the suggestions presented to date as effective mathematics teaching methods to use with Indigenous students, centers on the bias held by "reform" oriented mathematics teaching and learning advocates against the "traditional" way of teaching mathematics. As a secondary mathematics teacher, I see value in both reform and traditional teaching methods. As a math teacher of Indigenous students, I recognize the usefulness of grounding curriculum in the local context and using patterns of discourse found in the local community; this was something I did quite naturally. I also intuitively felt the need to foster positive relationships with my students, because I knew that a healthy relationship with students could be a way to help motivate the students themselves to learn. But I also realize the usefulness of clear explaining and direct instruction. I believe that, as a teacher, I should include all forms of pedagogy I think will be useful. In my estimation, different activities and varied mathematical concepts necessitate different approaches. Thus, mastering direct instructional techniques and coupling those methods with an ability to use joint productive activity and expert-apprentice techniques will enable teachers to meet the needs of Indigenous students' learning processes.

Another criticism I have of the teaching methods described in this chapter centers on the fact that none of the studies conducted on Indigenous pedagogy and curriculum were conducted at the secondary level. How effective are these methods when employed in classes with content set in higher forms of mathematics? I wonder, given the content-specific nature of high school mathematics and the set structure that high-stakes testing demands, whether a pedagogical strategy that is student driven and "time generous" is practical and feasible at the secondary level? It seems that successful implementation of these pedagogical practices will necessitate a change in the structure of the educational system itself.

That said, it is my hope that this discussion will help current and future mathematics teachers of Indigenous students think about the many ways in which they can improve their own teaching practices. At least, this chapter may offer a different way to approach mathematical content and students, and it may help teachers of Indigenous students realize that the solution to higher academic achievement may be quite simple. That, in the end, the type of teaching promoted as good teaching in the context of Indigenous mathematics actually requires us, as teachers, to trust our students more as learners.

5
Indigenous Knowledge and Science

WILLARD SAKIESTEWA GILBERT

An important focus in educating Indigenous students in the twenty-first century is Native language and culture. Historically, U.S. federal policy stripped Indian children of their language and culture in order to assimilate them into mainstream society (Gilbert 2009). A number of factors contributed to the suppression and elimination of Indigenous languages, thereby decreasing the number of fluent Native speakers. According to Reyhner and Eder (2004), one major contributor to Indigenous language loss has been coercive assimilative federal policies carried out through schools. One of the newest waves of these federal policies began with the passing of the No Child Left Behind Act (NCLB) in 2001. This law promised accountability, local control, parental involvement, and funding to improve the education of children across the nation. Unfortunately for many Indigenous children, this policy has had a negative effect on minority student academic achievement, owing to its promotion of "one size fits all" curriculum and instruction (National Research Council 2005).

When the current educational system neglects to accept, or dismisses, Indigenous students' own traditional knowledge, nurtured and taught in the home and within the local community, the educational system has lost a valuable educational tool to augment the school's existing science curriculum (Gilbert 2005). Historically, assimilative federal policies have aimed at separating Native students from their rich cultural heritage. Much of this suppression was accomplished through the educational system. Ironically, it is this same cultural heritage that for years the federal government was determined to eradicate that is now being recognized as a method by which Indigenous students may connect their cultural knowledge with academic disciplines, including Western science, and succeed academically. There have also been several attempts by the federal government to acknowledge and recognize the value of Indigenous languages and cultures, as noted in the 1928 Meriam Report and more recently with the passage of the Esther Martinez Native American Languages Preservation Act of 2006. In addition, according to the National Indian Education Study (Fuchs and Havighurst 1972), the lack of a curriculum supporting the language and cultural base of the Native community served must be rectified in the educational system.

Through a series of hearings, the National Indian Education Association identified key concerns related to how NCLB affected Indian education (NIEA 2005). Several witnesses testified that although accountability was seen as a positive factor for academic achievement, the law had not accomplished its intended results. Instead it was leaving Indigenous children behind. The hearings further determined that an unintended consequence of NCLB had been that culturally based instruction had come to be seen as a major disruption to the mainstream educational system, altering the educational potential of schools in Indian communities. The result was a major negative impact on culturally based education.

NCLB ignores how communities, parental income and education levels, language and cultural barriers, and teacher awareness of student cultural context and pedagogical approaches influence academic engagement for all students in ways that Davidson (1996) and others have found important. This neglect has affected the current use of culturally appropriate pedagogy and curriculum that is connected to the social, cultural, and linguistic heritage of Native children. Additional aspects of the hearings (NIEA 2005) focused on the culturally appropriate teaching approaches known to be highly effective for Native students. The emphasis on "highly qualified" teachers led to a growing concern that culturally based teaching would disappear from the schools, due to budget constraints, which raised the serious prospect of schools' diminished ability to provide a meaningful and effective education for Native students.

The original intent of the law was to "close the achievement gap with accountability, flexibility and choice, so that no child is left behind," which is considered to be a laudable goal. However, not only has NCLB created nationwide controversy, it has had an adverse effect among Native students, demonstrating that a single "one size fits all" pedagogical model in fact does not fit all students. It is my opinion that Native children, like any other children, are special and unique in how they respond to what they are taught in school. With this at heart, I suggest a solution that could help make a difference in how we teach Native children, utilizing culturally appropriate instruction, and begin to explore new and innovative ideas as to how we can make curriculum more culturally relevant with culturally based approaches to designing curricula appropriate for young Native students. The goal is to preserve and promote Indigenous "ways of knowing" within the existing science curriculum, to both enhance academic achievement and to foster a positive attitude toward science and science education among Native students. Current studies, including my own research, the Native Science Connections Research Project (NSCRP), have confirmed that dual benefit, which is not supported by federal NCLB policies. Further evidence to support my study appears in a number of research projects with similar hypotheses and outcomes (Gilbert and Carrasco 1999).

According to Lee (2003), recent efforts to provide culturally congruent science instruction demonstrate that when culture and linguistic background are used as intellectual resources, students have increased science achievement. In a similar study, Matthews and Smith (1994) concluded that when Native American students were taught science using culturally relevant materials, the students showed significantly higher achievement and more positive attitudes than did comparable students who were taught without the culturally relevant materials. In addition, Nelson-Barber and Estrin (1995) argued that not only is available, potentially important content knowledge from Native culture ignored, but well-developed Native ways of knowing, learning, and problem solving also go unrecognized. The result is that crucial opportunities to build on or draw from American Indian students' existing knowledge are missed.

Since the 1980s, educators have successfully incorporated local knowledge and languages into school curricula especially in the areas of literacy and social studies. However, the American school science and mathematics curricula have remained virtually unchanged in their cultural perspectives, under a false belief that these subjects are "culture-free" because they deal with absolute and universal sets of knowledge. The fallacy arises in that science in American schools is indeed funneled through Western European perspectives. For example, the elementary school science curriculum is somewhat standardized across North America. It varies only in terms of topic sequence and approaches to learning. The science topics by grade levels are generally standardized, as can be discerned by reviewing science textbooks and published state and national science education standards. However, an elementary school science curriculum that includes culturally appropriate knowledge can build on this mainstream curriculum. Traditional Native cultural knowledge and ways of knowing can be taught in ways that relate to the elementary science curriculum taught in schools today. Cultural knowledge can be culled from respective cultures of all students involved, and this knowledge can be connected to the existing elementary science curriculum. Cultural knowledge consists of legends, stories, beliefs, perspectives, and history, Native language, and values. It includes Native ways of interpreting and employing basic scientific knowledge.

For example, from the Euro-American perspective, students are taught the names, uses, and related iconic forms of the constellations, such as the Big Dipper (Ursa Major). Native Americans and other Indigenous peoples have for hundreds of years recognized and studied these same constellations, and like Euro-Americans, they too have attached special names and meaning to them. For example, among the Navajo, Orion is known as Átsééts'ózí (the Slim One), the Navajo hunter, protector, and provider of his people. The phenomenon is the same, but the perspectives regarding name, significance, and meaning of the constellation may differ. While most science concepts are absolute and universal, the cultural difference lies in their interpretation and applications. Science is science. However, the ways diverse cultures view, interpret, and apply knowledge of these universal scientific phenomena is, I believe, what can make science education more palatable and exciting for both Native American and mainstream students.

Researchers view this cultural component as a motivating factor for improving student achievement in science education. It is believed that if Native American children are grounded in their own traditional ways of knowing, they will learn the standard elementary school science curriculum as well, and they will also have a more positive attitude toward school science and toward science education in general. The increase in academic achievement and positive attitude is evident in a NSCRP study involving ninety-five Diné fifth-grade students. The experimental cohort who received instruction integrating traditional ways of knowing into their science curriculum significantly outscored students in the control group, who only received the standard science curriculum without the cultural component. Further evidence showed that the experimental students' attitudes toward science education improved, an indication that the students perceived their traditional cultural ways of knowing as being a valuable contributor to the learning of science and recognized that they themselves are thus "scientists" (Gilbert and Carrasco 1999).

In addition to the fifty-item survey questionnaire administered to the students before and after the twelve-week period of the study, the researchers also had the students draw a picture of a scientist before the study actively commenced. Results indicated that to the children, a stereotypical scientist was a white male with long, white bushy hair and thick glasses, wearing a lab coat with a pocket protector—in other words, the classic Einstein look. The problem with this image, when brought to mind by young Native American children, is that they do not perceive themselves fitting that picture, as being a scientist, but instead only view the profession of science as being unattainable. Sad to say, in some circumstances, somewhere along the way in their academic pursuits, they were told, or allowed to form the notion, that math and science were subjects that they might be better off avoiding, thus causing them to look toward other fields. On a positive note, after the twelve-week period of the study, the researcher again asked the students to draw a picture of a scientist. This time, a more positive view of themselves as being scientists was evident in their drawings, which showed the students themselves as scientists. On their own, students took out their crayons, and matched their own skin colors when they drew the scientists. Further evidence from this same extensive study indicated that Native students are more engaged in learning the concepts of science when their traditional ways of knowing become part of the existing science curriculum in the classroom. If the researchers could change the attitudes of young children within a period of a semester, just think what could be accomplished in a full academic year, and from grades pre-K through 12.

INQUIRY-BASED SCIENCE TEACHING

Hall and McCurdy (1990) document how *inquiry-based* curriculum has been shown to develop independent and critical thinking skills, positive attitudes, and curiosity toward the learning of science. This approach is a learning process or strategy that builds student knowledge. The process mirrors the stages of Bloom's (1985) learning phases, which can lead children to complete cognition by building on their previously learned knowledge (including, we would add, traditional ways of knowing). From the day children are born into this world, they try and make sense of the world around them. They become concerned about the surrounding environment in which they live, and which they experience on a daily basis. They try to understand and predict their world, and they begin doing this at a very young age. Early on, they are eager and willing to ask questions about different things they have experienced and have observed.

Among my recollections of my own young childhood on the Hopi reservation, in the village of Moenkopi in the northeastern part of Arizona, I remember my grandmother, So'o, putting me on her back, wrapped with a shawl. She would walk to the arroyo with a bucket in one hand and a stick in the other. When we had arrived at our destination, she would kneel down and dig into the earth with her stick, place a little bit of the soil in her mouth, and then move on to another spot and continue digging. Only after she had tasted a satisfactory batch of soil would she begin filling her bucket; when it was filled, we set off back to the house. It was not until a few days later until I finally learned the significance of her tasting the soil. A pottery maker's soil must have the right clay composition, or when the pottery is baked, the bowl will crack and break into pieces. So'o had taught me, a very young child, a valuable science lesson about the practical importance of soil composition.

Education should teach young children how to formulate questions, make observations and predictions, and develop the thought processes that will assist in solving problems. As young children become more mature in their own knowledge and education, they begin to learn how to figure out ways to investigate and answer their own questions about their specific surroundings and the environments they inhabit and experience. Their own inquiries offer the students a meaningful learning environment that allows them to satisfy their curiosity. They are more likely to develop closer ownership of the things that they are investigating if something sparks that curiosity.

Thus, inquiry-based learning allows students to start with their own curiosity—the things they wonder about, what excites them, and what prompts their questions. When children notice an event taking place in their own personal lives, and within their individual personal surroundings, it is related to specific things in nature as they experience it. Therefore, it is important to make the connection between curiosity and nature. Children come to the science classroom already prepared with curiosity about different things in life, and at the same time, they have virtually never had the opportunity to think about these things in a constructive manner. Children are known to carry out inquiry long before they start their formal education in a classroom setting. For Native children, development of inquiry-based skills is supported by their parents, family members, the community in which they reside, and other relatives as well as their own clans. Thus, education starts in the home, and parents and other community members are their first teachers.

Inquiry-based science is a process by which we can determine if what we see, hear, and read is in fact true. Unfortunately, what children see and hear in the broadcast and electronic media and read in books is often portrayed as being absolute, the truth. Children need to learn how to find out if the information they are exposed to is in fact true. Where is the evidence that proves this information is true? Without this, intellectual knowledge is not very useful in any given situation.

THE ROLE OF THE TEACHER IN AN INQUIRY-BASED SCIENCE CLASSROOM

In the majority of classrooms across the country, many teachers adhere to the direct method of instruction, with the intent of maximizing student achievement. This method includes teacher-led lectures, student completion of worksheets, and skill repetition, perhaps via computer programs (Thompson 2006). This approach was most evident in NCLB guidelines that established student achievement goals closely aligned with mastery of memorized content as the expected outcome of direct instruction. According to Heal, Hanley, and Layer (2009), "direct instruction is characterized by relatively simple and precise materials tailored to specific learning objectives, planned (and sometimes scripted) prompting procedures, provision of high-quality reinforcers for responding, and multiple trials conducted during brief teaching periods" (124). It is no secret that Native American children in schools who are subjected to this type of teaching approach are left farther and farther behind.

According to Hazari, North, and Moreland (2009), *constructivism* is inquiry-based, discovery theory of learning in which students construct new personal interpretations of knowledge upon their previous experiences and applications of prior knowledge, in a relevant context (189; see also Sanders, this volume, chapter 4). In a similar study, Thompson (2006) states that constructivist learning activities may involve using manipulatives, that is, hands-on materials, for incorporating inquiry, discovery, and problem-solving approaches into the learning process, and for applying science concepts to real-world situations. Therefore, the main role of the teacher is as a facilitator, ready to assist students in avoiding experiences that would limit their capability to respond intelligently and meaningfully to new and complex situations, while at the same time, leading them toward experiences and inquiries that will arouse curiosity and the learning of new concepts in a meaningful way. Teachers need to know how to draw on the student's natural surroundings, and utilize this rich, community based knowledge to the advantage of the student's curiosity.

DEVELOPING A CULTURALLY RELEVANT SCIENCE CURRICULUM

In assuring that science knowledge from Native cultures is integrated into existing elementary science curricula, curriculum developers must become well acquainted with local Native cultural science knowledge and then transform that knowledge into science curricula that can be connected to, or incorporated into, the existing elementary school science curriculum. Native educators, elders, medicine men and women, and other respected adults and students in the Native community need to contribute cultural knowledge toward the development of science curriculum. In developing such a curriculum from a Native American perspective, one must also be aware of the authenticity of the cultural information (ways of knowing) being presented.

A particular area needing further discussion is the appropriateness of the subject matter to be taught. In most Indigenous cultures, science and religion are intertwined. This can pose important questions in deciding what topics may be included in developing a supplemental science curriculum from a Native American perspective. For example, in Arizona, religion cannot be taught in public schools. Moreover, in Native American cultures, religion holds a special place in people's lives and community. Very importantly, religion is considered to be sacred knowledge that is only learned within the Native community. In my discussions with elders and medicine men and women, they have informed me that Native religious beliefs and rituals should not be taught in school classrooms, that instead these should be taught only at home and within the Native community. In addition, there are culturally specific times during the year for teaching and not teaching certain religious matters, and certain ages at which a child is expected to learn about certain Native cultural science topics. Even when the time is appropriate to address a science topic, I have learned, the manner of teaching and studying that topic may be inappropriate outside the Native community. For example, dissecting frogs, a common practice in American mainstream school science classrooms, is very inappropriate for the Hopi and Diné people and among other tribal nations.

Obtaining the appropriate background and pedagogy skills to respectfully integrate Native cultural science knowledge with established classroom curricula is, thus, not an easy task. But if thoughtfully included, culturally appropriate Native science knowledge can be transformed successfully into a curriculum that is connected to regular school science lessons.

Developing Culturally Appropriate Lesson Plans

As a major component of any attempt to develop and design curriculum that is culturally relevant, teachers must consider their own level of expertise and the amount of training they have in teaching science. The majority of teachers who graduate from teaching colleges with a teaching degree have taken the bare minimum of science courses required. I also believe that in most cases, if not all, teacher preparation programs across the United States do not require or provide training in how to teach science to Native American children. On the other hand, many colleges and private organizations do offer specialized training opportunities for teachers on appropriate approaches to use teaching science. For example, the Full Option Science System (FOSS) science curriculum provides not only teacher training and workshop opportunities, but the curriculum itself also furnishes a teacher's manual as well as a videotape on how to approach a specific science curriculum.

As the principal investigator for the Native Science Connections Research Project at Northern Arizona University's College of Education, I designed a culture-based science curriculum that incorporated Native cultural knowledge and ways of knowing into the existing science curriculum in classrooms for each of four different tribes in Arizona and New Mexico. The goal was to train teachers from these four tribes in how to teach science and also how to develop and teach culturally relevant science curriculum. Teachers were also taught how to develop culturally relevant science curriculum for each of the tribes represented (Gilbert and Carrasco 1999).

Designing Lesson Plans

Once the classroom science curriculum has been determined and the unit to be taught has been selected, teachers can then start to think about how to develop lesson plans. They will have to take into consideration the national science standards (National Academy of Science 1996), as well as state standards and in some cases tribal cultural standards. Many Native American tribes have already developed cultural standards that should be carefully respected. For example, in Arizona, the Diné Department of Education has developed and adopted cultural standards for all of the subject areas. My recommendation is that teachers seriously consider utilizing cultural standards when developing all lesson plans.

When deciding which units of study to teach and in what order, the teacher may already have a particular science curriculum to follow and apply in the classroom. Lesson plans integrating Native cultural science knowledge should be coordinated with these preplanned units. For example, in the Full Option Science System (FOSS) curriculum (see http://www.fossweb.com/), "Food and Nutrition" is one instructional unit for grades 4–5. I strongly recommend teaching this unit at the beginning of the school year, because it ties in very nicely with teaching students about healthy eating habits. In addition, that is the time of the year when Native people start to harvest their crops after a long, summer growing season. More importantly, as an educator, I know that we are all concerned about health issues in our communities, such as diabetes and the development of healthy eating habits among young children. A sample lesson plan can be found in Appendix B.

The Learning Cycle

The Indigenous way of life deals with the interaction of all the elements of the universe (and then some). There is harmony in the Indigenous perception of learning. This does not mean that Native Americans live untroubled lives; it means that the Indigenous understanding of life reflects cycles. The cycles of life, nature, and the elements are circles without beginning and without end.

When examined closely, all types of circles and cycles reflect the Indigenous perception of wholeness. It is intriguing that what educators call the "learning cycle" is so relevant to Native Americans' perception of a natural education, and that this concept parallels inquiry-based classroom and constructivist learning practices. It is also necessary that the knowledge and language of Native Americans be used as much as possible in this type of learning, in order for the relevance of these lessons to take root. The language must be appropriate for specific areas, the grade level, and the terminology for which it is intended. Again, the learning cycle rekindles the cyclical, harmonious Native American teachings that are natural for learning.

Each learning module's guidelines need to include a hands-on activities approach if it is to be successful. Teachers need to be knowledgeable in the concepts involved as a precautionary measure to insure that the questions students ask can be correctly answered. There will still be times when there are no fixed, correct answers. Renner and Marek (1988) describe the learning cycle in such a manner that the students become the main focus of learning: "The learning cycle, therefore, is not a method of teaching science, the learning cycle comes from the discipline itself; it represents science. If science is to be taught in a manner that leads students to construct knowledge, they must make a quest. The learning cycle leads students on that quest for knowledge" (170). Thus, the students are engaged in observing, measuring, interpreting, experimenting, model building, and predicting as they experience the learning cycle. These essential elements of learning science should be constantly implemented in all phases of the cycle.

The itemized paragraphs below offer a suggested overview of what a learning module can include. Again, appropriateness for the students, the grade, and the subject area is important. The learning cycle uses "teacher-friendly" terminology. Each cycle begins with an "Introduction" that allows the teacher and students to gain a general understanding of what is already known. Within the cycle, the terms for the steps of a lesson may vary: for example, *Exploration* may be called *Gathering Data,* or *Conceptual Invention* may be labeled *The Idea. Expansion* could be called *Expanding the Idea.* The learning cycle concludes with a *Teaching Suggestions* section that gives the teacher more information to allow diversity, and other alternatives to the concepts.

Introduction: The purpose of an introduction is (directly or indirectly) to motivate students' interest in a concept. This is accomplished through dialog in the child's first language (L1) or second language (L2), through a short excerpt of the lesson without mention of the concept at stake (which could be, for example, a web-making activity). The introduction needs to be relevant to the Native American child's environment in order for the general purpose of learning to take place.

Gathering Data (Exploration): It is at this juncture, that the module is thoroughly thought out and the materials, the lesson plans, the consultants, and all other resources have been gathered. The teacher must be well prepared in order to assist the children in collecting their own information. The directions to students regarding the new activities should provide them with guidance as to what they need to keep in mind, but must not tell or explain the concept to be taught. These directions are to be specific. The assimilation of the concept arrives through extrapolation of what is discovered during the activity. The children use their prior knowledge (traditional ways of knowing), gain information and insight from others, and learn in a more relaxed atmosphere. This part of the process requires time. It is necessary to allow time for all materials to be used that will lead to the concept.

The Idea (The Conceptual Invention): This phase of the module is a pathway into accommodating the concept to be learned. At this point the teacher centers action and discussion increasingly around the concept. Working toward total understanding is the key. The teacher must introduce the concept in the students' first language and refer to students' prior experiences. The students must also absorb any new language and/or definitions relating to what they have learned.

This could be done orally or in written form. It is up to the teacher to decide which method to use. Four factors need to be included in this process: (1) The findings of the exploration phase need to be debriefed and reviewed; (2) The students' findings, all of them, must be used in this process; (3) The students' language in achieving this must be relevant and proper; and (4) A rationale for the importance of the concept needs to be supplied, and it has to be relevant to the students.

Expanding the Idea (Expansion): During this phase, the students integrate the newly learned concept with others that relate to it. The language of the new concept needs to be used at this phase, to make sure that the students are accommodating the learned experience. It is important to expand the lesson with activities that are carefully related to the concept.

Checking Up (Evaluation): The evaluation of students' success must be included in how the teacher plans and organizes the module's structure. In this evaluation, the teacher may administer a teacher-made test, review portfolios of students' work, observe students' actions, check student notebooks, or devise other methods to document or monitor each student's progress in terms of meeting national, state, and tribal standards.

Teaching Suggestions (Additional Topics): Students' interaction with the presented materials is essential. It makes the difference between passive learning and active learning. Language considerations are highly important. The language in which the child engages with science makes the learning worthwhile. It is vital that Native American children be surrounded with their Indigenous language and learn to recognize its importance to school and education. Working in groups is another important factor in the learning cycle. Students need to interact with one another and learn from each other, to become teachers as well as learners in the classroom.

For hundreds of years, Indigenous peoples have relied upon their traditional ways of knowing as a basis for understanding the environment in which they live, and knowing how to manipulate their surroundings for survival. In Indigenous communities throughout the world, the concern for maintaining and revitalizing language and culture is a major issue for cultural survival. Through the efforts of tribal educational programs and state agencies, these traditional ways of knowing can be maintained through the development and teaching of culturally based curriculum in classrooms throughout the United States. Language and culture are a vital part of any child's educational experiences that can enhance their academic performance and foster a positive attitude toward science education.

6
Social Studies

CHRISTINE K. LEMLEY, JEREMY D. STODDARD,
AND LOREN HUDSON

In order to do your job effectively, number one, really care about the people that you're teaching. Know your students, know their community, and know their history. People identify with their history. There are certain things that are sensitive to people and we need to keep those in mind. No matter what culture they are in. Every culture has its own history. Every culture has its own values and we need to understand them as educators. And it must be an efficacy of care. A pedagogy of love. Understand what it really means to be a teacher. An educator is someone who's really there not only teaching, but also role modeling what we teach. So the advice I would give to teachers is pretty much the same I would give to students: be a lifelong learner who cares about modeling this for others.

Indigenous teacher

How and why you introduce yourself as a teacher is as important as what, how, and why you teach. Consider the next introduction, by a non-Indigenous middle school social studies teacher teaching on the Diné (Navajo) Nation:

I understand that many of you are Diné. Thank you for allowing me to be here on your land. And you all were here a long time before us and I'm going to teach you some things. And some things may be different. Let's bring those up for discussion. Let's learn from each other. And let's make each other better. And if there's anything that needs to be corrected, let's correct it. And I understand that books are often incorrect, let's challenge those inaccuracies to correct them.

white teacher

This teacher humbled himself from the beginning and opened up conversation. He acknowledged what existed and even noted that some of what existed as "knowledge" could be inaccurate. Throughout his practices, he approached social studies as a way to compare stories. Comparing stories was a way to acknowledge both Indigenous and non-Indigenous epistemologies, or ways of knowing. He would follow up with questions like, "What did you observe and come to know?" And he used these observations so that students could learn from each other. He chose materials that offered both Indigenous and non-Indigenous perspectives.

Both of these introductions to a social studies class identify the key components of the classroom environment, curriculum design, and instructional methods necessary for successful social studies pedagogy with Indigenous students. In this chapter, we focus on all aspects of pedagogy for the social studies, a key subject area for developing an understanding of the past and present, and learning how to act as a citizen. Then we identify the historical, social, and political contexts of how Indigenous peoples have been taught, and taught about, in the social studies classroom. Next, we present pedagogical frameworks that suggest ways of teaching social studies to Indigenous students and meld our knowledge of Indigenous worldviews and cultures. These frameworks include Culturally Relevant Pedagogy (Ladson-Billings 1994, 2001), Critical Indigenous Research Methodologies (Brayboy et al. 2012), and praxis. We then introduce pedagogical approaches to illustrate culturally relevant curricular design for American Indian students. These approaches include oral history, historiography and perspective recognition, place-based education, geography, ecology, and government and citizenship. Finally, we offer recommended approaches to consider when teaching American Indian students social studies. We urge teachers to integrate important topics in the curriculum, validate the knowledge students bring into the classroom, understand community value systems, seek Indigenous mentors, become involved in the community, and serve as role models.

THE SOCIAL STUDIES

"Social studies" is the term coined in the early twentieth century to identify a subject area in U.S. schools focused on the development of citizens. Conceptions differ regarding what social studies should include or what it means. For some, it is a broad examination of society in all its interactions. For others, it is the simple task of preparing citizens. As instantiated in policy throughout most of the United States, social studies refers to the collection of disciplines from history and the social sciences (for example, geography, economics, and government) with the overall goal of teaching the story of the nation and producing good citizens (Thornton 2008).

Historically, the core of social studies courses has been used to emphasize the teaching of the dominant narrative of American and Western history and to produce citizens who maintain the status quo. This westward expansion narrative emphasizes notions of progress and freedom seeking that ignore many controversial and destructive moments in American history as the United States expanded and colonized many of the peoples and much of the land of North America and beyond (Barton and Levstik 2004). There have been attempts to create social studies curricula and methods that focus more on cognitive models influenced by the social science disciplines, such as conducting historical inquiry or examining history and government through controversial issues and events. These attempts to change social studies curricula and pedagogy have taken effect in some schools and states and are part of what is known as the "New Social Studies" (Thornton and Barton 2010).

However, in the current era of standardization and high-stakes testing, social studies is again being constructed as a body of discrete facts to be learned, rather than as a process of forming an active and dynamic understanding of the past and present (Au 2009). This is occurring in part because, in addition to the thematic National Council for the Social Studies standards, each state has its own set of academic standards for social studies or the related social studies disciplinary courses, such as history and geography. These state standards vary widely, from Wisconsin's very minimal thematic standards emphasizing conceptual understanding to Virginia's very detailed outline of content that is assessed in high-stakes end-of-year exams. Yet, despite the emphasis on testing, the nature of standards, and the constraints of an "official curriculum" (Apple 1993), teachers still hold a great deal of power and decision-making discretion when it comes to how this content is taught and the particular narratives that are reinforced or challenged in the classroom (Thornton 2004).

AMERICAN INDIANS IN SCHOOLS AND IN HISTORY

The role of Indigenous peoples and their histories in schools is rife with tensions, including both the experiences of Indigenous children in schools and in what is being taught about American Indians and other Indigenous groups in the social studies curriculum. The history of assimilation and forced attendance at boarding schools has left a powerful and painful legacy of school mistrust in Indigenous communities (Ness and Huisken 2002). This painful past is perpetuated by the way that Indigenous history is currently included and/or excluded in the common history curriculum. Indigenous students often do not see their history, their perspectives, or themselves included in lessons in the social studies classroom. And the traditional lecture and textbook approach to teaching history or government does not represent the cultural and historical approach to understanding the past found in most indigenous groups, who instead favor learning more grounded in oral history and storytelling. Further, teaching a static textbook version of history often does not allow for multiple perspectives and a more interpretive examination of history. This textbook teaching approach rarely values perspectives from historically marginalized groups such as Indigenous peoples. In fact, the traditional lecture and textbook approach leads to a very narrow and often stereotypical inclusion of Indigenous history in national histories and social studies courses.

Historically, the inclusion of Indigenous history in textbooks and curricula has been problematic and has had real consequences for how both Indigenous and non-Indigenous students view this history. There are also real consequences for how Indigenous students view themselves as included in or excluded from American society. The narrative of history in the textbooks of a dominant culture is one of "progress" and striving for "freedom." These whitewashed narratives also tend to leave out much of what is controversial or negative in the dominant culture, including the treatment of Indigenous people. Events such as the original European colonization of North and South America, Asia, Africa, and elsewhere are viewed as part and parcel of destiny and progress, as in the case of Columbus's "discovery" of the "New World" in 1492 (Loewen 1995). For example, the first Thanksgiving in New England, in 1621, is portrayed as a harmonious connection of cultures, while other intercultural tensions from the period are left out.

As Sanchez (2007) discovered in his analysis of U.S. history textbooks that included Indigenous peoples, American Indians were portrayed less as savage and monolithic peoples, and there was increased inclusion of Native history overall in textbooks published from 1991 to 2004, as compared to textbooks from the previous thirty to forty years. This is positive evidence of improvement, given the emphasis on American Indians as "uncivilized" and "savage" in texts from the 1960s (Foster 1999). However, there is still little depth in the portrayal of American Indian history and culture; textbooks still fail to include discussions of American Indians as a diverse peoples with their own histories, governing structures, economies, and cultures. Instead, the Euro-American cultural narrative emphasizes that it was the Manifest Destiny of the United States to expand and take over unused or underutilized land in the West, as if it were uninhabited or only occupied by people who did not belong or were not worthy of it. Also, as Sanchez (2007) found, the focus of these texts is too often on the same iconic group of Indigenous individuals (Pocahontas, Sacagawea, Geronimo) and events, for example, the Battle of the Little Big Horn or the massacre at Wounded Knee, with little else offered to challenge the historical and cultural representations of American Indians nationwide. Other depictions of American Indian history, including Hollywood films and museum exhibits, do little to challenge or expand on these stereotypical aspects of American Indian history.

Too often the history of American Indians in U.S. history textbooks ends in the nineteenth century with the massacre at Wounded Knee. Very little reference is made to American Indians in twentieth- and twenty-first-century history, with a few recently emphasized exceptions such as the Navajo "code-talkers" of World War II and perhaps the inclusion of the American Indian Movement (AIM) within teaching on the Civil Rights era of the 1960s and

'70s (Sanchez 2007). This seemingly abrupt end to American Indian history, coinciding with the end of the nineteenth century, leads many to believe that American Indians also vanished at that time. In fact, Sanchez found that many books and textbooks refer to American Indians in the past tense, which further validates the view that they have simply disappeared. Similarly, there is often little Indigenous history after the nineteenth century included in many state history academic standards. Of course, that often depends on the region of the United States where the academic standards are set. Those in the upper Midwest, Southwest, Pacific Northwest, and plains states like Oklahoma, where there are long traditions of reservations and pueblos, will have a different view of American Indians than those in the Southeast or New England, where the presence of contemporary American Indian populations is sparse.

Additionally, social studies courses such as geography and government may clash with the experiences, culture, and worldview of American Indian communities. In these courses and textbooks, Euro-American conceptions of knowledge and institutions are reinforced, with little opening left for the inclusion of other perspectives. For instance, geography tends to be taught from a scientific and economic perspective, with a focus on topography, geographical features, and natural resources, while little attention is paid to either environmental or ecological issues. Similarly, U.S. Government courses rarely include much information about the roots of different governing systems that existed prior to the U.S. Constitution or the governing structures of American Indian nations that exist today. Instead, issues such as tribal hunting, fishing rights, and casinos are included, but are mostly viewed from a non-Indigenous perspective as legal concerns. Obviously, there is little agreement among teachers, schools, and states about how social studies courses are taught and what is to be included or excluded (Thornton 2008; Thornton and Barton 2010). While many teachers do a great job of including a wide variety of perspectives and challenging their students to consider different ways of knowing, the dominant narrative of Euro-American history and a static view of understanding the past and present are still evident in most social studies classrooms.

The challenge, therefore, rests with teachers to engage students in the study of the past and present with approaches that value different ways of understanding, multiple perspectives, and a broader range of cultural, social, and political histories. There are many curriculum resources available that teachers can incorporate in lessons in order to teach American Indian history that includes more nuanced and richer perspectives. Historian Dee Brown's iconic *Bury my Heart at Wounded Knee* provides a starting point, revealing perspectives not included in common history textbooks. This important book and other similar works by Indigenous and non-Indigenous authors, such as Howard Zinn's *A People's History of the United States* and Roxanne Dunbar-Ortiz's *An Indigenous Peoples' History of the United States,* have led to films and curricula developed for education both in and outside the tradition classroom (see references and Appendix C: Social Studies Resources). As convenient as it is to find better resources to teach about American Indian history, it is up to teachers to establish classroom environments for working with American Indian students in a way that values their cultural and historical perspectives and to engage Indigenous students through the use of pedagogies that instill value in cultural history, multiple perspectives, and Indigenous knowledge systems (Barnhardt 2005; Brayboy and Maughan 2009). The following section includes frameworks for developing a classroom culture and community that supports this type of pedagogy.

COMMUNITY-BASED PEDAGOGY

We suggest that teachers of Indigenous students draw on Culturally Relevant Pedagogy (CRP) (Ladson-Billings 1994, 2001), Critical Indigenous Research Methodologies (CIRM) (Brayboy et al. 2012) and praxis (Freire [1970] 1993), to build classroom learning environments through community-based pedagogy. Culturally Relevant Pedagogy includes three tenets: (1) *academic achievement,* from which teachers encourage all students to experience success in their content area, especially literacy, numeracy, and technology; (2) *cultural competence,* which uses students' traditional culture as a vehicle for learning through promoting awareness of students' own cultures, as well as fluency in at least one additional culture and (3) *sociopolitical consciousness,* which challenges existing individual and institutional inequities, especially in terms of race and ethnicity. Critical Indigenous Research Methodologies (CIRM) includes five notions: (1) *relationality,* to nurture relationships; (2) *responsibility,* to care for both ideas and knowledge; (3) *respect,* to know and honor communities, especially community members; (4) *reciprocity,* to take and give back in order to thrive and survive; and (5) *accountability,* to develop transformative outcomes for Indigenous communities.

"Praxis," defined as reflecting and acting on the world in order to transform it (Freire 1970), promotes acting on the identified sociopolitical consciousness and remaining accountable. Through praxis, with equitable transformation as an end goal, teachers make commitments to finding ways to counter dominant mainstream teaching trends that support only one way to create or adapt curriculum, lesson plans, and evaluations to meet the needs of learners. These commitments stimulate rich conversations about official knowledge (Apple 2000), focusing on curriculum and standards that pose questions like "for whom?" and "for what purpose?" in order to serve most students' needs and accommodate students best. We connect the theoretical concepts of CRP and the methodologies of CIRM and praxis to active civic engagement in order to encourage teachers to engage the communities in which they work in relevant, significant, and meaningful ways.

One way to begin to connect the classroom to the tribal community is to merge the school curriculum, often connected to Euro-American knowledge systems, with the culture of Indigenous communities, connected to Native knowledge systems. Barnhardt and Kawagley (2005) explain this connection in their proposed "converging streams of knowledge" as illustrated in figure 2 below.

Barnhardt and Kawagley underscore that, through collaboration and joint effort, a systematic integration of both Euro-American teaching initiatives and Indigenous knowledge systems can come to coexist, which makes the Native knowledge systems more accessible to schools and integrates more traditional local knowledge into the curriculum (2005). Considering these different ways of knowing, teachers working with Indigenous students acknowledge that Native cultures are much more than songs, music, and clothing. The understandings conveyed through the converging streams of knowledge represent ways for teachers to access deeper knowledge systems and to become involved in their community. These convergent streams tap into local knowledge and work with sources of this knowledge in holistic ways to encourage teachers of Indigenous students to become more involved in Indigenous communities in order to better understand how to integrate and weave tougher community understandings and school curricula.

Even within the pedagogical frameworks that we described, it is important for teachers to recognize their role and the power they hold in any classroom community. As Thornton (2004) argues, teachers maintain great power as "gatekeepers" to the classroom and in the nature of classroom culture, curriculum, and student engagement. Teachers of American Indian students may need to find gatekeepers in their Indigenous community in order to access traditional cultural knowledge. Informed by both community-based pedagogy and this "converging stream of knowledge," we will provide, in the following sections, several pedagogical approaches for social studies teachers to consider when working with American Indian students.

Instructional Approaches

Several different instructional approaches could be utilized to incorporate culturally responsive pedagogy, indigenous knowledge frameworks, and history and social science disciplinary inquiry. We will explore these approaches briefly and include references for more in-depth investigation of these approaches and the corresponding curriculum resources in Appendix C.

"Inquiry" is a way of viewing knowledge and the world as well as a specific method of learning. Inquiry involves active engagement in ill-structured problems and questions where there is more than one legitimate answer. Inquiry lessons lead students to hypothesize, question, collect, and analyze information and data, in order to construct evidence-based knowledge. This

NATIVE KNOWLEDGE STREAM

Academies of Elders/
   Elders-in-Residence

AISES Chapters/Science Fairs

Alaska Native Knowledge Network

Alaska Native Science Commission

Alaska Natives Commission Report

Cultural Standards/Organizers

Indigenous Graduate Studies

Regional Cultural Atlas

SPIRAL Framework for
   Curriculum Resources

WESTERN KNOWLEDGE STREAM

Alaska's Standards Adopted

AOTE/ARC Case Studies

Math/Science Curriculum
   Frameworks

Performance Assessment System

Performance Standards
   for Graduation

Quality Schools Standards
   (accreditation)

Teacher/Administrator Standards

SYSTEMIC INTEGRATION

AKRSI/ARC

Cultural Camps

Native Educators Professional Organization

Native Ways of Knowing

Rural Educators Partnership Program

Science Camps

Scientists-in-Residence

Village Science

Figure 2. Converging streams of knowledge.

pedagogical approach emphasizes the constructed nature of knowledge and values cultural perspectives and a wide range of evidence. This approach can also be used across the range of social studies classes and at all age levels.

An inquiry lesson begins with a good question or problem. These should not be questions for which there is a simple empirical or factual answer. Instead, these questions or problems should require interpretation, investigation, and the collection and use of evidence to construct a warranted argument. For example, a government teacher could begin a lesson with a scenario like, "If you were the president of your Indigenous community how would you solve _____?" Whenever possible, and especially at the beginning of a school year, select issues that are important to the students and their specific communities to fill in that blank. For this example, the teacher could explain that students will need to identify a solution that is equitable (fair and just) and one that follows correct procedures and protocols. Determining the best answer will require students to follow a process: (1) to find primary and secondary resources; (2) to learn the actual steps of how to pass proposed legislation; (3) to prepare an amendment; (4) to bring items up to their local Chapter House; and (5) to go through the proper channels to contact their legislative representative. The students are in charge of their own learning, and they solve problems that are significant and meaningful to their community. Thus, inquiry goes beyond learning simply a static government structure. Instead, students are engaged in both the process of identifying issues and the content of proposed solutions to those issues that are relevant and important to them. This approach emphasizes learning the process that produces knowledge and the development of students as empowered citizens.

Similarly, historical inquiry engages students in examining a historical issue or question that has multiple and competing answers or a problem for which there may be many different perspectives on what happened and why. Christine Rogers Stanton (2012) uses the example of "Chief Joseph" and the Nez Perces to demonstrate how critical Indigenous epistemologies may be used to engage students in an inquiry into the way Chief Joseph has become iconic in historical accounts of the American West and why this has occurred. Students engage in examining the historical context, the ways in which the U.S. soldiers misinterpreted Joseph's role in the Nez Perce tribe and the ways in which the historical record has been shaped by these misunderstandings and the desire to tell a compelling story that met the goals of the national historical narrative of the United States. Historical inquiry engages Indigenous students through asking them to challenge dominant Euro-American historical accounts, to develop skills in analyzing historical evidence, and to utilize indigenous theories of nature and knowledge to identify different perspectives and voices from a given time period.

Examples of Inquiry: Oral History

"Oral history is . . . a means for transforming both the content and purpose of history. It can be used to change the focus of history itself, and open up new areas of inquiry; it can break down barriers between teachers and students, between generations, between educational institutions and the world outside; . . . it can give back to the people who made and experienced history, through their own words, a central place" (P. Thompson [1978] 1988, 2). Integrating oral history into the curriculum, by having students collect the knowledge from community members, empowers students to do what many of them have always done growing up in their communities—to listen and learn from stories. In the classroom, the teacher could break this process down to include reading, writing, listening, and speaking skills, such as: (1) identifying a topic of interest; (2) considering appropriate primary and secondary sources to gain information on a given subject; (3) creating an overarching purpose/research question; (4) writing questions that will draw out answers to the larger inquiry; (5) practicing the questions; (6) conducting the interviews; (7) transcribing the interviews; (8) uploading the interview data in a repository for other people to access; (9) presenting the research data to the class ; and (10) providing feedback to one another.

Oral histories could foster a new way of learning in the classroom that supports an Indigenous epistemology, or way of knowing: stories. Indigenous students have acquired skills and knowledge in their communities through stories their whole lives. Highlighting the value of that knowledge through collecting and depositing stories in a community repository, would allow many more people to access this knowledge in the present and future. Many stories are of vital importance historically, especially to individual communities. Oral history accounts could provide access to these stories and could also serve to make connections between generations. Through these connections, Indigenous youth can acknowledge elders and the wisdom and knowledge they hold in tribally communal specific ways, and they can give back to the communities that have provided so much for them.

Some examples of oral history websites include: http://www.starschool .org/, a middle school program that provides demonstrations of student digital performances, and http://oybm.org, a filmmaking organization. Outta Your Backpack Media (OYBM) hosts youth filmmaking workshops. A documentary film produced by a young Diné girl participating in an OYBM workshop, *In the Footsteps of Yellow Woman* stars the young girl's grandmother. In the documentary, which received much praise, the grandmother teaches the young girl about her ancestral heritage (http://www.imdb.com/title /tt1504246/). Since today's youth live in the digital age, it is important to determine ways to use that format as a teaching tool to motivate young people to actively engage in learning.

HISTORIOGRAPHY AND PERSPECTIVE RECOGNITION

Another valuable inquiry approach to borrow from history is the historiographical lens. This approach asks students to not only focus on their own interpretations of the past from evidence, but also to analyze other representations of the past included in different text and visual forms (for example, textbooks, monuments, and films). Engaging students in historiography enables them to learn different perspectives from the past, but it also helps them to recognize the influence of the historical, social, and political context on how history is represented and how Indigenous representations, in particular, have changed over time. Students can be engaged in analyzing textbook representations of Indigenous peoples from different periods in history and then asked to identify the reasons why change occurs in the way Native people are represented, and what these changes mean in relation to the ways that American Indian history is taught and learned. Or the students can compare textbook representations to other pieces of evidence, such as primary sources, interviews, newspaper articles, or oral history stories collected during the time period. Students should be asked to consider textbooks as a concept and to think about for whom and for what purpose (Apple 1993) the textbooks are structured. The students could also engage in thinking about how certain events are selected to be included in textbooks and the limits of the perspectives those textbooks contain.

It is important for all students, but particularly for Indigenous students, to develop an understanding of historical perspective and the motivations and contexts of historical agents. This perspective helps students understand why events occurred and why they were allowed to occur. This deeper understanding of history could also include stories of marginalized groups who resisted colonialism, but whose stories are not included in the dominant historical narrative. For example, when studying an event such as the U.S.-Dakota War of 1862, also known as the Sioux Uprising, which took place largely in present-day Minnesota, students could engage in recognizing and understanding perspectives of the Dakotas who took up arms to attack settlers, the U.S. Army, and towns, as well as Dakotas who protected white settlers and did not join in the fight. What drove their decisions and what were the social and cultural contexts at that time in Minnesota that contributed to the conflict? Students need to engage in recognizing perspectives from the past and understanding the context of events, to inquire about other past and present events, and to seek out and evaluate alternative perspectives and primary and secondary accounts.

Because Hollywood films are often identified as a major culprit in perpetuating stereotypes of American Indians and Indigenous history, the historiographic analysis of film and other visual texts can also be a useful endeavor.

Seixas (1994) found that young people often do not view film from contemporary times as being stereotypical or inaccurate, only films from previous eras. Students can be engaged in analyzing the changing representations of American Indians on film, from early Westerns to films from the 1950s, and again in more recent decades. What similarities and differences do they see in what is represented? How are Indigenous people presented visually and as part of the film narrative? How accurate is the film when compared to historical sources? Who plays the American Indian characters, Indigenous or non-Native actors? Who writes the script and who produces and funds the film? How does the film represent the particular social, historical, and political era in which the story is set and those contexts when the movie was made?

For example, early films often included white actors in "red face" playing American Indian characters. Later films make greater and lesser attempts to include Indigenous perspectives, but they often either present American Indians as savages, as victims, or in a romanticized view that does not allow for depth in the characters or film narrative. Instead, historical inaccuracies and a lack of cultural understanding are perpetuated in film representations (Singer 2001). Similar types of analyses can also be applied to studies of historic monuments and other representations, by placing an emphasis on the historical and cultural context of the monument in order to understand the perspectives that it represents.

More recently, new films are being made by Indigenous filmmakers that feature American Indian casts and attempt to challenge the historical representation of Indigenous peoples on screen and include more accurate and culturally reflective stories. For example, *Smoke Signals* (1998) is one of the first films to feature an all American Indian cast and is also written by an Indigenous author. While adhering to some Western film genre components, *Smoke Signals* also challenges many of the stereotypical representations of Native peoples in Hollywood films. A more recent movie, *The Only Good Indian* (2009), was less critically acclaimed but attempts to portray the history of assimilation and American Indian boarding schools at the turn of the twentieth century, and acts of resistance on the part of American Indians to this cultural hegemony. In addition to Hollywood-style films, documentaries and more local productions are being used both to communicate and preserve Indigenous history as well as for other uses within Native communities.

Besides analyzing and critiquing historical representations of American Indian history, students should be engaged in producing their own media and representations. Advances in technology now allow students to create media, such as websites and digital videos, with little equipment or expertise. Projects centered on collecting oral history or creating a video that challenges stereotypical views of American Indians would help students apply what they have learned and create authentic products to share with their classes and their community.

PLACE-BASED EDUCATION

"Native people have begun to reintegrate their own knowledge systems into the school curriculum as a basis for connecting what students learn in school with life out of school . . . a pedagogy of place that shifts the emphasis from teaching about local culture to teaching through the culture as students learn about the immediate places they inhabit and their connection to the larger world within which they will make a life for themselves" (Barnhardt 2005).

Place-based education values students' local communities as an important and significant resource for learning. Land contains literal and figurative space. Basso (1996) writes: "What people make of their place is closely connected to what they make of themselves as members of society and inhabitants of the earth" (7). Indigenous tribal members revere their reservation land and the resources it affords them; the reservation has provided them a homeland and a means to survive and thrive as a community. Many American Indians express an obligation to maintain the land for future generations and want to learn its history in order to sustain its foundation. This approach shifts emphasis from teaching *about* culture to teaching *through* culture.

GEOGRAPHY AND ECOLOGY

Similar to the inquiry approach previously described for examining the past, another inquiry and deliberation approach can be used to examine geography and ecology through engaging Indigenous students in environmental and economic issues revolving around natural resources, sovereignty rights, and the Native relationship with the Earth. This approach focuses on issues that are relevant to American Indian students locally, but also serves as an examination of case studies of larger perennial issues, allowing for multiple perspectives, the use of different forms of evidence, and open dialogue, deliberation, and analysis. This approach can also integrate knowledge from history and Indigenous worldviews, policy and politics, environmental science, and geography.

Geography is vastly important to Indigenous history and culture, and it needs to include content from science (geology, geographic features, climate science, and social science data related to human geography), as well as an understanding of our historical and cultural relationship to geography. Therefore, geography should be integrated into history and civics courses, as well as taught as a separate course. American Indian students would also benefit from the study of their own nations' relationship to geography, the geographical relationships of other Indigenous peoples, and the role of geography in the history of colonialism. The key is to focus on geography as both a science and a social science, because geography is important for understanding many of the issues related to the environment and other public issues important to

American Indians, as well as understanding the personal and spiritual connections of Indigenous peoples to the Earth.

Deliberation of issues is also one way to engage young people as citizens (Hess 2009; Parker 2003); this pedagogical approach helps students develop the knowledge and skills necessary for successful citizenship in their community and beyond. For example, geography and environmental issues are fundamental issues for many American Indian groups across the United States. These issues include disputes over historic rights to hunting, fishing, and wild rice production lands granted in treaties. They also include current issues related to natural resource extraction and potential pollution, such as the "fracking" used to extract oil or natural gas, as well as perennial issues related to global warming and climate change. Engaging students in learning about these important issues helps them to develop expertise in important areas, as well as skills for participating as voters and citizens. Further, this deliberative approach to geography values Indigenous perspectives and also helps to tie issues of environment and geography to the study of government.

GOVERNMENT AND CITIZENSHIP

It is of fundamental importance that Indigenous students gain an understanding of the institutions and power structures of government in order to use that knowledge as active citizens. This is true of both their local government and national governments. Some American Indian students like learning about their local government and comparing it to other governments. Traditionally speaking, some Indigenous communities functioned as a direct democracy. Everyone had a voice and nothing moved forward until there was consensus. Ill feelings were lessened if you were not chosen to be a leader. Instead, people who were not elected looked at it as a personal challenge: "I'm not chosen this time. Not everyone agreed for me to become the leader. That means I just have to wait and continue to improve myself until I can become that person." This philosophy comes from a strong traditional understanding of the teachings that exist in Indigenous communities about being patient and improving oneself until it is time to be whatever is chosen for you. In addition to community members, this applies to outsiders being invited to participate in community activities; until one is invited, the outsider must wait because it is not yet time for them to become involved.

As part of the curriculum, teachers should engage students to examine their Native community government structure and see how it is similar to and different from the United States government. Provide students with specifics on how things work, like how to pass a law and how to campaign. Consider hands-on learning, in which students can learn how to campaign, for example, by having them run for a certain position. Within a government unit like this, have the students research the positions, the qualifications for each office, and the contemporary issues important to voters. Using this information, then have the students: (1) write a speech showing how they meet these qualifications and make statements about contemporary local issues they are ready to address; (2) present the speech to the class; (3) debate issues other student "voters" present; (3) vote for one candidate versus another; (4) justify their votes; and (5) write a reflection on how it felt running for office or voting for one candidate versus another.

Students learn much more when they realize that they have power and a voice, and that there are many ways for them to act as citizens within and outside of formal government structures. As Levinson (2012) advocates, young people from groups who have been historically marginalized from the dominant culture need to be able to understand and value their own culture and history, but they also must be able to understand the history of the dominant culture in order to be able to take action and use their power as citizens and as a nation.

TEACHING RECOMMENDATIONS

In addition to pedagogical frameworks and approaches, it is also important for teachers to understand how and why Indigenous ways of knowing translates into value systems to include in daily practices, throughout their entire curriculum. In this final section, we offer six recommendations utilizing Indigenous perspectives that teachers should consider incorporating through content (*what* to teach) and pedagogy (*how* and *why* to teach) when working with American Indian students.

1. INTEGRATE TOPICS INTO YOUR CURRICULUM THAT ARE SIGNIFICANT, MEANINGFUL, AND RELEVANT TO THE COMMUNITY AND THE STUDENTS. Students need to identify issues and topics of interest so teachers can build from this knowledge and motivate the students to learn. The teacher also guides students to know which skills, issues, events, and topics are important for students to study at particular grade levels. At this point, the teacher could use knowledge of the students' interests and backgrounds to help them discover these additional topics of interest and integrate them into lessons in a relevant way. The key is to guide students to understand *why* this content or issue is important and why it might be relevant to them.

2. VALIDATE THE KNOWLEDGE AND TRUTH STUDENTS BRING INTO THE CLASSROOM. An important consideration when teaching American Indian students social studies is to validate where the students come from and what they know. Social Studies curricula is most often relayed to the students through textbooks. And most of the authors of these texts have a different background from the American Indian students. Therefore, a teacher working

with American Indian students must understand the history and culture of the students and their communities. Teachers should identify important historical and contemporary community events and be ready to integrate those into the curriculum. They should also seek out multicultural resources and texts (see Appendix C for a sampling) that provide a wider array of relevant perspectives than the common textbook.

For example, consider countering the common narrative of Manifest Destiny by having the students look at the reasoning behind that concept, how it was used for political and economic gains, and how the Indigenous people in these colonized areas were affected by westward expansion. Furthermore, it is important for students to understand why events happened the way they did in the past, what the motivations and circumstances were, and the historical context in which the events took place. The questions "For whom?" and "For what purpose?" an event occurred often lead to deeper knowledge about topics.

Equally important, however, is for teachers to seek out and present counter narratives and perspectives that have been historically marginalized and are important and valuable. Internet resources such as *The Zinn Education Project* and books like *A People's History for the Classroom* (Bigelow 2008) provide articles and evidence to support discussion topics like "Discovering Columbus," "The People *vs.* Columbus, et al.," and "Teaching about Unsung Heroes" (Bigelow 2008). Consider including lessons from *Rethinking Columbus* (Bigelow and Peterson 1998) to help Indigenous students re-read the past and gain a sense of how history is constructed and who constructs it.

Empower students to use evidence to construct their own accounts of history. Understand that Indigenous students are constantly negotiating two world perspectives, Indigenous and non-Indigenous. As teachers, explore ways to value and validate their Indigenous communities and understand how they interface, both in harmony and in tension with, national and global worldviews. Through cultural competence (Ladson-Billings 1994), find ways to support the students' quest to know their culture and to understand the perspectives from other dominant and non-dominant cultures.

3. UNDERSTAND COMMUNITY VALUE SYSTEMS. Indigenous students have their own varying levels of connection to traditional values, ethics, morals, and teachings that guide them in all the things they do. Traditional knowledge is something that is practiced daily, a system that creates their identity and shapes how they interact with the world around them. A teacher of Indigenous students must have a good understanding of the Indigenous community's value systems. And this teacher must know what those Native teachings are to truly touch the heart of the child and be able to guide them in the learning process.

To be effective with American Indian students, teachers must have a good understanding of their community's value system, the value system that their students' "home teachers" have. These home teachers are usually their grandparents or parents, or other relatives and community members. Value systems evolve from a traditional and historical standpoint. And they include more than one value. It's important to be up early, to bless yourself with the dawn, to run, to be thankful, to be humble, and to give back to your community. All these things are understood by children in Indigenous cultures. In order to teach an American Indian student history, instructors should check what they are teaching, and ask, "Is this knowledge coming from their Native value systems or from an entirely different viewpoint?" An effective teacher would validate and value what the American Indian students already know and then build from that knowledge, using the text as a secondary source.

Teachers should validate the Indigenous students' knowledge because they already hold it as true, as truth. When they are being taught stories in their Indigenous culture, a lot of times the speakers begin with the words, which translate in English as, "A long time ago it was said. . . ." And a lot of Native people hold these teachings as truth because they come from a primary source. An elder or a grandparent is often telling the story, and they are saying it because their elders or grandparent said it. And they are able to say it because that person was there. That person was at the Long Walk or the Trail of Tears or was a Navajo Code Talker during World War II. That person fought in that war. That person was the chief at the time. So, it's almost like the students are learning from the primary source, because their people hold on to those stories.

4. SEEK INDIGENOUS MENTORS. Some communities have people who are ready to share Indigenous knowledge openly and others will guard this knowledge as sacred. The keepers of knowledge have been chosen to be leaders, and they will determine with whom they can share this knowledge. Invest time with people in school and the broader educational and societal community to show that you are committed to them and to the success of their children. Go to the community chapter meetings or school board meetings. See who the people are that hold the power in these gatherings. They hold the power because of the respect that they have earned. Making connections with those leaders is a good idea because, once they trust that you are invested in the community, they can guide and direct you in communally accepted ways. Perhaps not right away, but know, that as time goes on, you will eventually meet someone who is knowledgeable and can guide you in important ways.

5. BECOME INVOLVED IN YOUR COMMUNITY. In every case, becoming involved in the community shows your authentic dedication to it and may enable you

to ask questions to help you better understand its philosophies. You may eventually be invited to participate in ceremonies and other events, but understand that some knowledge may be too sacred to share with an outsider. Respect for these interactions is most important. Some ceremonies are tied to oral stories, tied to what is called "the beginning," meaning the beginning of all things, the creation. Understand that all Indigenous knowledge and teachings are tied to that origin story.

Realize that you must earn your place within the community, which could take months or years. To earn this place, you must be involved, show respect, and help out. An American Indian student described his grandmother's house as a place where everyone is accepted, where people feed each other before they are hungry, where everyone loves each other unconditionally, and where there is no translation for "I'm sorry" because they live a life never needing to use that term. Knowing and participating through these philosophies will demonstrate your understanding of community ways. So, if a family invites you to dinner, accept, bring food, and help out. The more teachers do with the community, the better their chances will be for the people to welcome them, want to teach them community ways, and want to learn with and from those teachers.

6. Serve as a role model. And finally, we complete the circle within this chapter by returning to the advice shared in the opening quote: "So the advice I would give to teachers is pretty much the same I would give to students: be a lifelong learner who cares about modeling this for others." As a teacher of social studies, it is important for a teacher to be a good role model both in the school and community. Show the students that you are doing what you are telling them to do. So, if you are an advocate for learning, show them that *you* are learning. Explain the educational choices you have made and are still making today. Show them that you read and research and make connections with people to build relationships and gain knowledge. In brief, if you teach social studies, show them that you are a teacher *as well as* a student of social studies.

Explain how much there is to know and how there are multiple opportunities to learn by listening, observing, reading, and researching. Illustrate how learning opens new doors and creates more questions. Demonstrating these actions will show students that you are interested in knowledge, that you are interested in them, that you are interested in their education, and that you are interested in their success. Explain this in a manner that demonstrates a culture of caring (Valenzuela 1999) that uses additive schooling practices, which view Indigenous languages and culture as assets to build on, to validate and value their identities and understand where they come from. When you do this, the students will meet you half way. These are important considerations to keep in mind when designing curriculum and selecting materials to use in teaching social studies, while also incorporating Indigenous knowledge systems, culture, and community values.

CONCLUSION

Following the advice attributed to Sioux leader Sitting Bull, "Let us put our minds together and see what life we can make for our children," it is important to take the education and content knowledge you have and find ways and means to continually merge it with the Indigenous knowledge of your community. While recognizing the culture and worldviews of their students, teachers must also recognize the skills and knowledge the students will need to participate as citizens in their nations and globally. They will need to understand the nature of power and the institutional structures used to maintain that power. They will need to know how to engage as active citizens to advocate for change in the best interests of their communities. This work is challenging, both for teachers and students, but necessary, necessary for the preservation of Indigenous cultures and no less important for the survival of democratic education and our global society.

7
Music

CHAD HAMILL

Although ethnomusicologists long ago abandoned the notion of developing a universally applicable definition of music, there is one conclusion on which we can readily agree: music is a human necessity. Every culture possesses something that can be called music, utilizing melody and rhythm as a form of cultural expression that shapes individual and collective identities. Although music remains mysterious, powerful, and resistant to quantification, recent studies in cognitive science and neuroscience have shed new light on music's multifaceted role in human development and behavior.

In a study designed to measure cognitive transfer among children learning instrumental music (transfer is the effect that skill acquisition in one domain has on skills and cognitive performances in other domains), it was found that in addition to improving melodic and rhythmic discernment and fine motor skills, children with at least three years of musical training outperformed their control counterparts in verbal ability and nonverbal reasoning (Forgeard, Winner, Norton, and Schlaug 2008). Other studies have demonstrated the relationship between the development of musical skills and phonological processing, reading ability, and increased full-scale IQs (Anvari et al. 2002; Schellenberg 2004). Utilizing neuroimaging technology (MRIs), ongoing studies have shown that multiple areas of the brain are fed by music, an indication of why the brains of adult professional musicians are larger than those of nonmusicians (Gaser and Schlaug 2003). Music occupies quite a bit of cognitive real estate, and despite the perpetual marginalization of music programs in public schools, it appears that music continues to make students smarter.

For millennia, music has been at the center of American Indian lifeways, facilitating connections between people in social and spiritual contexts. Across Native Nations, traditional song has been part of a larger matrix tied to ceremony, in which many facets of spiritual expression—dancing, singing, and drumming—are viewed as functionally indistinguishable, operating holistically to contribute to the manifestation of spiritual power. Songs sung outside of a ceremonial sphere, such as those sung at powwows, often have a spiritual dimension as well. For Native peoples, songs have always been much more than "music" in a conventional sense. Songs are seamlessly woven into the social, cultural, and spiritual fabric of Native communities, so much so that one would be hard pressed to find a word in any of the hundreds of Native American languages that can be translated simply as "music."

In the first week of teaching my Native American Music class at Northern Arizona University, I am quick to make this distinction, emphasizing that culturally embedded forms of traditional Native American songs are not performances, they are prayers. I also inform students that in addition to traditional songs, they will hear a variety of contemporary Native American musical genres that utilize performance, including rock, metal, jazz, and rap. In this chapter, I will outline my pedagogical approach to teaching this broad spectrum of Native American music, with a particular emphasis on employing culturally relevant methodologies in the classroom. Native American students will be part of the discussion, offering critical perspectives on what they feel works best for them. Although I teach at the college level, my approach can easily be applied to upper-level elementary, middle, and high school students.

SINGING

In addition to playing recordings, assigning readings, and facilitating in-class discussions, I teach the students songs. Native ways of knowing have never relied on the printed page or a cursory, one-way transmission method from teacher to student. Learning to sing a song requires embodiment, a process by which a song is taken in and given back in a way that reflects the unique voice and constitution of the individual. A student who embodies a song and sings it has a relationship to it, one that often awakens within Native students an innate sense of knowing, rooted in ancient lifeways. One of my students, Dustin Rector, expresses this in terms of the Chumash welcoming song, a song I learned to sing in the context of ceremonies in Chumash homelands (a region along the coast and inland territories of what is now referred to generally as Santa Barbara, California):

> It's like the Chumash welcoming song. I'm not Chumash but I felt something, I really liked it. . . . Like this summer we're going to do a Sunrise Dance, and this class helped me to connect with myself. When we were singing the songs, you felt harmony—connecting with that harmony within yourself. I'm sure I'll need that this summer and the summer after that. (April 27, 2012)

For Native American students, singing traditional songs can play an important role in strengthening identity. Another of my students, Burrell Jones, described how he walked away with a voice. Just hearing those songs that you play and teaching us music. Hearing them on a different level, especially with the spiritual connection to it. I walked away with something to believe. . . . I don't have much experience with traditional ceremonies, but this class brought me to understand the significance of it. The class made me want to learn some Navajo songs. (May 7, 2012)

Even when the songs taught are not from a student's home culture, Native American students often relate to them on a visceral level. Traditional Native American songs are not homogenous, differing widely from one culture to another in terms of vocal range, melodic complexity, and tempo. Yet there is an intangible quality that remains consistent within songs that have developed over time and on lands that, despite the innumerable state lines that crisscross them, remain continuous and unbroken. Like language, songs are at the essence of who we are as Native people. The act of singing collectively as a class erases divisions fueled by an overly individualistic and hypercompetitive society, quickly creating a unified circle that mirrors the cooperative and communal qualities of Native communities.

Regardless of the benefits, there are a number of reasons why teachers might feel reluctant to bring traditional Native American songs into the classroom. Songs are often "owned," and it is up to the person in charge of that song or ceremony to decide whether to grant permission for its use out of context. Many traditional singers, including medicine people, have stated that a song can lose its spiritual power or even cause physical harm if used improperly. (In my teaching I sing only songs that qualify for classroom use, keeping songs of a more sacred nature to myself.) In cases where teachers do not have the option of singing traditional songs, they might consider inviting traditional singers to the classroom. For students, learning songs taught by a community culture bearer can have the added benefit of reinforcing processes of enculturation historically reserved for life outside the classroom, providing another context by which tradition can be passed on. Inviting cultural leaders from the community also has the potential to reframe their role in the eyes of young Native students, who might otherwise view the keepers of *old* traditions as old-fashioned. In Native communities where traditions are at risk and young and older generations struggle to find common ground, the classroom can be another important site of cultural immersion and sustainability.

LISTENING

The landscape of Indian Country is vast. For the purposes of bringing into view its broad cultural strokes, I begin the semester by discussing tribes in terms of geographic regions: the Northwest, the Southwest, the Plains, and the East. Doing it this way (which is by no means comprehensive) provides a level of cultural contrast for students as they begin to grasp the enormous diversity found among Indigenous groups of North America. I focus primarily on tribes south of Canada. We take one region at a time, exploring select cultures through readings, recordings, and discussion. For recordings, I have students keep a listening journal. For every song played, students not only listen, they write. Because listening is an individuated task that takes place exclusively between the ears, an instructor has no idea of the extent to which listening is actually happening in each student. By writing while listening, students are focused and engaged in the listening process, picking up the nuances of melody, instrumentation, and tonal quality that might be lost during passive listening, when the mind is prone to wander. Writing also puts students directly in touch with how they feel about a song, helping them to articulate their thoughts in class discussions that follow each recording. Like singing, listening can help Native American students connect with cultural and ancestral taproots in a way that can be personal, immediate, and powerful. Referring to recordings of traditional songs, Shanicey Pinto, another of my students, says, "When I hear the beating of the drum and the voice that was passed down so many years, I hear my ancestors' voice[s]" (April 30, 2012).

As with songs, choices in recorded music should be made carefully. Teachers should avoid anything that feeds stereotypes, such as the myriad of songs written by non-Indigenous composers inspired by romantic, Hollywood-style notions of Native Americans. Inauthentic and misappropriated images, movies, and music can be terribly damaging, undermining the development of a healthy identity for the student. As a final caution, when searching for authentic recordings of traditional music, make sure they do not contain songs reserved for sacred ceremonies. There are many recordings of traditional Native American music in circulation that should never have been made, another reason why working with a Native cultural leader or tribal consultant is wise.

CONTEMPORARY NATIVE AMERICAN MUSIC

In addition to learning and listening to traditional music, students in my Native American Music class are introduced to a range of contemporary Native American recording artists. This has had a palpable effect on Native and non-Native students alike. For non-Native students, it pulls their conceptions of Native Americans into the present, an important step for students who—through years of exposure to biased, ethnocentric histories—have been conditioned to view Native Americans as relics of a bygone era. Familiar instrumentation (guitar, bass, saxophone, drum set, etc.) and genres (jazz, rock, classical, country, metal, folk, and rap) make contemporary Native American music more accessible to non-Native students, who typically become more engaged and enthusiastic, and occasionally unsettled, by what they hear during this section of the course. Native American students also enthusiastically embrace contemporary musical styles, but often from a more personal and informed perspective:

> I really love the old traditions and I wish that was the way it was, but I think that the contemporary music is more inspirational because it's Native American musicians, and they have to adapt to this newer society. By just going backwards they are only putting themselves in more struggles, but by putting it out there and trying it their way but also using their beliefs—that's what the Native Americans need to do. That way it kind of shows the best of both worlds. We can play contemporary music, but we still have our traditions. (Tya Manygoats, April 4, 2012)

Tya commends musicians for simultaneously looking forward *and* looking back, using contemporary musical forms as a vehicle in the present while referencing a Native American worldview rooted in the past. Although Native people have perhaps grown tired of the oft-used "walking in two worlds" metaphor, it persists for a reason. Tya suggests that Native American artists have perhaps bridged the gap, forming through their music a new—but no less Native—identity.

JOHN TRUDELL

One of the artists I feature in my Native American Music class is John Trudell (Santee Sioux), a courageous poet, activist, musician, and actor who has been a critical voice of truth and resistance in Indian Country since the late 1960s. During the All Tribes occupation of Alcatraz from November 1969 to June 1971, Trudell became a spokesperson for the movement, wielding words that deftly cut through media noise and misinformation with surgical precision. Following the occupation, Trudell was the last active chairman of the American Indian Movement (AIM). After a personal tragedy in 1978 in which he lost his wife, mother-in-law, and four children in a suspicious house fire, he began writing lines of poetry, lines he would "hang onto" to help him find a way forward. Those lines became *Tribal Voice* (1983), a collection of spoken-word poems interspersed with traditional Native American singing and drumming. (Originally released as a cassette recording, *Tribal Voice* became part of the 2011 box-set release *John Trudell: The Collection 1983–1992*.) Selections from *Tribal Voice* and Trudell's many other records can be streamed online at www .johntrudellarchives.com.

Trudell's recorded performances have an immediate impact on students, Native and non-Native alike. Prescient, provocative, and penetrating, his songs are often followed by a period of contemplative silence in my classroom, during which students appear to be processing what they have just encountered. Using the official AIM song as a backdrop, the piece *Look At Us* captures the eloquent and uncompromising quality of Trudell's art. When I play it in class, I ask students to write down lines that jump out at them, giving us a starting point for discussion. Although some of my non-Native students may be initially "surprised at [his] anger," it provides the opportunity to have an important conversation about the epic five-hundred year cultural clash of the Americas and its many casualties. Trudell often aims his poetry squarely at the elephant in the room, firing a shot that flies directly into the heart of the matter. Free of ambiguity, his words allow for an uncluttered and meaningful discussion involving the whole class.

Among Native American students, the effect of Trudell's work cannot be underestimated. For Tya Manygoats, it changed the direction of her course-work as well as her life:

> When I first came into NAU [Northern Arizona University], my major was set. But someone informed me that I needed a minor. I started with Visual Communications, but I also wanted to take Navajo classes because after my grandfather passed away I kind of made it a goal of mine to learn Navajo so I can talk to my grandma more. I don't want both of my grandparents to go without me getting to know them. So I was thinking about Visual Communications as my first choice and Native American studies my second, but after taking this course I realized how—especially after going into the Trudell stuff—to change the reservation and make a difference, with the Navajo Nation and sovereignty. That's what changed my mind. The music course made me have more passion for my people, and I wanted to do something with my education. (April 4, 2012)

From the beginning, the education of Native American students in the United States was designed to indoctrinate, in an effort to sever the ties that bound them to their culture and family, and to reconstitute them as pseudo–white Americans. As the chapters in this volume indicate, much has changed. But in imparting the tools with which to compete in the dominant culture, K–12 schools and colleges still create—irrespective of intention—an assimilation effect. For Native students, the music of John Trudell can be a powerful beacon for Native identity, quickly bringing into focus what can become lost in the din of the non-Native world that surrounds them:

> With John Trudell I thought it was interesting because he incorporated a history of Native Americans that probably isn't written, but just this oral kind of tradition. It's very poetic. It sounds like if you translated any Native language into English it would sound just like that, fluid, power-ful, and captivating. It's in the tone. He wrote a poem about a lady, I like the way he talked about her, how she was connected with the Mother

Earth, seeing the beauty of it. Not being able to capture it but just looking at it from a distance. (Burrell Jones, May 7, 2012)

The "poem" Burrell refers to is Trudell's "See the Woman" (1992). Our Native American students—perhaps now more than ever—need exposure to
positive representations of women. We currently live with the tragic statistic
that one in every three Native American women will be raped during their
lifetimes. For countless centuries before European contact, women were the
heart, soul, and backbone of Native communities. The cruel victimization
they endure is a symptom of a much broader problem. When Native communities are healed, women will once again occupy the center of our lifeways.
For now, music can quickly illuminate what a discussion alone cannot, the
"eyes," the "heart," and the "spirit" of our timeless Native women, who remain,
as Trudell's song tells us, integral and beautiful "in all ages" (line 4).

Another song that Native American students readily connect with is "NDN
Kars" (1992). Written by Keith Secola (Ojibway), it has become a classic in Indian Country, a catchy rock and roll number with traditional Native singing
that has a way, as Burrell Jones puts it, of "playing in your head over and over":

I've been driving in my Indian Car
Hear the pound of the wheels drumming in my brain
My dash is dusty, my plates are expired
Please Mr. Officer, let me explain
I got to make it to a Pow Wow tonight
I'll be singing 49, down by the riverside
Looking for a sugar, riding in my Indian Car

Got my T-bird in the glove box, I ain't got no spare
Got a feather from an eagle, I ain't got no care
The road is empty in my bottle of desire
Daylight is breaking, the sun touches fire
I got to make another Pow Wow tonight
I'll be singing 49, down by the riverside
Looking for a sugar, riding in my Indian Car

My car is dented, the radiator steams
One headlight don't work, the radio can scream
I got a sticker says "Indian Power"
I stuck it on my bumper, that's what holds my car together
We're on a circuit of an Indian dream
We don't get old, we just get younger
When we're flying down the highway
Riding in our Indian Cars

We're on a circuit of an Indian dream
We don't get old, we just get younger
When we're flying down the highway
Riding in our Indian Cars
Riding in our Indian Cars
Riding in our Indian Cars

Hoka . . .

"NDN Kars" speaks directly to the contemporary Native American experience, conveying the unique character of the "Indian car," a symbol of perseverance that, like the indomitable Native American spirit, just keeps on rolling. It addresses the issue of discrimination ("driving while Indian") and the daunting socioeconomic reality of most Native people while speaking to a unique set of values that transcends both. There is a sense that, despite the roadblocks, in the end the eagle feather will help the driver to prevail, confirming the sweet irony of the "Indian Power" bumper sticker and getting him to the powwow to sing the 49. Ultimately the car is just a vehicle for the Native spirit, which doesn't grow "old," it "just get[s] younger," eternal, vibrant, and free. The song ends with "*Hoka*" followed by a war whoop, urging the listener to keep on rolling, defiant and strong in the face of adversity.

CO-TEACHING

In my Native American Music class I emphasize discussion rather than a standard lecture format. As Swisher and Deyhle point out, Native American students "are predisposed to participate more readily in group or team situations" (1992, 89). Singling out students individually can have a stifling effect, whereas an open discussion can lead to collective understandings. Student Burrell Jones found that:

The class was different, more of a discussion-based class. Because most classes you go to, you have to bring a notebook, take notes. With this class you did take notes, but on the songs that you heard, what you thought of those songs, and what they meant to you, and what it meant to Native culture. I kind of believe that Native languages were orally learned, orally spoken, and I thought the class had the same way of teaching students. I enjoyed going through that process. (May 7, 2012)

For Dustin Rector, "the listenings were very interesting, having an open discussion about them. It was just really nice and relaxed as we talked about the music" (April 27, 2012). For Native students and, arguably, students in general, the one-way transmission model of teaching has limited value. It treats the human brain like a silo within which the teacher deposits information. Absent substantive dialogue, much of that information is lost. By helping students to come to their own understandings, knowledge becomes fixed through a process of direct engagement and experience.

During discussions, I indirectly encourage Native American students to participate as co-teachers, asking questions of the class that I suspect will invite individual input. Referencing the affirmation of her Native identity, Shanicey Pinto says she was "proud to actually help someone learn about cultural aspects and stuff. I felt pretty important" (April 30, 2012). Through the co-teaching of non-Native students, Native students often cross a cultural divide that can be mutually beneficial:

> Giving my input helped me feel a lot more comfortable with other non–Native Americans learning about the music and the culture. I don't want them to misinterpret the information given to them, so what I would do is make little comments, further explaining things. If their minds are kind of straying I kind of want to get them back on track, because I think things are misinterpreted all the time and I want them to have the right idea about who we are. I left the class feeling comfortable knowing that they have a better idea of Native American culture. And it's coming straight from Native Americans, not from the media. (Tya Manygoats, April 4, 2012)

During one class I played a recording of a Navajo Corn Grinding Song. Shanicey recognized the song, which led to a broader discussion on the importance of grandmothers in passing down tradition and language. Shanicey shared that she wished her grandmother was still around, to teach her not only the words to the Corn Grinding Song, but many other words she was unable to grasp before her grandmother passed. It had a powerful effect on non-Native students. Shanicey eloquently conveyed to the class the gravity of a loss that was both personal and cultural, emphasizing the importance of the link between the generations. Music helped flesh out these insights for her, leading her to conclude that "music made me feel connected to my own culture. That was big because it was my first semester of college and I needed that. I still wish I was in that class, I really did get a cultural understanding" (April 30, 2012).

CONCLUSION

Across hundreds of Native American cultures and countless centuries, music has been essential to the formation and expression of Native identity. Rather than an "extracurricular" activity or cultural addendum designed to entertain or amuse, it has been as critical as language in the ongoing communication that strengthens who we are in the world. Any curriculum designed to support personal and academic development must include music, which has the unparalleled capacity to solidify the students' sense of themselves and open cognitive pathways that will give them every opportunity to succeed academically. In schools where music is valued, it prepares students to be successful lifelong learners. However it is used in the classroom, the more music resonates with the Native heart, the more potential it has to enlighten, empower, and transform. Some recommended recordings for use in the classroom are listed in Appendix D.

DISCOGRAPHY

Secola, Keith. "NDN Kars." *Circle.* AKINA Records. ©1992 by Keith Secola.
Trudell, John. "Tribal Voice." *Tribal Voice.* Peace Company. ©1983 by John Trudell.
———. "See the Woman." *Child's Voice: Children of the Earth.* Peace Company. ©1992 by John Trudell.
Trudell, John, and Bad Dog. *Crazier Than Hell.* Sobeit Recordings/Asitis Productions. ©2010 by John Trudell.

8

Physical Education

WILLARD SAKIESTEWA GILBERT

The historical background of Indigenous peoples has a significant importance in their culture. The rich cultural identity of any group of Indigenous
people can be expressed in many forms. One way in which this is expressed is
through traditional sports and games of the people themselves. Through these
activities, whether the identity is expressed in dance, music, art, or sports and
games, one may become aware of and respect the diversity of all humanity.

Over the past years, there has been an abundance of research related to
sports and games of North American Indians. In particular in the Southwest
United States, Matz (1970) found that sports and games of the Hopi Indians
of northeastern Arizona have been influenced by historical events over the
years, and the role of education cannot be overlooked as one of the major
transmitters of the Hopi culture. We have learned that sports and games differ significantly among North American Indian tribes as compared with the
European sports and games. The study of sports and games from an anthro-
pological perspective deals with their meaning and description; the cross-
cultural definition and analysis of sport; sport as a factor in acculturation;
enculturation, and cultural maintenance; and sport as a perspective on other
facets of cultural behavior (Blanchard 1981). Therefore, according to Gilbert
(1987), the anthropologist is involved in more than finding a ball game in
progress, but instead is interested in understanding it more clearly in terms of
what it "does" rather than what it "is."

Thus, it is important that a people should be interested in knowing and
understanding their cultures and identifying and expressing themselves in
them. As Navalta (1978) stated, an important application of anthropology is
the preservation of cultural identity in areas such as language, religion, and
tradition, which enhances the student's probability of educational success, according to studies conducted by educators.

This is especially true for the Hopi people of northeastern Arizona because
of their traditional ceremonies, agricultural cycle, and the land itself, all of
which are woven into an intricate tapestry of cultural beliefs, customs, lifeways, and behavior. At the same time, it is just as important not only to preserve one's own culture beliefs, but also to be able to share chosen aspects of

that particular culture with others. The preservation of worthy aspects of all cultures can add to the richness of the American educational system, where a diversity of children coexist in the classroom. Ultimately, the traditional sports and games of Indigenous peoples of the world could contribute to the enrichment of American culture by increasing mutual understanding of all cultures.

THE DEFINITION OF PLAY

There have been many attempts by well-known scholars in the field to explain the concept of play and the fact that play is a part of everyday human behavior. Play is a phenomenon that is not only universal to all humans, but is also common among other animals. In his classic book *Homo-Ludens,* Johan Huizinga defined play as a "free activity" outside "ordinary" life, as being "not serious" but at the same time absorbing the player intensely and utterly (1950, 8). It is an activity "connected with no material interest, and no profit can be gained by it. It proceeds within its own proper boundaries of time and space according to fixed rules and in an orderly manner. It promotes the formation of social groups which tend to surround themselves with secrecy and to stress their difference from the common world by disguise or other means" (13). It is evident from this definition that Huizinga did not concern himself with the biological significance of play as a trait of the species *Homo sapiens.* Instead, he was more concerned with the major study of play in cultural and social anthropology. In doing so, he included the relationships between play and other elements of culture that include values, deals, law, politics, and ritual as being acted out. Therefore, play must be a voluntary activity having two basic concepts: a contest for something, or a representation of something. Thus, according to Huizinga, we can only conclude that play is essential to culture.

TRADITIONAL SPORTS AND GAMES OF AMERICAN INDIANS

Culin (1902) stated that the interrelationship of Indian games within the same area, and of each game to its counterpart among all Indian tribes, is dependent upon the origin of the games. American Indian names of games are descriptive, although they vary from language to language even though the games are sometimes identical among tribes of the same lineage. Therefore, it is evident that many Native American games are related either directly to each other or to a common source. For example, a game played with a die or dice appears to be universal throughout the North American continent. Such games exist among 61 tribes, comprising 23 linguistic stocks, and represent 90 specimens of implements from 41 Indian tribes.

It is also evident that games have been classified among Native American Indians into two general classes: games of chance, and games of dexterity. Games of chance fall into two categories: (1) games in which implements with the nature of dice are thrown at random to determine a number or numbers, and the sum of the counts is kept by means of a stick or pebbles, or upon an abacus or counting board; and (2) games in which one or more of the players guess in which of two or more places an odd or particularly marked lot is concealed, with their success or failure resulting in the gain or loss of counters. Games of dexterity may be enumerated, such as archery, sliding javelins or darts upon hard ground or ice, shooting at a moving target consisting of a netted wheel or a ring; or ball playing, in several highly specialized forms, and racing, more or less related to the ball games (Culin [1907] 1992).

MULTICULTURAL EDUCATION

The United States has always been a multicultural society in which a great variety of different cultures exist. It is also evident that our educational system consists of a multicultural population of children representing many different cultural backgrounds. Thus, multicultural education is not just the observation of Native American Week or the celebration of Cinco de Mayo. Instead, it is an educational movement that builds on basic American values that encompass the freedom to choose, justice for all, and opportunity and equality for everyone regardless of ethnicity or religious preference. Multicultural education includes well-defined strategies that classroom teachers can utilize to help students address the increasing ethnic diversity in many countries of the world today. It also affirms that our schools are to be oriented toward the cultural enrichment of all children through programs rooted in the preservation and extension of cultural alternatives, along with the maintenance and preservation of one's traditional culture, which enhances a student's probability of educational success. Multicultural education also recognizes cultural diversity. According to Hogg and McComb (1969), the American educational system has long been held up as a model, free and open to children from all social and economic levels, all religious and cultural backgrounds.

One of the challenges for education in the twenty-first century has been the development and implementation of multicultural classroom instruction that recognizes and celebrates a diversity of cultures. The need for multicultural education is based on the premise that the United States is a nation comprised of cultural pluralistic groups. Gibson (1984) stated that the purpose of multicultural education is to teach children not only to value cultural differences but also to accept the rights of others. In addition, Swisher and Swisher (1986) point out that teachers must recognize that for some culturally diverse children, the implicit aspects of cultural identity, while not always visible, are strongly embedded and guide the attitude and behavior of the individual.

Thus, teachers must be prepared to meet the individual needs of all students regardless of the color of their skin, or their language, socioeconomic status, and cultural practices. Furthermore, Geneva Gay (2010) contends that teachers must build bridges between what their students already know and the new ideas and experiences to which they are exposed. In the same manner, Siedentop (2000) observes that students cannot develop and thrive in a pluralistic society unless they acquire understandings, values, attitudes, and behavioral skills that demonstrate an appreciation for cultural differences and overcome the stereotypes acquired by children raised in an area dominated by one culture.

Thus, multicultural education curricula should be designed to assist students to develop an understanding of and acceptance for the vitality of cultural pluralism (Gilbert 1987). Gay (1990) states that curriculum designs for the multicultural classroom must reflect a real sense of purpose and a clearly articulated philosophy. These designs must be organized around clearly desirable goals and objectives that can easily be translated into instructional lessons. Multicultural curricula should address many different dimensions: not only of the lives of ethnic group members, but also their cultural characteristics.

In the application of multicultural games and activities within such a curriculum, we must keep in mind that addressing only one culture is far from the goals and objectives of multicultural education. Instead, educators must focus their attention on the promotion of multiple cultures. This application of games is not restricted to any particular culture or group of content areas being taught in the school curriculum today. Instead, the integration of multicultural games and activities can be applied to a variety of content materials.

For example, in the content area of physical education, games and activities can become part of the curriculum through the study of culture(s) that have similar games. Playing games similar to those from other cultures can help children understand that they share similar forms of play with many other children from around the world. In addition, playing games from other cultures also enables children to experience some cultural differences that will foster and enhance their knowledge base. Teachers of physical education who encourage their students to appreciate rhyme and music through specific sports skills and dance, or who employ form and color in creative activities, are helping to develop the cultural person. They are helping students by getting them involved in actual participation, perhaps in dance, thus augmenting awareness of the art and culture of people in different parts of the world.

Multicultural education is no less critical a concern in the physical education classroom, in sports, and in recreation than in any other subject field. It can be argued that it is even more vital to physical education because of the emotions and interactions that occur in gymnasiums and on playgrounds and athletic fields. Without a doubt, physical education can become multicultural if it is oriented toward the enrichment of youth through the preservation of cultural diversities.

Multicultural education as applied to the teaching of physical education, recreation, and dance is the framework of cultural pluralism in all schools that focus upon the intention of promoting knowledge of, and a supportive philosophy for, the entire spectrum of American society. Baptiste and Baptiste (1979) state that cultural pluralism involves the mutual exchange of culture within a state of equal coexistence in a mutually supportive system. In the United States, this system comprises one nation of diverse groups of people with significantly different patterns of belief, lifestyle, race, and language. Therefore, we can conclude that multicultural education provides boys and girls with an understanding of the heritage of all ethnic groups, including European Americans, and of contemporary social and cultural patterns among these groups.

According to Willgoose (1979), the development of the cultural person is the least considered objective of physical education, because it is the least understood. It involves a deep appreciation for life's activities—associated with a rich and full life for an individual. Thus, a cultured person experiences a concern for a number of facets of multicultural education, such as the production of learning that enrich appreciative attitudes toward all the arts.

Teachers, coaches, and administrators must support and respect the ethnic attachments of their students and make positive use of these cultural values. In addition, Freischlag (1978) stated that it is essential that the physical education educator be concerned with two contrasting ideologies: assimilationism and cultural pluralism. The assimilationist approach involves the promotion of full socialization of all individuals and groups into the common culture; the cultural pluralist approach, by contrast, argues that an individual can learn different languages, and change his or her diet, yet, at the same time, maintain integrity with their original cultural heritage and values. An element common to all of this is that individuals are permitted to maintain their own ethnic identity—ethnic differences are respected, but the social status of the individual is not tied to ethnicity. It is also important to emphasize that all students should know, understand, identify with, and be proud of their own heritage.

JUSTIFICATION FOR MULTICULTURAL GAMES AND ACTIVITIES

One of the most exciting innovations in the study of cultural aspects of ethnic games in bilingual/multicultural education today is the idea of "preserving" the individual's cultural heritage through classroom instruction. For example, traditional games of the Hopi people of northeastern Arizona have existed since the era before their contact with Euro-Americans. Such games were played not only as amusements, but during certain seasons of the year. These games also played an important role in the Hopi culture. For example, it is well known that historically and today, the Hopi Indians have always been excellent long-distance runners. Before Europeanization, Hopi men were known for their endurance in running from the village of Oraivi (Third Mesa) to the village of Moencopi, in what is now the western part of the Hopi reservation. Hopi men would rise early in the morning, before sunrise, and run to Moencopi to tend their fields, then return home on the same day, approximately one hundred miles round trip. Not only was running cherished by the Hopi people as a way of life, it was also believed to bring the rain for their crops.

Gilbert (1987) conducted interviews with several elders living on the Hopi reservation who were representative of the three different Hopi mesa villages. The purpose of the interviews was to determine whether traditional Hopi games and activities were being taught to the children by their parents or grandparents, and if so, whether the children were playing these games and activities today. One of the questions posed was, "How do you [elders] feel about the idea of having the traditional games played by the Hopi children of the villages of today?" The elders responded with a general consensus, stating that "the Hopi children of today are playing the white (*bahana*) man's games, and our fathers and/or grandparents told us that these [Hopi] games would never be played in the future because the children have never been taught to play these games" (1987, ix). They also expressed their concern that these games of the Hopi people were not being played or taught to the younger generation for fear that if children were in fact taught the traditional games, they still would not play them, and also would not pass the games down to their own children in the future. In addition, when asked how they felt about Hopi games and activities being played off the reservation, outside the the Hopi Nation, by non-Hopi, they all replied that this would be a good idea to do, because non-Hopi people could learn about Hopi games and activities and have a better understanding of the Hopi way of life.

The preservation of games in any culture is vital to the culture that the games represent, and this aim could offer students from various cultural groups an opportunity to share and possibly defend various customs, beliefs, and practices from their respective cultural heritages. As Navalta (1978) stated, the preservation of the worthy aspects of all cultures can add to the richness of America, where a diversity of people exist. Thus, it is suggested that preservation of games and activities of any culture can add to the richness of the American society in which we live.

A second reason for preserving traditional games is the promotion of the "cultural identity" of any group of people, which may be expressed in many forms. Whether identity is expressed in dance, music, art, or games, people can increase their awareness and respect for the world's cultural diversity. Navalta (1978) reported that studies by educators found that the promotion of cultural identity through participation in areas such as language, religion, and tradition enhances students' probability of educational success. Studies such as those by Gilbert (1987) and Navalta (1978) reveal that games play a vital part in the promotion of cultural identity. For example, the Hopi have been influenced by American historical events over the years, and the role of education cannot be overlooked as one of the major transmitters of that culture. One important prerequisite for understanding other cultures and behaviors is to become aware of one's own cultural identity and the nature of one's culture or cultures. Therefore, it is vitally important that each individual should understand, identify with, and be proud of his or her culture(s).

A third reason for preserving traditional games is to help students develop an appreciation of other cultures. Understanding cultures other than their own can increase their self-knowledge and objectivity. We all live in a society in which we are surrounded by different ethnic groups, which necessarily brings us into interaction with or among these groups. Whether we identify with one or more ethnic groups, we still are often engaged in some form of cross-cultural contact. In schools today, appreciation of cultures has been demonstrated through programs such as the celebration of Indian Day, Culture Day, or Native American Heritage Week. But although this may satisfy the multicultural requirements of state or local school districts, the recognition of cultures through programs with this "tourist" approach—here one day, gone the next—should be avoided. The idea is not to make the celebration of cultures into a one-time appearance on the school calendar, but instead to make such a celebration become part of the ongoing school curriculum. In reality, we as educators have to dig deeper and present multicultural identities in more meaningful ways to keep in mind the ultimate goals of our educational institutions.

Too often when teachers, administrators, and school personnel are called upon to participate in such activities, the true meaning of the activities is overlooked, and misunderstood. In some instances, teachers may find it very difficult to fully engage themselves in promoting cultural games and activities. They may only be going through the motions, and satisfying the minimum requirements for their own efforts at participation. These "doers" are people who are, perhaps, in conflict with themselves, or it may well be that they have never been introduced to the concept of multicultural understanding, or they have not received any formal training regarding it. In any case, the doers are those who may participate because it is required of them, or they may feel pressure from community and other school personnel to comply or cooperate. On the other hand, "participants" are those who see this activity as being very crucial to promoting cultural sensitivity and placing value on the culture(s) of all children represented in their school. Perhaps they are more aware of cultural sensitivity issues, or they have had some training or background in cultural understanding.

It is common to see teachers who are members of the specific ethnic group(s) outside the mainstream always called upon to develop and implement such multicultural awareness programs for the entire school. This misunderstanding by the administration of the point of such programs is all too common. Just because I may be a Native American, doesn't mean that I should have to be responsible for coordinating all the activities during the celebration of Native American Week. Instead, teachers who are sincere, and who are advocates for cultural pluralism, are the people who should be involved, regardless of their ethnic backgrounds. Since the quality of multicultural programs and instruction depends largely on teachers' attitudes, teachers must become aware of their own competencies in educating children from different ethnic backgrounds. Teachers must be free from cultural ethnocentrism, and instead accept diverse cultures as being valuable contributors to the classroom.

A first step that teachers can take to have a better understanding of different cultures is to understand their own culture and self-identity. Perhaps a more plausible approach is to ask yourself the following questions: First, can you describe the earliest memory you have of an experience with a person (or people) of a culture or ethnic group different from your own? For some people, this question can be very easy to answer; for others, it may be a very difficult task to accomplish for whatever reason(s). The more common experiences that people identify are those associated with the school, foreign travel, attending school in another country, or a teacher who was of different ethnicity than their own.

The second question is to ask yourself who or what has had the most influence in the formation of your attitudes and opinions about people of different cultural groups? One of the main goals of multicultural education is to reduce racism and discrimination and stereotyping in schools and to promote cultural understanding. But too often, schools are actually promoting the opposite. For example, children are very smart, and when schools concentrate on focusing on the "differences" among peoples, all too often, children begin to form negative opinions of one another. The better practice would be to simply acknowledge differences but to promote the similarities and to expound on the positive aspects of all cultures. If you ask a group of children to list the differences and likenesses they recognize among one another, what you will find is that they are all too eager to give an extensive list of their differences and they will have a short list, if one at all, of the likenesses they perceive among one another. Children learn about stereotypes at a very early age, before they enter school. Derman-Sparks (1989) stated that even as early as two years of age, children start to notice the color of people's skin. Usually, this awareness stems from the types of television shows they watch, the media, and the home and community environment. Let us not contribute to promoting stereotypes, prejudice, or racism to children at an early age, but instead let us promote positive feelings about who we are and an appreciation for one another.

CURRICULUM DEVELOPMENT AND IMPLEMENTATION

The development and implementation of units of instruction that focus on ethnic games and activities for the physical education classroom has attracted great attention over the years. One of the justifications for the inclusion of multicultural games and activities is an appreciation for other cultures. The experience of playing these games provides an opportunity for students to learn about other cultures and to express their own cultural heritage with pride. This experience is important for children of all cultures, because in today's globalized society we will, most likely, be surrounded at various times by people of different cultures. And in order to function in society positively and without biases and ignorance, children need to develop their own understanding of cultures. In some cases, the value of diversity is not stressed in the home, and consequently, children may come to school already believing some stereotypes. It is easy to say how interesting and important a culture is, but it is a greater challenge to model behavior appropriate to that culture and to demonstrate true acceptance of other peoples to students in a classroom.

Appendix E provides a sample format to aid in the development of instructional materials for physical education classrooms. Much of the material used in the preparation of information on a specific culture, such as the Hopi people, can be found by searching the Human Relations Area Files at Yale University (http://www.yale.edu/hraf/). Additional information on traditional games of American Indians can be found in Stewart Culin's *Games of the North American Indians* ([1907] 1992). Some examples of games that students could play can be found in Robert W. Grueninger's chapter on physical education in *Teaching American Indian Students* (Reyhner 1992).

CONCLUSION

Based upon the results of research conducted to determine whether multicultural games and activities should be part of the existing physical education curriculum, it is evident that the concept of multicultural education, in general, should be a required block of professional training for those who are entering the field of education. For example, instruction at the university or college level should include a class that could be cross-referenced between the departments of education, physical education, and multicultural education. It should be made available to all educators, and it would include instruction in the sports and games of many cultures and furnish aspiring teachers with the skills necessary to promote cultural pluralism in their classrooms. One key to becoming a successful educator is to embrace diversity, to be someone who is not afraid to incorporate several different teaching methods in a classroom.

Among all Indigenous cultures, sports and games are an important part of the daily lives of the people themselves. For example, the Hopi game of kickball was played during a particular time of the year and during a particular ceremony. Studying the relationship between the two reveals that the game was an integral part of the ceremony. Cultural values are also an important ingredient in shaping people's lives. It was necessary for Hopi men to run long distances, not only to tend their fields but also because this demonstrated that the individual was not to be considered lazy in fulfilling the daily duties within the household. Contemporary values such as cardiovascular fitness, well-being, and cooperation among group members were also demonstrated by playing these traditional sports and games. Whether or not players themselves were aware of these contemporary values, the fact remains that they incorporated these values into their daily lives through participating in traditional games.

Every culture has a rich cultural identity that could be shared with others easily in an educational setting. Survival of a culture is dependent upon the perpetuation of its customs, traditions, values, and religion. When this is accomplished through the avenue of education, it may enrich the lives of many who are not regularly exposed to cultures other than their own. It may also allow individuals to take pride in their own heritage. Teaching cultural awareness will help augment a greater understanding and respect for our differences.

9

The Fourth Generation

The Sustainability of Native American Art Education

MICHAEL HOLLOMAN

> No other race in America is confronted by such unrelenting stereotyping as Native Americans. The relationship between native people and white America is fraught with dichotomy. The dominant culture molds, reshapes and packages the portrait of native people to whatever image best suits its needs at any given time.
>
> Mike Leslie, "Native American Artists"

Recently I participated in a symposium on sustainability in one's community. Inevitably, a colleague—in this case Tom Salsbury, an associate professor in teaching and learning at Washington State University—presented the concept of the Seven Generations. As a Native American, I sighed, expecting another clichéd appropriation of a particular indigenous concept to support a New Age agenda. Surprisingly, what Salsbury presented offered a fresh view of a continuum between past and present. The focus was not the usual linear, cause-and-effect scenario, but instead an exercise in visualizing oneself in the middle, hence the fourth, generation. The idea was that we have a better ability to truly imagine and understand ourselves connected to our great-grandparents, while at the same time imagining our own great-grandchildren. Here, we are posited in our own time, while feeling the impact of past generations and acknowledging our own direct impact on future generations. This profound interpretation kindled in me the enthusiasm to articulate some of the challenges of Native American arts and education in an ever-changing America.

Teachers of Native American and other Indigenous students are too often on their own when it comes to responsive ideas that can be applied to teaching culturally appropriate art lessons (and art appreciation) to their K–12 students. Inability to locate quality resource materials and curricular activities adds to this dilemma. Recently many tribes have identified a central pedagogical issue as being the lack of a formalized agreement on what is culturally appropriate and who designates this.

These issues derive from ongoing paternalistic U.S. governmental over-sight that has seen generations of Native students' art education being deliv-ered by non-Natives. Government boarding schools were the most prominent vehicle in this respect. Their original focus upon continuing the promotion of cultural assimilation has led to arts education for Native students that is still directed primarily at the importance of Western art history and its tech-niques. In time more humane arts education programs sought to empower the Native students, yet somehow they could not overcome educators' im-pulses to dictate to Native students how best to create and or preserve "In-dian Art." Too often it was the authoritative non-Native who defined to the students what this artwork was to look like. As a result, generations of Na-tive students have endured a systematic process of cultural genocide, while simultaneously being burdened with the expectation to remain authentic In-dians. Native American author Gerald Vizenor and performance artist James Luna have both addressed the negative impact of how being held in the past has forced American Indians to continually portray a fictionalized identity not of their own making and subsequently to relive the unresolved histori-cal trauma that has ravaged their tribal communities (Vizenor 1990, quoted in Townsend-Gualt 1999). These issues of identity can only be recognized as important factors that significantly contribute to the devastating attrition rate of tribal students nationwide.

The last few decades have seen tribal nations exert their sovereign rights to work with states and local school districts to ensure that all students in schools be provided with more accurate and culturally acceptable curricu-lar activities pertaining to the Indigenous peoples in their respective regions. Because of this development many teachers today are sincerely conscious of what is no longer acceptable when it comes to the education of Indigenous students. Still missing, however, are some simple concepts and tools that con-cerned and committed teachers can acquire to help them develop culturally appropriate activities and projects that students can engage in.

Author Lucy Lippard stated in her book *Mixed Blessings; New Art in a Mul-ticultural America* (1990) that "art speaks for itself only when the artist is able to speak for her or himself" (21–22). Issues of identity and self-determination have been one of the major conceptual frameworks of contemporary Native American artists for a number of generations. This political/artistic response to the historic motif of colonization has been an important step for many Na-tive American artists.

By its very nature art history posits itself in the past, and for many this is where the comfort zone of studying American Indians remains, particularly regarding their arts. However, for the Native American student today, being relegated to the past or bound to invented images of what Indians and their art should be makes pursuing art that much more of a challenge. My own transformation, from student artist to collegiate faculty member, and then from being a museum director working with Indigenous collections back to a position in academia, has only reinforced these concerns regarding the perpetuation of a non-Native audience's expectations of Native American art-making as I engage with my own students.

"Native Americans didn't have a term for art" is one of the most overused axioms offered by academics who have sincerely attempted to introduce Native American art in an independent and respectful manner honoring unique Native cultural conventions. I recall when Betty Edwards, in her popular book *Drawing on the Right Side of the Brain* (1998), relieved art students nationwide who, pointing to her definition of the analytical versus the intuitive hemispheres of our brains as an excuse to articulate why they could not or would not pursue certain required activities such as proportion and perspective in their drawings, explained: "I can't because I am more right-brained!" What was lost was Edwards's simple explanation that, yes, the left side of the brain will dominate the imaginative right side if allowed; but what is optimum is an equality and synchronicity between the two. Along similar lines, academic efforts to discern formal qualities inherent in the Western art canon, such as design and composition, within Indigenous creative works and aesthetics too often segregate Native art to the domain of the "primitive," with attendant constrictions and definitions that Native students and artists need to avoid. Janet Berlo and Ruth B. Philips in *Native North American Art* (1998) articulate the negativity implicit in such judgments, which reduce Native American art-making to a lesser value than Western practices. They point out that "though specific criteria vary, Native Americans, like people everywhere, value the visual pleasure afforded by things made well and imaginatively. They also value many of the same attributes that make up the Western notion of 'art,' such as skill in the handling materials, the practiced manipulation of established stylistic conventions, and individual powers of invention and conceptualization" (9).

One only needs to see the master basket maker's or beadworker's pride in their work to recognize that deft skill, precision, and observation are required for the success of these art forms. Berlo and Philips provide a potent example of this in their discussion of the similarity between arts of the Plains Indian warrior societies and women's artistic activities (115). The need to create cultural distinctions is evident if one is to better understand the arts of Native America, yet it should not be at the expense of overarching implications of "high" and "low" art. More importantly, although the significance of similarities in common approaches is noteworthy, particular cultural nuances are equally worthy of interpretation and distinction. As Richard W. Hill, Sr., wrote in *Uncommon Legacies: Native American Art from the Peabody Essex Museum* (2002):

The lack of the word *art* in Native language does not mean that art did not exist in its own terms in that society. Most tribes do not have a word for religion and prefer to refer to it as "their way of life." There is no word for culture, because you cannot isolate culture from the rest of life. The objects created by Native artists pull us towards them because we share a common identity with their creators. Across tribal boundaries, we can feel the emotional and spiritual intent of the artists without knowing the specifics of those feelings. There is a belief in many Native communities that objects such as these need to be part of people's lives in order to be useful. They were meant for use, not necessarily to last forever. (2002, 191)

C. Adrian Heidenreich notes in his 1985 exhibition catalogue *Ledger Art of the Crow and Gros Ventre Indians: 1879–1897* that a history of pictorial art forms among the Crows and "other Native Americans of the West" extends from prehistoric images in pictographs and petroglyphs to nineteenth-century representational images on buffalo hides, tipis, and other objects. It is from this interest in visually defining "what no longer is there" in a multitude of two-dimensional media that the Crows and other Native Americans pursued a natural transition to new formats, such as ledger paper that was introduced by Europeans and Americans. The tribes also interacted personally with a variety of traveling Euro-American visual artists who ventured into their territories hoping to document the Indigenous peoples before Western civilization obliterated their way of life. "Observation of the work of all these artists, combined with their traditional interest in realistic pictures, no doubt influenced other warrior-artists. Younger Crow were encouraged, and sometimes forced, to go to boarding schools, including the famous Carlisle Indian School in Pennsylvania. There, they learned other artistic conventions from their teachers" (1985, 10).

This period of federal policy toward Native American culture and education became known as the Allotment and Assimilation Era, initiated by the Dawes Act of 1887 and extending until 1943. President Chester A. Arthur stated on December 6, 1881 that "a resort to the allotment system would have a direct and powerful influence in dissolving the tribal bond, which is so prominent a feature of savage life, and which tends so strongly to perpetuate it" (quoted in W. N. Thompson 2005, 217). The Dawes Act provided for the allotment of lands to Indians with the intention of transforming them into a civilized people focused on farming the land. The author of the act, Congressman Henry Dawes, once expressed that such a transformative endeavor in the pursuit of private property would ultimately encourage Indians to "wear civilized clothes . . . cultivate the ground, live in houses, ride in Studebaker wagons, send children to school, drink whiskey [and] own property" (quoted in Blackman 2013, 23). Edwin L. Wade acknowledges in his article "The Ethnic Art Market and the Dilemma of Innovative Indian Artists" that "the intellectual justification for this system was the nineteenth-century philosophy whereby Anglos assumed the right and responsibility to direct the internal affairs—including the art traditions—of other cultures. By the 1900's official policy at Indian boarding schools was that traditional arts would be suppressed and utilitarian handicrafts encouraged" (1981, 11).

The closing decades of the nineteenth century witnessed the end of the Indian wars, the extension of railways into the western frontier, and the crowning jewel of the Industrial Revolution: the completion of the Panama Canal, which let to rapid Euro-American settlement of the Pacific coastal areas of the nation. The invention of new technologies such as the incandescent light had American envisioning a future well beyond the Wild West. James Earle Fraser's iconic sixteen-foot sculpture, *The End of the Trail* won a gold medal at the 1915 Panama–Pacific International Exposition in San Francisco. It portrayed an Indian on horseback, head and shoulders bent down in resignation (along with his impotent spear), representing the Indian's imminent demise in the face of Manifest Destiny. This artwork has been one of the most frequently reproduced images of Native Americans in the decades since its creation. However. its origins, longevity, and pathos might owe more to imperialist nostalgia than to genuine respect for the subject. Renato Rosaldo defines this as "a mood of nostalgia that makes racial domination appear innocent and pure; people mourning the passing or transformation of what they have caused to be transformed. Imperialist nostalgia revolves around a paradox: A person kills somebody and then mourns the victim; or someone deliberately alters a life form and then regrets that things have not remained as they were. . . . Imperialist nostalgia uses a pose of 'innocent yearning' both to capture people's imagination and to conceal its complicity with often brutal domination" (1989, 69–70).

Contemplating this alarming frame of reference, one might be forced to reinterpret the attitudes that inspired Dorothy Dunn. Any academic discussion of the history of Native American arts applies a significant amount of attention to what was initiated by Dunn as the art teacher at the Santa Fe Indian School in 1932. As a product of her time, she was obliged to pursue educational goals that promoted an empowering atmosphere for Native student artists as they were enduring governmental campaigns of assimilation. This direct oversight saw a pragmatic approach to engaging students in the modern mediums of painting and sculpture. By all means, the students were learning much that assisted in their image-making. Attached to these studies, however, were realistic concerns about student artwork being marketed for a potential consumer audience.

The Southwest by this time had become a major tourist attraction, and the Native students' artworks were in high demand. The collecting culture, including acquisition of American Indian artifacts, had been established for decades, and from this developed a pursuit of "authentic" Indian materials. Responding to potential economic opportunities, many artists became very interested in this commerce, as the era of the trading post and government agent was redefining the social structure that equally depended on that economic model. This transformation of Native America into the modern era witnessed the integration of non-Native materials and influences into tribal communities, even as an emphasis on Native artists' maintaining a "primitive existence" was still coveted in the arts. This was witnessed in the collecting of Southwest pottery, its immediate value being proportionate to whether it was of "traditional" origin. Ethnographers and anthropologists were complicit in this definition, to the point of actually providing historic designs from archaeological sites to contemporary potters such as the Hopi artist Nampeyo, therefore ensuring higher commodity values for their creations.

The public's appetite was voracious, including private collectors and museums. The ethnographic interpretations of Native America, which paid the most attention to a sense of aesthetic purity, unsoiled by modern civilization, leaked into the training of Native students. The Euro-American medium of paper had long since replaced the sole focus of Indigenous image-making on hides or other traditional surfaces. Canvas was encouraged now, as was the use and appreciation for modern materials such as gouache and tempera paint. Still it was imperative that the work remain authentic. Therefore as mediums and materials inevitably changed, the emphasis on authenticity turned to the content of the artwork. Here the ideal of preserving what was left of vanishing peoples and their customs became the goal. This, combined with the commodity value of the work created, prominently influenced the styles and techniques that were taught. John Richard Grimes notes, "Dunn's premise was that encouraging Indian art fostered student self-esteem, self-sufficiency, and increased English proficiency. Dunn's Studio School and its graduates became widely known. While it succeeded for a time, the school eventually sowed seeds of its own demise, as graduates such as Allen Houser began to react against Dunn's view that Indian art, to be genuine, should adhere to 'traditional' styles" (2005, 180). For all of Dunn's great accomplishments, she will equally be remembered for her paternalistic oversight of her students' work, particularly for dictating to Indian students what Indian art should be.

In 1962 Lloyd Kiva New (Irish, Cherokee) became the artistic director of the newly created Institute of American Indian and Alaska Native Arts Development, now known as the Institute of American Indian Arts (IAIA), and he brought with him a new central vision. As John Richard Grimes explains: "Breaking with the notion that Native art and culture are static entities, New championed a radically different vision. Instead, he argued that contemporary Indian art should be inspired by the past but grounded in the demands of the present; and, moreover, that Indian art should be individual, that it should be expressive, and should utilize the full range of available mediums, 'traditional' or otherwise" (2005, 180).

Harrison Begay's painting *Navajo Yei'bichai Dancers* (see Figure 3) illustrates one of the main points of criticism of Dorothy Dunn's teaching while at the Santa Fe Indian School. There is no doubt that she was committed to providing her students with the formal skills and understanding to employ and excel in new mediums such as watercolor and tempera painting. In this regard Begay was one of her most outstanding pupils, and yet this painting shows so poignantly the other influence she was later ridiculed for, particularly by Native scholars: the imposition of thematic content. This scenario of paternalism urged Indian students to paint images from their traditional culture. The preservation in image of vanishing lifeways motivated Dunn and others at a time when the imagined complete assimilation of Native America seemed inevitable. Years later, artist Kay Walkingstick (Cherokee) selected one of Begay's early paintings, of the Enemy Way ceremony, for the exhibition *So Fine! Masterworks of Fine Art from the Heard Museum* (2002–2003); in the catalogue (2001) she acknowledged that recent criticism of the content of Begay's work, as being focused on an ethnographic interest, had allowed viewers to lose sight of his highly skilled artistic talents.

Perhaps no other contemporary American Indian artist epitomized refraining from being labeled an Indian artist as much as Fritz Scholder (Luiseño) (see Figure 4). He was traditionally educated in fine arts at Sacramento State College and later at the University of Arizona. His faculty position at IAIA, beginning in 1964, provided a fertile ground for his artistic expression. He was inspired as much by his non-Native contemporaries, such pop artists Wayne Thiebaud and Richard Diebenkorn or the notorious Irish painter and cultural icon Francis Bacon, as he was by his Native culture. Scholder took advantage of the dynamic and culturally transformative times of the 1960s to expand, possibly more than any other artist at the time, the definition of Indian art. He chose to become known as an artist who happened to be Indian. His willingness to paint as an American Indian living in the present time, and not just an artist portraying a romanticized past, was instilled through his early training in South Dakota by the renowned Indian artist Oscar Howe (Yanktonai Dakota), who once remarked, "One criterion for my painting is to present the cultural life and activities of Sioux Indians; dance, ceremonies, legends, lore, arts. . . . It is my greatest hope that my paintings may serve to bring the best things of Indian culture into a modern way of life" (quoted in *Contemporary Sioux Painting,* 1970, 48).

The 1960s and 1970s saw dramatic changes in Native America, as the pursuit of sovereign rights for tribal self-determination pushed the people into armed conflict against the federal government for the first time since the Wounded Knee Massacre in 1890. Scholder's artwork equally rebelled against the expected norms of what American Indian art should look like and who determines what it is. He did not paint vestiges of the past, such as noble red men, bloodthirsty savages, or Indian maidens; he painted Indians (often

Figure 3. *Navajo Yei'bichai Dancers*, by Harrison Begay, watercolor on paper, n.d. Courtesy Fred Jones, Jr., Museum of Art, University of Oklahoma, Norman; James T. Bialac Native American Art Collection, 2010.

Figure 4. *Indian, Dog and Teepee,* by Friz Scholder, acrylic on canvas, 1973. Courtesy Fred Jones, Jr., Museum of Art, The University of Oklahoma, Norman; The James T. Bialac Native American Art Collection, 2010.

renditions of himself) existing in a complex world. His work is a visual statement asking the viewer to reconsider the stereotypes imposed on American Indians and American Indian artists. His influence has inspired generations of Native painters ever since.

Native American art education in the era of self-determination (inaugurated by the Self-Determination Act of 1975) is a story of Native Americans reclaiming their own artistic traditions and the stories that are attributed to them. Joe Feddersen and Elizabeth Woody articulated this in their essay "The Story as Primary Source: Educating the Gaze" (1999):

Native art has a history different from that of Western culture and serves its purpose differently in a Native Community. At times it runs in tandem with Western art and at other times runs its own course. In mythic history and oral history the presentation of the story reveals our shared histories. The rendition simultaneously provides specific descriptions of what sets us apart from our neighbors and defines our relationship with other participants in the environment, such as the animals, plants, and regional geographic markers. (1999, 174)

The Montana Office of Public Instruction and its K–12 curriculum, described in *Indian Education for All: Connecting and Classrooms* (Fox 2006), have been seen as torch bearers for culturally appropriate teaching materials that have gone through an impressive vetting process by regional tribes. The importance of a tribal voice that is empowered and invested in the curriculum is not surprising, given the fact that Montana's Native population is very prominent and diverse.

Julie Cajune's essay "Developing Culturally Integrated Content Lesson Guidelines for American Indian Content" (2001) illustrates the desirability of tribally specific cultural oversight of Native American arts education. She begins by differentiating between general descriptions of Native America as opposed to the need to present specific tribes' culture and history. This speaks to an important aspect of tribal sovereignty and raises the important question of who historically has spoken for specific tribes. Too often an independent tribal voice was generalized into a larger panorama of Native America at the expense of particular tribal histories and locations. Cajune offers a specific example to this as it relates to art projects:

> Lessons need to provide real meaning and understanding. What has been published as multicultural curriculum has often been shallow activities that revolve around a food, craft or holiday. Some of these activities may be authentic, but if there is no substantial learning about the people they come from, real understanding has not taken place. Two examples are the ever popular pictograph paper bag writing and the decorated tag board tipi. Many well-intentioned teachers confuse pictographs and winter counts. Because the activity is art oriented, students usually enjoy the drawing aspect of the lesson, but rarely learn anything about actual winter counts, or tribes that specifically used them to document events. (2001, iii–iv)

This description offers a dramatic example of the need for better cultural understandings, a topic addressed by Feddersen and Woody (1999), mentioned above. In a state as large as Montana, and with many distinctive tribes, with their own languages, cultures, and histories, how to accommodate such an important issue might seem overwhelming. Herein lies the challenge for teachers who want to do the right thing in presenting culturally appropriate materials. In short, local school districts and their teachers need to work with local tribes.

Washington State and its Office of the Superintendent of Public Instruction have worked with regional tribes whose historic traditional lands reside within the state, to uphold the tenets of the 2005 House Bill (WSHB) 1495. The bill mandates that each school district teach tribe- and district-approved history and culture of the tribes that reside within its boundaries. It took a full seven years, until 2012, for the state to offer a common curriculum to teachers that can be embellished at the school district level in partnership with individual tribes. The importance of this model is that it acknowledges each tribe's sovereign identity and history as well as the need for school districts to provide committed teachers with resources to better teach their students regarding tribal histories and culture. Unfortunately the arts remain minimally addressed in such endeavors.

The National Museum of the American Indian (NMAI) in Washington, D.C., opened in 2004, almost immediately became a leader in the presentation of Native American material culture while maintaining the integrity of the Indigenous peoples whose cultural legacy the museum preserves. Beyond the exhibition of ancient and traditional artifacts and contemporary arts, the museum is also a fabulous resource for American Indian educational programming. Of note is the museum's Artist Leadership Program for Individual Artists, which is available to indigenous artists of the Americas. This program provides eligible artists with access to the museum and its collections (850,000 artifacts) as a resource for research, artistic development, and skill development. The NMAI website states that "this program aims to rebuild cultural self-confidence and to enable artists to think more broadly about themselves and their art while perpetuating Indigenous cultures and reflecting artistic diversity." The program utilizes specific tribal objects in the museum's collections as touchstones of cultural inspiration and education for established and emerging artists. The opportunity for Indigenous young people to interact culturally with historic material objects from their own tribes nurtures a continuum of spirit and creativity. This program or any museum program that engages tribal youth with their historical legacy can become a wonderful intergenerational art project. Art instructors and administrative curriculum planners might benefit from the development of a localized project modeled on NMAI's, utilizing ancient and traditional Native American cultural materials at a regional museum or interpretative center.

Recently I have been involved with tribal elders, traditional tribal artists working in traditional mediums, contemporary tribal artists working in contemporary mediums, and Native American youth to engage in a project utilizing historical tribal materials in a regional museum. The objective of the program is to present these objects as a reference point for discussion, inspiration, and cultural understanding, including exploration of the materials' temporal contexts, construction, and spiritual importance. An art exhibit based on new work by the students, artists, and elders is planned as a one outcome of the project. The students represent the Fourth Generation.

The Third Generation would be represented by the Native American artists (often parents themselves) who work directly with the students. Beyond their artistic skills they can offer personal views of their own artistic education and of cultural influences that began in the last three to four decades of the twentieth century. Specific to his group of Native artists are the contemporary influences that speak to their own work as much as traditional connections. Many of these artists have left their reservations to pursue arts education in tribal colleges, art schools, or universities.

The Second Generation is the elders, many of them elderly traditional artists (often grandparents) who share and demonstrate the tribally specific knowledge of craft and culture. Many of these mentors lived in the era of self-determination, which tremendously transformed life and culture on the reservations. These individuals offer a unique impression of history and the resurgence of tribal culture.

The First Generation (great-grandparents) are often represented through sharing their stories and the legacy that they have passed on to present generations. Those still living can recall a transformative era in the arts and the liberation from extensive educational paternalism (boarding schools, policies of relocation and termination). The cultural continuity of tribal identities through the generations, particularly in the arts, was cherished and honored by all participants. These elder knowledge-bearers, who are held in great esteem in tribal communities, define the strength of tradition, as it historically it was the grandparents and great-grandparents who educated tribal youth while parents were immersed in the daily duties of survival and tribal leadership.

Tribal youth today are situated in a wonderful position to learn, to become empowered, and to accept their responsibility for future generations. Therefore, it is also important to recognize the specific time frame in which most tribal youth exist. This recognition demands an understanding of the individual's historic legacy as referenced in the model of multiple generations, yet it also requires that tribal youth be allowed to exist in their own time and not be expected to relive a past that was someone else's. This is a delicate balance for tribal youth, because their identity is still so connected to who their people were.

One impressive example of engaging tribal youth in contemporary artistic projects can be seen in a recent Museum of Indian Arts and Culture exhibit called *Comic Art Indigène* (2008–2009; catalogue 2008). Here the importance of tribal oral traditions and storytelling is exemplified through comic book art that expressed present-day themes. The exhibit utilized the ongoing interest in animé art as a medium to address the contemporary Native American experience. The Mashantucket Pequot Museum in Connecticut, which hosted the exhibit in 2012, expanded the description: "*Comic Art Indigène* explores how American Indian artists today articulate identity, art, worldview, politics, and culture through sequential comic art." The exhibit also highlighted the tradition of narrative art in the Native American tradition as represented in rock art, ledger art, and traditional ceramics. Of importance here is the artistic programming that was offered to youth, featuring participating Native comic artists and their willingness to promote this art form for Native students (see, for example, Figure 5).

Figure 5. *Protector of Innocence* (2007), by Jolene Yazzie (Navajo). Digital print courtesy of the artist.

Interest in this type of artistic opportunity among Native youth is mirrored in the Native Comic Book Project (NCBP) developed by Michael Bitz and hosted by the University of Washington's Partnership for Native Health (Montgomery et al. 2012). The program's objective was the development of a curriculum that would train educators in the use of comic book art to enhance healthy decision making for Native youth. The success of this project was reflected in the participation of Native youth and their engagement with the content of the work, which empowered understanding of contemporary Native identity in the context of issues that youth are confronted with today. The authors reporting on the program acknowledge that "few studies of comic books have assessed their effectiveness as educational tools" (S42). The scarce data available revealed increases in the awareness of healthy life choices among the youth targeted in the studies. What has made a distinctive difference in Bitz's work (and specifically the NCBP) is that the comics were created by the young participants themselves, not just made for them. Bitz's efforts confirm the significance of this hands-on involvement for Native youth, whose cultural realities still uphold the traditions of storytelling and image making.

In Sherman Alexie's illustrated novel *The Absolutely True Diary of a Part-Time Indian* (2007), his protagonist is a Native American cartoonist, making for a great bookend to curriculum that Bitz developed for the University of Washington project. The cartoons drawn by Ellen Forney (non-Native) reflect a lot of interesting identity issues that are common among today's Native youth, while self-referencing author Alexie's impoverished childhood on the Spokane Indian Reservation in Eastern Washington State.

Native Americans remain an enigma to most non-Natives. They are so close to everyday American life in terms of regional history, town names, even casinos, and yet they are so far away. Reservation communities are still places where outsiders rarely venture in, while urban Indian communities often go unnoticed. For too long the definition and identity of an Indian was controlled by non-Natives. By the time the consequences of the legal battles of the 1960s self-determination era took hold, most Americans' empathy for Native America was sincere, yet sadly still uninformed. Learning to allow Native Americans their own voice in defining themselves and their artwork has been an ongoing challenge for academics, curators, and art collectors. This has left a distinctive divide even in Native communities as to what Native arts and which Native artists are traditional, compared to who and what are contemporary (and nontraditional).

The tribal battles for sovereignty also were executed on the artistic landscape. Typical coursework on contemporary Native American art history would follow a linear analysis, identifying a progression from Dorothy Dunn's controversial objectives for the art programs of Indian students at the Santa Fe Indian School in the 1930s, through celebrated Institute of American Indian

Arts icons such as Fritz Scholder and T. C. Cannon, and on to Luiseño performance artist James Luna's transformative *Artifact Piece* (1987) at the San Diego Museum of Man. All reveal a rejection of the paternalistic oversight that dictated who and what Native art is and should be.

Artist Suzi Gablik states, "The pre-condition for any human effort is the vision of success. One way to make art into a culturally useful tool might be, then, to implant images of hope, images that can empower, into the collective unconscious" (quoted in Matanovic 1985, 13). It is here that the Fourth Generation of Native student artists exists in real time, looking through the windshield toward future generations and not confined to the past. This empowerment of one particular Native student (and their tribal, clan, or band) offers great opportunity for healing, and the creative activity of the visual arts is encouraged as a foundation of this success. The model of engaging Native students with local resources, such as historically relevant tribal collections and connections with tribal elders, can provide a great opportunity to promote artistic continuity and innovation, a hallmark of all creative peoples. The comic book project is a wonderful opportunity for Native art students to remain engaged in a contemporary culture and to continue the narrative traditions that are so vitally important to tribal communities.

Recently, I worked with the U.S. Department of Education's Office of Indian Education to host their exhibit *Tradition Is My Life, and Education Is My Future* (2009). This installation featured selected student artwork from a national art competition that had asked Native students to consider the connection between their education and their culture. Part of an annual art competition series that focused on themes of Native inspiration and identity, the 2009 exhibit drew participants from all over the United States. Native and non-Native educators encouraged these students to illustrate their pride in their Native identity. This emphasis on empowerment, which was promoted at the national level, was sadly lost when budget cuts and federal spending reductions, during the economic downturn of the time, terminated the program.

In conclusion, once again I encourage concerned teachers to utilize their own resources and personal commitments to inspire their Native students in relevant art projects. It is imperative in these challenging times that Native students be allowed to exist in their own time, stable and inspired academically and culturally, as the soon-to-be Fourth Generation leaders of their communities. Given such opportunities, the next generation of students can look with pride toward the future, where their confidence and accomplishments will inspire and continue to provide a sustainable Native American culture as the Fifth, Sixth, and Seventh Generations await.

10

Immersion Education

JON REYHNER AND FLORIAN JOHNSON

One of the most promising trends in Indigenous education is the recent establishment of Indigenous-language immersion schools, which are playing a role in improving the quality of education for Indigenous students and helping heal the historical trauma inflicted by colonialism that still disrupts many Indigenous homes and communities. In this chapter we will describe support for immersion schools among Indigenous leaders and explore how these schools reflect the spirit of the United Nations' human rights declarations. Immersion schools utilize place-, community-, and culture-based education to make education relevant to students' lives. Apache, Ojibwe, Diné (Navajo), Hawaiian, and Blackfeet examples illustrate how traditional Indigenous values are infused into these schools to help build strong positive identities in Indigenous students and their communities.

Indigenous language immersion schools are becoming a key part of the post-colonial healing process that seeks to strengthen Native families and communities. These schools reverse the suppression of Indigenous languages that was historically carried out by assimilationist colonial schooling, and they use the power of Native languages to convey Indigenous values. A key feature of Indigenous immersion schools is that they are voluntary, allowing parents who choose to enroll their children in them to exercise basic human rights, as upheld by the United Nations' initiatives and declarations on human rights and Indigenous peoples.

For much of the history of colonialism, Indigenous peoples have been denied basic human rights delineated by the United Nations. In fact, it was government policy to exploit, marginalize, or assimilate Indigenous peoples through schools in which their languages and cultures were suppressed. Schools were used for centuries to help eliminate Indigenous languages. Students who spoke their Native languages were punished, and all students were indoctrinated into believing in the superiority of English and other "world" languages as compared to their "barbarous dialects" and the superiority of Christianity as compared to their "barbarous beliefs" (D. W. Adams 1995; Reyhner and Eder 2004). Dating back to the 1928 Meriam Report, which documented the findings of an independent, comprehensive investigation of the U.S. Indian Office by the Brookings Institute for Government Research at John Hopkins University, research studies have shown the harm that assimilationist policies have done to Indigenous students and their academic achievement, which has lagged far behind U.S. national averages.

When an Ojibwe (also known as Anishinabe or Chippewa) high school student on the Red Lake Reservation in Minnesota shot and killed a teacher and seven students in 2005, Navajo Nation President Joe Shirley emphasized how poverty and the breakdown of traditional tribal culture helped make such a tragedy possible, writing:

> We are all terribly saddened by the news about our relatives on their land in Red Lake in Minnesota. Unfortunately, the sad truth is, I believe, these kinds of incidents are evidence of natives losing their cultural and traditional ways that have sustained us as a people for centuries.
>
> Respect for our elders is a teaching shared by all native people. In the olden days we lived by that. When there was a problem, we would ask, "What does Grandpa say? What does Grandma say?"
>
> On many native nations, that teaching is still intact, although we see it beginning to fade with incidents like this.
>
> Even on the big Navajo Nation, we, as a people, are not immune to losing sight of our values and ways. Each day we see evidence of the chipping away of Navajo culture, language and traditions by so many outside forces.
>
> Because we are losing our values as a people, it behooves native nations and governments that still have their ceremonies, their traditions and their medicine people, to do all they can to hang onto those precious pieces of culture. That is what will allow us to be true sovereign native nations. This is what will allow our people to stand on our own. The way to deal with problems like this one is contained in our teachings. (Shirley 2005, 5)

However, any effort at revitalizing Indigenous cultures in schools needs to overcome the deep suspicion that some Indigenous people harbor toward schooling. Many American Indians and other Indigenous peoples distrust schools because historically government boarding schools were designed to eradicate Native languages and to assimilate Indians into the white, Euro-American, and Christian culture (Adams 1995; Reyhner and Eder 2004). Whether government- or missionary-run, the primary goal of schools for American Indian students was to replace Indigenous community and family values with a new set of ideals. While government-sponsored institutions saw education and suppression of native languages as a means of assimilation, religiously affiliated schools viewed the imposition of English as a means to convert students to Christianity. Conversion and assimilation tore tribal communities and families apart as some members hung on to cherished traditions, whereas others rejected those traditions as outdated, the work of the devil, and/or "savage." The results of this cultural damage can be seen in Dillon Platero's description of "Kee," a Navajo boarding school student, and in Lori Arviso Alvord's description of her father's punishment for speaking Navajo (see chapter one of this book).

Speaking at the U.S. Office of Indian Education's Language and Culture Preservation Conference in Albuquerque, New Mexico, in 2004, former Menominee Tribal Chairperson Apesanahkwat recalled that in Catholic school the nuns, in effect, told their students "to throw stones at the elders." He opined that Indians today "have tasted cherry pie [the good things of modern America] and we like it." However, Indians today are "like fish lying on the beach . . . we need to be in that water" of their culture. Apesanahkwat, like Alvord and Platero and others, argues that Indigenous cultures are inextricably intertwined with the survival of Native peoples, and that when their cultures suffer attacks, Indigenous peoples' survival is jeopardized.

SUPPORT FOR THE REVITALIZATION OF INDIGENOUS LANGUAGES

Many American Indian leaders have expressed support for their Indigenous languages. At the 2005 annual meeting of the National Indian Education Association, Cecelia Fire Thunder, president of the Oglala Sioux at Pine Ridge, testified, "I speak English well because I spoke Lakota well. . . . Our languages are value based. Everything I need to know is in our language." She declared that language is more than communication: "It's about bringing back our values and good things about how to treat each other" (NIEA 2005). Sisseton Wahpeton tribal college president Dr. William Harjo LoneFight declares, "When people spoke Dakota, they understood where they belonged in relation to other people, the natural world, and to the spiritual world. They truly knew how to treat one another" (quoted in Ambler 2004, 8).

Sally Midgette writes, "I have heard several Native Americans speak feelings about their sense of rootlessness and despair, and how they recovered when their grandmothers taught them to speak Tolowa, or Navajo, and they regained a sense of themselves and their heritage" (1997, 39). Interviewing Navajo elders in their own language, Dr. Evangeline Parsons Yazzie found, "Elder Navajos want to pass on their knowledge and wisdom to the younger generation. Originally, this was the older people's responsibility. Today the younger generation does not know the language and is unable to accept the words of wisdom." She concluded, "The use of the native tongue is like therapy, specific native words express love and caring. Knowing the language presents one with a strong self-identity, a culture with which to identify, and a sense of wellness" (1995, 3). An elder told Yazzie, "television is robbing our children of language" (1995, 135). As Indigenous children learn English or other "national" languages and cultures through the media and in schools, they increasingly become separated from their heritage, and some cannot speak to their grandparents. One of Yazzie's informants told her, "Older people who speak only Navajo are alone" (1995, 4). Many American Indians see language as the key to their identity, and they question whether one can be Cherokee, Navajo, Crow, Seminole, and so forth without speaking their tribal language. Northern Cheyenne educator Richard Littlebear found,

> Our youth are apparently looking to urban gangs for those things that will give them a sense of identity, importance, and belongingness. It would be so nice if they would but look to our own tribal characteristics because we already have all the things that our youth are apparently looking for and finding in socially destructive gangs. We have all the characteristics in our tribal structures that will reaffirm the identities of our youth. Gangs have distinctive colors, clothes, music, heroes, symbols, rituals, and "turf." . . . We American Indian tribes have these too. We have distinctive colors, clothes, music, heroes, symbols, and rituals, and we need to teach our children about the positive aspects of American Indian life at an early age so they know who they are. Perhaps in this way we can inoculate them against the disease of gangs. Another characteristic that really makes a gang distinctive is the language they speak. If we could transfer the young people's loyalty back to our own tribes and families, we could restore the frayed social fabric of our reservations. We need to make our children see our languages and cultures as viable and just as valuable as anything they see on television, movies, or videos. (1999, 4–5)

THE FOCUS OF IMMERSION SCHOOLS

Indigenous educational reformers advocate immersion schools that teach subject matter in the Native language. It is not enough, however, to simply introduce the Indigenous language if a school's curriculum remains unchanged (Nevins 2004). Merely translating a non-Native curriculum into the Indigenous language and focusing on vocabulary and grammar is in no way part of a decolonization agenda. In fact, coopting Native language to promote a non-Native curriculum could be viewed as nothing more than a new approach to colonization. On the other hand, if the non-Native curriculum is ignored as language revitalization programs are implemented, Indigenous students will be denied access to the skills they need to learn in order to negotiate the larger society and participate in the modern economy. In addition, reversing longstanding assimilationist policies may engender confusion and deep suspicion among Indigenous peoples who have accommodated to the pressures they faced by assimilating into the dominant culture, for example by converting to Christianity. The concerns of some Christian Native peoples, who see language revitalization programs as possibly leading to the revitalization of Native religions, need to be considered (see e.g., Yazzie 2003). One example that can be viewed as a compromise comes from Hawaiian activists, whose goal in language revitalization is to restore the "Hawaiian philosophy of life" and incorporate its values into the curriculum instead of teaching traditional Hawaiian religion.

Some educators, however, are uncomfortable with the premise that curricula can be balanced so that students "can live in two worlds." LaDonna Harris (a member of the Comanche Nation) remarks, "It drives me crazy when people say we have to live in two worlds. We can't live in two worlds. We have to live in one world and carry those values with us and live them every day wherever we live. People become dysfunctional when they adopt situational values" (quoted in Mankiller 2004, 68–69). Oglala Sioux educator Dr. Sandra Fox also hates "the 'walk in two worlds' idea; the time you should be most Indian is in the white world" (quoted in Reyhner 2006b). Like Harris, Fox wishes to foster traditional tribal values, which usually include cooperation, generosity, reciprocity, respect, and humility, and emphasize relatedness to all things and the need for balance and harmony. These cultural values cannot be taught as only a thing of the past, because children are growing up in and must live in the present. Wilkins (2008) describes how, with the help of an elder, her school district put together a values curriculum based on her Yakama Nation's values of honesty, compassion, caution, courage, taking care, respect, thoughtfulness, humility, and service. Lipka et al.'s study of Alaska Native education pointed out how Yup'ik teachers rejected the profuse "bubbly" praise promoted by outside [non-Native] teachers because traditional Yup'iks believed "overly praising will ruin a person" (1998, 126).

PLACE-, COMMUNITY-, CULTURE-BASED EDUCATION

Any successful Indigenous language revitalization school curriculum must address the questions raised in the preceding section regarding what subjects will be taught using the medium of the Native language. Will school studies reflect the standard state curriculum or will the curriculum be indigenized and contextualized to reflect a particular Native community? As Wayne Holm, former director of the Navajo-English bilingual Rock Point Community School, noted, "If school is to be relevant, it has to deal with the realities of the land, the animals, and the people" (2006, 2). While such an education can be accomplished largely in English, as shown in the publication *Between Sacred Mountains: Navajo Stories and Lessons from the Land* (1982) written by "storytellers and teachers" at Rock Point and transcribed by Sam and Janet

Bingham, it makes sense to teach these same concepts in the Indigenous language as well.

In a series of alternating essays in *Power and Place: Indian Education in America*, Vine Deloria, Jr., and Daniel Wildcat (2001) outline a rationale and framework for Indigenous language revitalization efforts. Deloria writes, "power and place produce personality" (27). He contrasts the "Native American sacred view" with the "material and pragmatic focus of the larger American society" (v), and draws a distinction between a "unified" Indian worldview wherein everything is related versus a "disjointed sterile and emotionless world painted by Western science" (2). Wildcat takes Deloria's vision of Indian education and proposes "an indigenization of our educational system" (vii). As a way of emphasizing our interconnectedness with the environment and relationship to the world, Deloria and Wildcat advocate experiential learning, involving example and observation, as well as learning the importance of reciprocity/giving back. Both educational approaches not only reflect Native American worldviews, but also are deeply embedded in tribal values. Deloria notes that "human personality was derived from accepting the responsibility to be a contributing member of a society" (44) and that "education was something for the tribe, not for the individual" (84).

In presenting their framework for indigenizing education, Deloria and Wildcat (2001) are directly challenging problems associated with non-native education and societal values. Wildcat describes the United States "as a nation of homeless people" who have places to live but don't know their neighbors (67). Deloria goes on to write that Americans "live within a worldview that separates and isolates and mistakes labeling and identification for knowledge" (133). They believe that instead of just learning skills and facts, students in Indigenous schools should develop a positive identity that includes having a sense of place both physically and socially; in fact, as Wildcat points out, the word "Indigenous" means to be of a place (31). Children are to be educated to "find home in the landscapes and ecologies they inhabit" (Deloria and Wildcat 2001,71). Sandra Fox's (2000 2001a, 2001b, 2003) K–12 Creating Sacred Places for Students curriculum guides, published by the National Indian School Board Association, focus on the type of curriculum called for by Deloria and Wildcat.

SOME REVITALIZATION EFFORTS

M. Eleanor Nevins found that "awareness and participation in activities sustaining of family life" was viewed by the White Mountain Apache community as "central to knowing the Apache language" (2004, 280). "Knowing how to speak Apache is an index of the child's involvement in the intimate moral universe of family life" and "language loss is therefore interpreted as an indication of problems within the family." She notes that "Apache family-centered pedagogy teaches language by cultivating a child's awareness of the social world in which speaking is possible" (278). The community felt "that computers [used in the Apache language program] in the schools should not be allowed to take the place of parents and grandparents" (282). They wanted the Apache language program to strengthen families. Because the language program Nevins studied failed to focus on what the community saw as important, the tribal government ended it.

Bowen (2004) describes an Ojibwe language maintenance program created to address not only language loss, but also the social problems linked with it. An Ojibwe band saw the decline in the use of their language as correlating "with a loss of Ojibwe traditions, the unraveling of the extended family, depression among Band members, high drop out rates among Ojibwe students, and an increasing amount of gang activity among youth" (4). An Ojibwe commissioner of education argued, "By teaching the language we are building a foundation for a lifetime of productive citizenship. . . . Ojibwe values are inextricably linked to the language. These values, such as caring for the environment, healing the body and mind together, and treating all creation with respect are taught most effectively when they are taught in Ojibwe" (4). The Ojibwe Advisory Board "firmly believed that writing Ojibwe was not as important as speaking it" (8). They wanted two fluent speakers in each classroom so conversation could be modeled for learners. And to make Ojibwe relevant to students' daily lives, they used music to make Ojibwe "cool."

Similarly, there are several Navajo examples of culture-based American Indian education programs that have been implemented as part of the healing efforts to restore traditional Diné family values. These efforts show that the "either-or" idea that one must either restore their traditional values or assimilate into the non-Indian dominant society in order to achieve academic and economic success is a false dichotomy. In the 1970s, to counteract a perceived breakdown in children's behavior, the Rock Point School Board established a Navajo-English bilingual program in their school that emphasized Navajo social studies and Navajo beliefs about kinship. For the Navajo people and other tribes, kinship through family and clans establishes rules for interacting in a respectful manner. And this interaction is reflected in the language itself. The Rock Point bilingual program was modified and transported to the Window Rock Public School. Studies of this program found that the Navajo language immersion students showed more Navajo adult-like, responsible behavior than Navajo students not in the immersion classes (Arviso and Holm 2001; Holm and Holm 1995). In addition to the Navajo social studies component of the immersion curriculum, a hands-on approach to math and science, using manipulatives and experiments, allowed students to understand and talk in Navajo about what they were learning (see e.g., Reyhner 1990).

The Window Rock Navajo immersion school started in 1986. The two hundred students in the school, most of whom are English dominant, are immersed Navajo during kindergarten and first grade with curriculum based on the Navajo Nation's Diné cultural content standards, as well as Arizona State academic standards. Some English instruction is started in second grade, and by sixth grade half the students' instruction is in English (Johnson and Wilson 2005). Besides the improvement in student behavior reported, the immersion students showed higher English-language test scores than the non-immersion students in the same school district (Johnson and Wilson 2005; Johnson and Legatz 2006). Observing Window Rock's immersion program Kathryn Manuelito (Navajo) and Daniel McLaughlin found that, "Navajo values are embedded in the classroom." A parent whom they interviewed, "noticed a lot of differences compared to the other students who aren't in the immersion program. They [the immersion students] seem more disciplined and have a lot more respect for older [people], well anyone, like teachers. They communicate better with their grandparents, their uncles. . . . [It] makes them more mature and more respectful. I see other kids and they just run around crazy" (quoted in Reyhner 2006a, 79–80).

In the table, Johnson and Wilson (2005) list the lessons learned in implementing the Window Rock immersion program, which teaches the first two grades in Navajo and then introduces English as the students' Navajo proficiency develops further.

The Navajo Nation's Education Division lists its preschool through college cultural learning goals (approved in 2000 by the Navajo Nation's Education Committee) in *T'áá Shá Bik'ehgo Diné Bí Ná nitin dóó Íhoo'aah*, which translates as Diné Cultural Content Standards. The preface to the standards states, "The Diné Cultural Content Standards is predicated on the belief that firm grounding of native students in their Indigenous cultural heritage and language is a fundamentally sound prerequisite to well developed and culturally healthy students" (Office of Diné Culture 2000, v). The empowering values of the Diné individual to be taught include being "generous and kind," "respecting kinship," "being a careful listener," and "having a balanced perspective and mind" as well as not being lazy, impatient, hesitant, easily hurt, shy, or mad. Diné individuals are to respect the sacred, have self-discipline, and prepare for challenges (80).

At the U.S. Office of Indian Education Program's Third Symposium on Language and Culture Preservation, the theme of which was "Journeying Home: Creating Our Future From Our Past," Navajo elder and statesman Jack Jackson summed up the goal of values-based Diné language programs in his March 9, 2004, address. He noted that, at Diné College, the Navajo Nation's tribal college, students and educators are "in a search to create our future based on our past." He emphasized the importance of teaching Navajos the Navajo philosophy of "Ké," of being a balanced person. This involves examining beauty before oneself, beauty behind oneself, beauty underneath, beauty

Lessons Learned from Navajo Immersion at Window Rock

WHAT WORKS

- Learning Diné language (speaking, reading, and writing) helps the students to increase skills in English.
- Exposure to Diné language increases language learning by providing a language base for academic learning.
- Using Diné language to learn state academic standards increases rate of Diné language learning.
- Constant exposure to Diné culture provides a feedback system to Diné language learning.
- Using and reflecting on student's life experiences makes learning relevant for students.
- The use of Diné language and integrating the Diné culture validates students' identity.
- Standards-based system (curriculum, instruction, assessment, grading, reporting)

RESULTS

- Language proficiency in Diné/English
- Literacy in Diné/English
- Retention and high school graduation rate
- Teacher Retention
- Family involvement in responsibility for student learning
- Diné values
- Language revitalization/ maintenance

WHAT MAKES THE DIFFERENCE

- Use of Diné (heritage) language as medium of instruction
- Consistent integration of Diné (heritage) culture in instruction
- Strong parent involvement motivates student learning (child and parents learning culture knowledge together).
- Visionary leadership

above, and beauty around, with the goal of becoming a balanced person who walks in beauty.

Like many Indigenous languages, Navajo is agglutinative, meaning that most words are made by joining morphemes together and the language is built around verbs. The Window Rock immersion school uses a classroom tested instructional approach called Situational Navajo:

> In "Navajo Immersion," we attempt to recreate—to the extent that we can in a classroom setting—a situation in which the student *needs* Navajo to communicate. Not only all instruction but all interaction goes on in Navajo. "Situational Navajo" is intended as a relatively simple approach to Navajo Immersion in which we take the recurring situations that occur during the class as the curriculum. It is not necessarily a total Navajo language program, but it would be the core of such a program.
>
> The teachers select a recurring situation in which they think it is important for their students to be able to communicate. The teachers identify the verb(s) most needed in that situation. They block out—for themselves—the imperfective paradigm of that verb, identify which forms they will teach, and when they will teach them. They then set out to teach those forms of that verb in such a way that they add only one form at a time, contrasting each new form with the forms already taught. The teachers insist that students speak verb-fully and that they use the appropriate form of the verb in all but the most trivial utterances. They lead students to use and contrast those forms in statements, negations, *aoo'/dooda* [yes/no]-type questions, *ha*[who/what]-type questions, and responses (including corrections).
>
> Over time, the students begin to accumulate more and more Navajo. (Holm, Silentman, and Wallace 2003, 45)

The Window Rock immersion program also used "Accountable Talk," in which students are asked to explain their reasoning behind their answers to questions in order to get them to elaborate, thus developing students' reasoning skills and more sophisticated language usage.

Native Hawaiians have also been very active in seeking to restore their traditional values through language immersion programs. The *Pūnana Leo* (Hawaiian Immersion Language Nest) movement begun in 1983 in Hawai'i is built around reestablishing the Hawaiian philosophy of life. From their start with Hawaiian preschools in the 1980s, Hawaiian language immersion classrooms were extended into successively higher grades until the first five K–12 immersion students graduated from high school in 1999. Students entering the program are mostly English speakers and they are immersed in Hawaiian from kindergarten to fifth grade with some English introduced after grade five. In a case study of a new immersion teacher at a Hawaiian immersion school, researchers Keiki Kawaiʻaeʻa and Angayuqaq Oscar Kawagley observed the interaction between approaches to teaching and the values being transmitted:

> One feels comfortable in entering the [immersion] school. Everyone is friendly, paying attention to the task at hand. The students work cooperatively on various projects. One project was developing a story using the Hawaiian language to describe what is happening and drawing a picture to go with it. The finished products are hung outside the classroom for everyone to see and enjoy. The few teachers observed were easy going, moving around from one individual or group, giving suggestions, answering questions, all done in a conversational tone even when correcting a child. Everyone is engaged in an easy going but disciplined process. Self-discipline becomes obvious as one observes, which is the desired outcome. (Quoted in Reyhner 2006a, 80).

Kawaiʻaeʻa and Kawagley found that "people have realized that they have to revitalize their language and culture for healing to begin" (quoted in Reyhner 2006a, 69). They observed:

> At the Hawaiian immersion school, the day began and ended with traditional Hawaiian protocol—a Hawaiian chant, a positive thought, and a prayer to open and close the day. Included in the morning protocol was the formal request chant and reply in Hawaiian to enter the school. This opening protocol set the mood for the day by helping all to focus and reflect on the task of learning, teaching and leading with good thoughts, intentions and feelings, and a cooperative spirit. The school day ended with a chant to attune them to another realm, that of home, family, friends, and place with all its different idiosyncrasies. The well-being of the whole group through active participation at the *piko* (a spiritual gathering place) was a part of the healing, health and lifelong learning daily experiences for the total learning community—students, teachers, support staff, families and guests. (Quoted in Reyhner 2006a, 78)

The researchers commented, "The Hawaiian language is the living language of the school," noting the pivotal role it plays in the curriculum:

> The language best expresses the thought world of the ancestors and thrusts them into the Hawaiian worldview. This is the language of connectedness, relatedness and respect. The language provides the cultural sustenance and the lens from which the dynamics of the school community has evolved. The language is formed by the landscape with its soundscape and therefore, conducive to living in concert with Nature. The families working together as part of the total learning community

become an integral part of the learning environment. . . . The language shapes and nurtures the school learning community as a complete and whole entity. (Unpublished case study by Keiki Kawaiʻaeʻa and Anga-yuqaq Oscar Kawagley 2006)

According to Kawaiʻaeʻa and Kawagley, "The program is family-based, en-rolling the families rather than the individual student for an overall program of language and cultural development." The seven guiding cultural pathways for Hawaiian educational success developed with the assistance of *kūpuna* (elders) from sixteen cultural guidelines are:

1. *ʻIKE HONUA* (Value of Place): Developing a strong understanding of place, and appreciation of the environment and the world at large, and the delicate balance necessary to maintain it for generations to come.
2. *ʻIKE HOʻOKŌ* (Value of Applied Achievement): Measuring success and outcomes of our learning through multiple pathways and formats.
3. *ʻIKE KUANAʻIKE* (Value of Cultural Perspective): Increasing global understanding by broadening the views and vantage points from which to see and operate in the world. (Developing the cultural lens from which to view and operate in the world.)
4. *ʻIKE MAULI LĀHUI* (Value of Cultural Identity): Strengthening and sustaining Native Hawaiian cultural identity through practices that support the learning, understanding, behaviors, and spiritual connections through the use of the Hawaiian language, culture, history, traditions, and values.
5. *ʻIKE NAʻAUAO* (Value of Intellect): Instilling and fostering a lifelong desire for knowledge and wisdom, while strengthening a thirst for inquiry and knowing.
6. *ʻIKE PIKOʻU* (Value of Personal Identity): Promoting personal growth and development, and a love of self, which is internalized and develops into a sense of purpose/role. (Growing *aloha* and internalizing *kuleana* to give back.)
7. *ʻIKE PILINA* (Value of Relationships): Enriching our relationships between the people, places and things that influence our lives through experiences that ground us to our spirituality and connect us to our genealogy, culture, and history through time and place. (Hawaiʻi Guidelines 2002, 1)

On a smaller scale, the Cuts Wood School on the Blackfeet Nation in Mon-tana immerses its students in their Blackfeet language. Its web site declares: "Cuts Wood School is nationally recognized as a successful and effective model for Native language immersion with a multi-generational approach. Cuts Wood School's mission is to use the Blackfeet language as the tool (not object) of instruction within a local context to produce fluent speakers of the

Blackfeet language. In operation since 1995, Cuts Wood School offers full day programming for children age 5–12. Our objective is to develop highly skilled learners who are knowledgeable in both Blackfeet and world academia" (Piegan Institute 2010).

Values are also emphasized. The Cuts Wood School avoids competition, "a form of violence," as well as hierarchal concepts, ranking, and punitive designations. According to Darrell Kipp (2009), a cofounder of the school, "What the students learn being taught in Blackfeet transfers to English."

At Rough Rock Community School in Arizona the Diné (Navajo) language is used as a primary language of instruction across the curriculum and integrates a multilingual approach to learning in other school and community activities in ways that promotes the distinctive spiritual, cultural, and social mores of the community. Rough Rock's culturally based pedagogy—instructional strategies, teaching activities, classroom management strategies, and physical environments—are organized in ways that reinforce the distinctive spiritual, cultural, and social mores of the community. The culturally based curriculum has been integrated into all grade levels and subject areas, and it addresses the relationship of academic content to both traditional and local community knowledge, as well as the historical, social, political, and economic experiences of the community in a modern context. The curriculum also provides students a rich foundation of multicultural, national, and international content from which their knowledge may grow and mature.

The Rough Rock community served as a partner in decisions regarding school vision, philosophy, mission, goals, curriculum, and the assessment of student progress and in the articulation of values for the program. The sociopolitical processes associated with decision-making reinforce traditional and contemporary spiritual, cultural, and social mores of the community in a modern and expanding context. Assessment of student progress is carried out in the language of instruction, is based on the local curriculum, and is used to adjust pedagogy and curricular approaches for individual students and to adjust classroom practices. Schools monitor the progress of both students and teachers in order to make decisions on curricular management, using an Indigenous Cultural Well-Being Continuum that includes traditional values for students, such as:

1. Strong, positive Indigenous identity and active involvement in cultural community.
2. Active and practical traditional spirituality.
3. Understands and demonstrates responsibility to family, community, and broader society.
4. Shows continuing development of cognitive and intellectual skills.
5. Knows, understands, respects, and applies kinesthetic activity for physical development.

The curriculum promotes a strong, positive Indigenous identity, along with active involvement in the cultural community, so that each student:

- Knows and affirms direct lineage to Indigenous community
- Knows and participates in tribal/community mores, customs, and social practices
- Knows and respects traditional stories, legends, and oral histories
- Knows the socio-historical and political experiences of one's people
- Knows and appreciates traditional practices for preparation and use of Indigenous food, clothing, and material culture
- Knows and honors connections to heavens, land, and sea; affirms connections to ancestral homeland
- Recognizes the unique status of Indigenous languages in the U.S. and to the world in general
- Knows and appreciates major contributions to national and international communities

Proponents of Indigenous language immersion emphasize teaching culture through the language with a goal of preparing Indigenous children for life, not just jobs.

CONCLUSION

Students of any race or culture who are disconnected from their traditional values are only too likely to pick up unhealthy values of consumerism, consumption, competition, comparison, and conformity from the barrage of popular culture and advertising transmitted in our modern world by television, movies, and the Internet. In 1998 the National Research Council reported that immigrant youths tend to be healthier than their counterparts from nonimmigrant families. It found that the longer immigrant youths are in the U.S., the poorer their overall physical and psychological health becomes. The more "Americanized" they became, the more likely they were to engage in risky behaviors such as substance abuse, unprotected sex, and delinquency (Hernandez and Charney 1998). There is evidence that this pattern holds true for Indigenous youths, with those young people who are less assimilated into the dominant culture doing better in school and in life. As Vine Deloria wrote, "A society that cannot remember and honor its past is in peril of losing its soul" (1994, 272). A primary goal and impetus of Indigenous language revitalization programs is to reestablish this lost link to traditional values and culture.

While academic knowledge and test scores are important, it is students' behavior toward others that is of paramount importance because it will determine how individuals use the knowledge they have gained. The future of Indigenous individuals, communities, and nations, as well as that of the world, depends on our ability to get along with each other and work together for a better future. Well thought-out and implemented Indigenous immersion programs can restore positive traditional values, develop students' reasoning ability, and teach solid academic content. Janine Pease concluded her research of immersion schools in "New Voices, Ancient Words" by stating that "immersion improves overall educational achievement, strengthens family ties, and increases retention rates, keeping Native students in school who might otherwise drop out" (2004, 16).

Note: This chapter is partly adapted with permission from Jon Reyhner's article "Indigenous Language Immersion Schools for Strong Indigenous Identities," published in the *Heritage Language Journal* 7, no. 2 (2010): 138–52.

Appendix A

Sources of Information on Children's Books

Debbie Reese's (Nambe Pueblo) American Indians in Children's Literature web site (http://americanindiansinchildrensliterature.blogspot.com/) provides critical perspectives and analysis of indigenous peoples in books for children and young adults, the school curriculum, popular culture, and society, including book reviews, Native media, and more. The Oyate web site (http://oyate.org) provides reviews of American Indian children's literature and Jon Reyhner's web page (http://jan.ucc.nau.edu/~jar/AIE/ICB.html) provides recommendations and sources for Indigenous children's books. Tim Tingle's (Choctaw, http://www.timtingle.com/) favorite books written by American Indians for children include:

Shi-shi-etko by Nicola Campbell (Salish/Metis): Shi-shi-etko awakens four days before she must leave for boarding school. She strives to remember her home, with the help of her family. This quiet, poignant story provides young readers with unique insight into the fate of many Native children in Canada and the United States (Groundwood Books, 2005).

Beaver Steals Fire: A Salish Coyote Story by the Confederated Salish and Kootenai Tribes: Coyote devises a plan to steal fire from the people above and bring it to the Earth. Through teamwork, Bear, Snake, Frog, Beaver, and other animals risk their lives and achieve their goal (Bison Books, 2008).

The Good Luck Cat by Joy Harjo (Muskogee Creek): Harjo is one of Indian Country's most respected poets and an accomplished jazz saxophone player. In her first children's book, Joy shares the alarming mishaps of Woogie, "a stripedy cat with tickling whiskers and green electric eyes." Woogie has nine lives and pushes the limit (HMH Books for Young Readers, 2000).

Thanks to the Animals by Allen J. Sockabasin (Passamaquoddy): While his family is moving to the woods for the coming winter, baby Zoo Zap tumbles from the sled. His cries are heard by the animals—furry and feathered, large and tiny—who surround and protect him till his father appears. A Passamaquoddy storyteller, Sockabasin, offers a powerful glimpse of the bond between Natives and the natural world (Tilbury House, 2005).

Jingle Dancer by Cynthia Leitich Smith (Muskogee Creek): Jenna, a modern Creek girl, wants to dance at the next powwow and needs tin jingles for her dress. She borrows jingles from four Creek elders and proudly represents her people at the powwow. Cynthia's modern story, set in suburbia, is a beautiful crossing of modern life with traditional ways (HarperCollins, 2000).

The Birchbark House by Louise Erdrich (Ojibwa): Omakayas, a baby Ojibwa girl, survives an outbreak of smallpox and is adopted by a tribal family on Madeleine Island. Erdrich's novel follows the family through four winters, and presents in fascinating detail the daily life of an Ojibwa family of 1847, as seen from an Indian perspective (Disney-Hyperion, 2002).

Skeleton Man by Joseph Bruchac (Abenaki): Her parents disappear one night, and sixth-grader Molly comes under the care of a man claiming to be her distant uncle. Locked in her room at night, she dreams of Skeleton Man, from an old Mohawk tale. The frightening conclusion pays tribute to both the ancient and the contemporary in Mohawk culture (HarperCollins, 2003).

Muskrat Will Be Swimming by Cheryl Savageau (Abenaki): A young mixed-blood (Seneca and French) girl is called a Lake Rat by taunting classmates. Her Seneca grandfather shares an old tale of muskrats, giving her a newfound sense of pride and identity (Tilbury House, 2006).

The Christmas Coat: Memories of My Sioux Childhood by Virginia Driving Hawk Sneve (Lakota Sioux): This deeply moving holiday tale, based on the author's childhood, begins with a Lakota girl hoping for warm clothing for Christmas. A simple act of giving turns disappointment into a sacred moment (Holiday House, 2011).

A Coyote Columbus Story by Thomas King (Cherokee): King has written the most original and outside-the-box book ever to appear in Native American literature, but it is filled with little-known truths. Trickster Coyote takes on a red-headed Columbus, and the results are hilarious! (Groundwood Books, 2007).

Appendix B
Sample Science Lesson Plan Format

Strand: Earth Science
Module Unit: Earth Materials
Unit Lesson: Cultural Uses of Rocks and Minerals
Grade Level: 5th Navajo

Concept and themes (concepts to be learned): Investigation and functional Navajo uses of three rock minerals

Science thinking processes (reasoning skills): Observing, recording, relating, communicating, inferring, identifying, and comparing

Introduction: This lesson will . . .

Performance objectives:
 a. Cultural: (1) Describe the functional uses of rock minerals using at least four Navajo terms; (2) Name and describe three rock minerals used for cultural purposes: red ochre, white clay, red sandstone; (3) Compare and contrast properties of red ochre and white clay, rocks, and minerals common to the Navajo; (4) Prepare (create) a sunscreen remedy using red ochre.
 b. Affective: The student will (1) respect Mother Earth, Sky, parental and community knowledge, and (2) demonstrate appreciation and enthusiasm toward science.
 c. Science objectives (embedded in the classroom science curriculum)

PHASE ONE: Exploration (inquiry and students' perceptions)

Activity 1: Inquiry

Getting Ready: (materials needed for this activity)
 • Chalkboard or large sheet of butcher paper
 • Pictures of rock formations from posters and magazines
 • Quiz A: Cultural Uses of Minerals (answer key included)
 • Samples of red ochre, white clay, and red standstone
 • Student journals, pencils

Doing the activity: Show samples of red ochre, white clay, and sandstones, and point to pictures of rock formations and canyons to focus on minerals. Ask the following . . .

Culminating activity:
1. Oral discussion of the lesson
2. Distribute Pre-Quiz A: Navajo Cultural Uses of Minerals. Instruct students to do their best.

PHASE TWO: Explanation of Concept: Cultural Perspective

Activity 2: Cultural information

Getting Ready: (materials needed for this activity)
- Sample of soils and rocks: Ground and solid chunks of red ochre, chunks of white clay, pieces of sandstone
- Student Sheet 2A: Rock Minerals
- Student reflections Worksheet 2A: Rock Minerals (a cultural teaching assistant may be asked to help pronounce the Navajo words)

Doing the activity:
- List the Navajo vocabulary words on the chalkboard and instruct students to write the Navajo words in their science journals.
- Have students pronounce Navajo words with a Navajo TA's help.

Vocabulary Words: (5–8 words per lesson)

Navajo vocabulary	*English translation*
chííh	red ochre
dleesh	white clay
tó	water
kǫ	fire
tsé	rock, stones
łeezh	soil
nítch'i	air
nahosdzáán	earth (soil)

Cultural perspective: Distribute Student Cultural Sheet 2A for a reading session.

PHASE THREE: Expansion (scientific explanation)

The Navajo Cultural Rock Mineral Unit is supplementary to the regular classroom science text. The classroom science is a text by Britannica Science System's *Full Option Science System* (FOSS), an up-to-date text coordinated with the National Science and Math Standards in education.
Materials:
- FOSS

- FOSS teacher's guide titled *Earth Materials*
- Student sheets, assessments, FACTS, and
- Student inventory sheets

Activities: 1–4: Concepts
- Mock rock test
- Scratch test
- Calcite test
- Take It for Granite test

Procedure: The learner is provided with a student activity sheet. The teacher's guide has a lesson with each activity.

Evaluation: Hands-on assessments, pictorial assessments, and reflective questions assessment are at the objective of the activities.

Unit pre-test and post-test: A pre-test is given before instruction begins early in the year. A post-test is given upon completion of the Earth Materials unit.

PHASE FOUR: Cultural Science Connections (expanding the Idea)

Activity 4: The scratch test

Getting ready: (materials needed for this activity)
- Materials for testing rocks and minerals from the FOSS kit
- A balance scale
- Student science journals
- Samples of solid and ground red ochre, chunks of white clay
- Pieces of red sandstone (one solid piece for each group)
- A tube (about 7 grams) of lanolin or zinc nitrate (purchased at drugstore)
- Spoons or sturdy tongue depressors (for each cooperative group)
- 1 or more liters of water

Doing the activity: Give a piece of red ochre to each group of students. Instruct student groups to do the following, according to FOSS:
- Make a prediction: Is red ochre a rock, or is it a soil type?
- Observe red ochre for color, feel, smell, size, and texture. Record your observations of characteristics of red ochre on FOSS worksheet and in your student science journals.
- Do the scratch test according to FOSS, with red ochre.
- How close were your predictions? Record scratch test findings on FOSS test sheets and in your student science journals.
- Do the scratch test on chunks of white clay and pieces of sandstone.
- Record findings on FOSS test sheets and in student science journals.
- Which earth material is hardest? Which is not very hard? Which is the softest material?

Culminating activity (create a sunscreen preparation):
First, demonstrate the mixing of lanolin with the finely ground red ochre by following steps 1 through 3 below, before giving each student group a plastic lid, tongue depressor or spoon, lanolin, and some ground red ochre. Next, instruct student groups on how to prepare a sunscreen remedy using the following instructions.

- Using a tongue depressor or spoon, measure and place 3 grams of lanolin on a plastic lid.
- Using a balance scale, weigh 5 grams of ground red ochre and add the ochre powder to the lanolin on the plastic lid. Mix ingredients well.
- The sunscreen salve is ready to apply to the face.
- Reflections: Have students complete Activity 4: Reflections Worksheet.

Appendix C
Social Studies Resources

BOOKS

Amerman, S. K. 2010. *Urban Indians in Phoenix Schools, 1940–2000*. Lincoln: University of Nebraska Press.

Bigelow, B., and B. Peterson, eds. 2002. *Rethinking Globalization: Teaching for Justice in an Unjust World*. Milwaukee, Wis.: Rethinking Schools.

Bruchac, J. 1997. *Between Earth and Sky: Legends of Native American Sacred Places*. New York: Harcourt, Brace and Co.

———. 2005. *Code Talker: A Novel about the Navajo Marines of World War II*. New York: Dial Books.

Caduto, M., and J. Bruchac. 1994. *Keepers of Life: Discovering Plants Through Native American Stories and Earth Activities for Children*. Golden, Colo.: Fulcrum Publishing.

———. 1994. *Keepers of the Night: Native American Stories and Nocturnal Activities for Children*. Golden, Colo.: Fulcrum Publishing.

———. 1997. *Keepers of the Animals: Native American Stories and Wildlife Activities for Children*. Golden, Colo: Fulcrum Publishing.

———. 1997. *Keepers of the Earth: Native American Stories and Environmental Activities for Children*. Golden, Colo.: Fulcrum Publishing.

Crow Dog, M. (1990. *Lakota Woman*. New York: Harper Perennial.

Dunbar-Ortiz, Roxanne (2014). *An Indigenous Peoples' History of the United States*. Boston: Beacon Press.

Kerner, K. 1995. *They Taught You Wrong!: Raising Cultural Consciousness of Stereotypes and Misconceptions about American Indians*. Yorktown, Va.: J and R Graphics Services.

Lee, E., D. Menkart, and M. Okazawa-Rey, eds. 2002. *Beyond Heroes and Holidays: A Practical Guide to K–12 Anti-racist, Multicultural Education and Staff Development*. Washington, D.C.: Teaching for Change.

Mander, J. 1991. *In the Absence of the Sacred: The Failure of Technology and the Survival of the Indian Nations*. San Francisco, Calif.: Sierra Club Books.

Mander, J., and V. Tauli-Corpuz. 2006. *Paradigm Wars: Indigenous Peoples' Resistance to Globalization*. San Francisco: Sierra Books.

Qöyawayma, Polingaysi. [1964] 1992. *No Turning Back: A Hopi Woman's Struggle to Live in Two Worlds*. Albuquerque: University of New Mexico Press.

Slapin, B., and D. Seale, eds. 1998. *Through Indian Eyes: The Native Experience in Books for Children*. Berkeley, Calif.: McNaughton and Gunn.

Wilson, W. A., and M. Yellow Bird, eds. 2005. *For Indigenous Eyes Only: A Decolonization Handbook*. Santa Fe, N.Mex.: School of American Research Press.

FILMS/MOVIES

Council on Interracial Books for Children/Rethinking Schools (producer). 1977/2008. *Unlearning "Indian" Stereotypes* [documentary]. Milwaukee, Wis.: Rethinking Schools.

Eyre, C. (director), and S. Alexie (writer). 1998. *Smoke Signals*. Seattle, Wash: ShadowCatcher Entertainment.

Singer, Beverly. 2001. *Wiping the Warpaint Off the Lens: Native American Film and Video*. Minneapolis: University of Minnesota Press.

Willmott, K. (director), and T. Carmody, (writer). 2009. *The Only Good Indian*. TLC Films.

WEBSITES

American Indian Curriculum Services, University of Wisconsin–Madison School of Education: http://aics.education.wisc.edu/

Minnesota Department of Education: Indian Education Curriculum: http://education.state.mn.us/MDE/EdExc/StanCurri/Curri/

Zinn Education Project: https://zinnedproject.org/

ORAL HISTORY WEBSITES

Pre-Contact Culture Areas, interactive map by P. Giese. (1993) 1997: http://www.kstrom.net/isk/maps/cultmap.html. Explores how North America before first contact can be divided into several different cultural areas.

STAR (Service to All Relations) School, Flagstaff, Ariz.: http://www.starschool.org/, Demonstrations of student digital performances.

Saskatoon Public Schools, Saskatchewan, Canada: http://schools.spsd.sk.ca/curriculum//blog/category/first-nations/. Using First Nations and Métis materials in the classroom.

Appendix D

Recommended Music Recordings

BLUES

Indigenous: *Things We Do*. Pine Creek Entertainment, 1998.

CLASSICAL

Brent Michael Davids: *Bright Circle*. Blue Butterfly Group, 2007.
Carl Fischer: *Reflections of an Indian Boy: A Tone Poem*. CBS, 1974.

COUNTRY

Apache Spirit: *Native Country*. Alta Vista, 1994.
Edward Gamblin: *Cree Road*. Arbor, 2006.
Floyd Westerman: *The Land Is Your Mother*. Full Circle, 1984.

FOLK

Sharon Burch: *Yazzie Girl*. Canyon Records, 1989.
Jack Gladstone: *Buffalo Café*. Hawkstone Productions, 2008.
Medicine Dream: *Tomegan Gospem*. Canyon Records, 2002.
Buffy Saint-Marie: *Coincidence and Likely Stories*. Chrysalis, 1992.

JAZZ

Mildred Bailey: *The Complete Recordings of Mildred Bailey*. Mosaic, 2000.
Russell Moore: *Russell "Big Chief" Moore's Powwow Jazz Band*. Jazz Art, 1973.
Jim Pepper: *The Path*. Enja Records, 1988.
Keely Smith: *Keely Sings Sinatra*. Concord, 2001.

POWWOW

Arawak Mountain (Northern Style): *Honoring the Ancient Ones*. SOAR, 1996.
Bad Canyon Wellpinit (Northern Style): *Powwow Songs*. Canyon Records, 1980.

Bad Medicine (Southern Style): *Southern Style Powwow Songs*. Canyon Records, 1996.
Bear Creek (Northern Style): *The Show Must Go On*. Arbor, 2003.
The Best of Hinckley Powwow Northern and Southern Style: 11th Annual Powwow Grand Celebration. Arbor, 2003.
Blacklodge (Northern Style): *Veterans' Honor Songs*. Canyon Records, 2003.
Blacklodge (Northern Style): *Powwow Songs for Kids*. Canyon Records, 1996.
The Boyz (Northern Style): *Life and Timez of TBZ*. Arbor, 2000.
Cozad (Southern Style): *Live at Red Earth*. Sweet Grass, 1996.
Eyabay (Northern Style): *Miracle*. Arbor, 2002.
Midnite Express (Northern Style): *Band of Brothers.* Pow-wowJamz, 2012.
Northern Cree Singers (Northern Style): *Still Rezin': Powwow Songs Recorded Live at Saddle Lake*. Canyon Records, 2002.
Pipestone (Northern Style): *Tribute to the Old Timers: Powwow Songs Recorded Live at Prairie Island*. Canyon Records, 2011.
Poor Boys (Southern Style): *Oklahoma*. Arbor, 2003.
Porcupine Singers (Northern Style): *Songs from Porcupine: Honoring Irving Tail*. Turtle Island Music. 1997.
Schemitzun 2000: Hand Drum Songs. Sweet Grass, 2001.
Southern Boys (Southern Style): *Live at St. Croix*. Arbor, 2003.

RAP/HIP HOP

Litefoot: *Native American Me*. Red Vinyl, 2003.
Supaman: *Crow Hop*. Rezawrecked Music, 2008.
Trurez Crew: *Tru 2 Da Rez*. [Independent], 2009.

REGGAE

Casper Lomayesva: *Sounds of Reality.* Third Mesa Music, 2000.
Marty Dread: *The Hits (1993–2003)*. Five Corners Records, 2003.

ROCK

Arigon Star: *Backflip*. Wacky, 2002.
Bezhig: *Tonto Was Cool*. [Independent], 2002.
Jimmy Carl Black: *When Do We Get Paid?* Divine, 1998.
Blackfire: *Silence is a Weapon*. Tacoho, 2007.
Jim Boyd: *First Come Last Served*. Thunderwolf Records, 2004.
Jesse Ed Davis: *Keep Me Comin'*. Epic, 1973.
Robert Mirabal: *Indians Indians*. Silverwave Records, 2003.
Redbone: *The Best of Redbone*. Epic, 1974.
Robbie Robertson: *Contact from the Underworld of Redboy*. Capitol, 1998.

Keith Secola: *Circle.* AKINA, 1992.
XIT: Silent Warrior. SOAR, 1973.

SPOKEN WORD

Joy Harjo: *She Had She Some Horses.* Mekko Productions, 2006.
John Trudell: *AKA Graffiti Man.* Peace Company, 1986.

TRADITIONAL

American Indian Dances: Great Lakes Indians. ARC Music, 1995.
Chief Jimmy Bruneau School Drummers: Drum Dance Music of the Dogrib.
　　Canyon Records, 1998.
Flathead Stick Game Songs. Canyon Records, 1973.
Haida: Indian Music of the Pacific Northwest. Folkways, 2001.
Hopi Butterfly. Canyon Records, 1998.
Kiowa Gourd Dance Songs. Canyon Records, 1973.
Kwakiutl: Indian Music of the Pacific Northwest. Folkways, 2001.
Peyote Ceremonial Songs. Canyon Records, 1998.
Traditional Music from Warm Springs. Canyon Records, 1998.
Traditional Apache Songs. Canyon Records, 1998.
Traditional Lakota Songs: William Horncloud. Canyon Records, 1998.
Traditional Navajo Songs. Canyon Records, 1998.
Traditional Voices: Historical Recordings of Traditional Native American Music.
　　Canyon Records, 2012.

TRADITIONAL/CONTEMPORARY

R. Carlos Nakai: *Sanctuary.* Canyon Records, 2003.
Joanne Shenandoah: *Covenant.* Silverwave, 2003.
Ulali: *Ulali.* [Independent], 1992.

Appendix E

Sample Format for Development of Instructional Materials

NAME OF TRIBE/NATION: HOPI (PEACEFUL ONES)

LOCATION: The Hopi people, also known as the Hopitah, which means "peaceful people," live in northeastern Arizona. Most of their settlements are on high mesas. At first, the Hopis did not build their homes on the top of the mesas but, instead, at the bottom, where their cornfields are now located. Atop First Mesa are the villages of Hano, Sichomovi, and Walpi, and below the mesa is Polacca. Second Mesa holds three villages, Shipaulovi, Mishongnovi, and Shungopovi. Farther west is Third Mesa, which until September 1906 contained only the unofficial "capital," Oraivi, at its tip. Thereafter, successive splits led to the founding of the villages of Hotevilla and Bacavi. Another village, Moenkopi, lies some forty miles west of Third Mesa, and on the plain between Third Mesa and Moenkopi is the village of New Oraivi, or Kykotsmovi.

LANGUAGE: The Hopi people are the only Pueblo Indians speaking a Shoshonean dialect of the Uto-Aztecan stock; they are therefore linguistically related to the Comanche, Ute, Paiute, and various other tribes in the southwestern United States.

POPULATION: At the time of Spanish contact, the Hopi population was about 10,000. By 1900, it had dropped to 2,000 due to the smallpox epidemics. The Hopi population according to the 2010 U.S. Census was 12,580.

FOOD: The principal Hopi industry is agriculture. Corn is still the chief food of the people. Early Hopis grew melons, squash, beans, and peas. Currants, prickly pears, cactus fruits, and other berries were the only local native fruits. Later, Europeans introduced pumpkins, onions, peppers, beets, cucumbers, apricots, and peaches. The Hopi people hunted for food such as deer, elk, doves, rabbits, prairie dogs, and quail. Today they own flocks of sheep, goats, and a few head of cattle.

HISTORY: The Hopis' origin story states that their ancestors climbed upward through four underground chambers, called kivas, and lived in many places before reaching their present locations.

The Europeans first contacted the Hopi in 1540, but the history of the Hopi goes back many hundreds of years prior to Spanish entry. Juan de Oñate, the Spanish colonizer of New Mexico, obtained the formal submission of the Hopi in 1598, and between 1629 and 1641 the Catholic religion and missions were imposed on the Hopi. When the New Mexico Pueblos revolted in 1680, the Hopi destroyed the Catholic missions. Thereafter the Hopis remained free from foreign domination until the mid-nineteenth century, when American military groups and settlers from the eastern United States began to make contact with them. In 1882 the Hopi Indian Reservation of 3,863 square miles was set aside by executive order during the presidency of Chester A. Arthur.

GOVERNMENT: The village is considered to be the unit. There is a house chief, a kiva chief, a war chief, the speaker chief or town crier, and the chiefs of the clans, who are likewise chiefs of the fraternities. All these make up a council that rules the pueblo, the town crier publishing its decisions. Laws are traditionally unwritten.

RELIGION: The Hopi are peace-loving and center their lives on their religion, which involves morning and evening prayers and participation in many seasonal ceremonies. Because of European influence, the Hopi people practice the different Christian dominations on the Hopi reservation as well.

ARTS AND CRAFTS: The Hopi are considered to be skilled craftsmen. The women on each of the three mesas make different crafts. The women of First Mesa are known for their pottery, those of Second Mesa for baskets made of yucca leaves, and those of Third Mesa for their weaving of sumac and rabbit brush into wicker baskets. The men carve and paint kachina dolls, weave blankets and belts, create paintings, and are skilled at silversmithing.

GAMES AND ACTIVITIES: Hopi games depend upon the sex and, to a large extent, upon the age of the players. Boys and girls play different games, and this division persists into adulthood, because these games are preparation for adult tasks. The majority of the games the Hopi play have counterparts among other Indian groups in North America. For example, girls utilize animal knuckle bones of various sizes to represent the members of a make-believe family. Miniature cradle-boards and dolls are used for make-believe, and even occasional kachina dolls (*tihu*). Boys play with bows and arrows in endless efforts to sharpen their skills with these weapons. There is a two-person game called *totolopsi* that is every similar to the American game of Parcheesi (which is based on a traditional game from India). One of the more interesting aspects of games and activities among the Hopi is the almost complete lack of ceremonial game playing. The Koyemsi or Mudheads play guessing and skill games with members of the audience during ceremonial dances, but other than these stimulators being part of the ceremony, there are no ritual overtones. Plaza races with elaborate punishments for the losers seem to have the most obvious ceremonial content.

GAME: *NA-HOY-YA-TA-TA-SE-YA*
(A FORM OF SHINNY, OR STREET HOCKEY)

AGES: 8 years to adult

PLAYERS: 4 to 15 (an equal number of players on two opposing teams)

PLACE: Outdoors (a field of play can be 100 to 400 yards long).

EQUIPMENT: Sticks measuring from 17 to 30 inches in length and curved at one end are decorated in a variety of colors—green, white, red, purple, and black—with encircling stripes. The ball is made of buckskin and stuffed with animal hair or other materials such as cloth, cotton, or wool. Goals for each team are formed by placing rocks at each end of the field to create goals measuring approximately 12 inches across, 8–10 inches high, and 12 inches deep.

DESCRIPTION OF THE GAME: Mainly played by young boys, this game starts out with one player from each team standing in the middle of the playing field. The object of the game is to hit the ball through the opposing team's goal, which scores 1 point. When the starting signal is given, both players begin to hit the ball, and other players join in. The ball can be struck only with the stick or feet (it can be kicked at any time). The players kick and hit the ball toward their designated goal. The first team to score 4 points is the winner of the game. Once either team wins a game, the game begins again. Rounds of the game may continue for up to four days.

SKILLS OF THE GAME: (1) Cooperation with teammates, (2) agility, (3) sportsmanship, (4) well-balanced control of major body parts (eyes, legs, and hands); (5) cardiovascular development.

LEGEND OR FACTUAL STORY: The ball is stuffed with the seeds from different plants and the Hopi considered it to be an omen. If the ball does not tear apart in the four days of playing the game, it is said that it "will not be well," indicating that the Hopi will not have good crops the coming year.

References

Adams, B. L., A. S. Adam, and M. Opbroek. 2005. "Reversing the Academic Trend for Rural Students: The Case of Michelle Opbroek." *Journal of American Indian Education* 44(3):55–79.

Adams, David Wallace. 1995. *Education for Extinction: American Indians and the Boarding School Experience, 1875–1928.* Lawrence: University Press of Kansas.

'Aha Pūnana Leo. *Mission Statement.* Accessed August 4, 2010, http://www.aha punanaleo.org/eng/about/about_mission.html.

"Alaska Native Ways of Knowing." *Anthropology and Education Quarterly* 36(1):8–23.

Alexie, Sherman. 2007. *The Absolutely True Diary of a Part-Time Indian.* New York: Little, Brown.

Allen, R. V., and C. Allen. 1982. *Language Experience Activities.* Boston: Houghton Mifflin.

Allen, T. D. 1982. *Writing to Create Ourselves: New Approaches for Teachers, Students, and Writers.* Norman: University of Oklahoma Press.

Allington, Richard L., ed. 2002. *Big Brother and the National Reading Curriculum: How Ideology Trumped Evidence.* Portsmouth, N.H.: Heinemann.

Allington, Richard L., and H. Woodside-Jiron. 2002. "Decodable Text in Beginning Reading: Are Mandates and Policy Based on Research?" In *Big Brother and the National Reading Curriculum* (Allington 2002, 195–216).

Alvord, Lori Arviso, and E. C. Van Pelt. 1999. *The Scalpel and the Silver Bear: The First Navajo Woman Surgeon Combines Western Medicine and Traditional Healing.* New York: Bantam.

Ambler, M. 2004. "Native Languages: A Question of Life or Death." *Tribal College* 15(3):8–9.

Anderson, R. C., E. H. Hiebert, J. A. Scott, and I. A. G. Wilkinson. 1985. *Becoming a Nation of Readers: The Report of the Commission on Reading.* Washington, D.C.: National Institute of Education, U.S. Department of Education.

Anvari, Sima H., Laurel J. Trainor, Jennifer Woodside, and Betty Ann Levy. 2002. "Relations among Musical Skills, Phonological Processing, and Early Reading Ability in Preschool Children." *Journal of Experimental Child Psychology* 83(2):111–30.

Apple, M. W. 1993. "The Politics of Official Knowledge: Does a National Curriculum Make Sense?" *Teachers College Record* 95(2):222–41.

ARBIC [*Annual Report of the Board of Indian Commissioners*]. 1869. Washington, D.C.: U.S. Government Printing Office.

Arviso, Marie. 2000. *Official Knowledge: Democratic Education in a Conservation Age*, 2d ed. New York: Routledge.

Arviso, Marie, and Wayne Holm. 1990. "Native American Language Immersion Programs: Can There Be Bilingual Education When the Language Is Going (or Gone) as a Child Language?" *Journal of Navajo Education* 8(1):39–47.

———. 2001. "Tséhootsooídi Ólta'gi Diné Bizaad Bíhoo'aah: A Navajo Immersion Program at Fort Defiance, Arizona." In *The Green Book of Language Revitalization in Practice*, edited by Leanne Hinton and Ken Hale, 203–15. San Diego, Calif.: Academic Press.

Ashton-Warner, Sylvia. [1963] 1971. *Teacher*. New York: Bantam.

Atkins, J. D. C. 1866. *Annual Report of the Commissioner of Indian Affairs to the Secretary of the Interior for the Year 1886*. Washington, D.C.: U.S. Government Printing Office.

Au, Kathryn. 2001. "Culturally Responsive Education as a Dimension of New Literacies." Accessed August 17, 2013, http://www.readingonline.org/newliteracies/au/index.html.

Au, W. 2009. "Social Studies, Social Justice: W(h)ither the Social Studies in High-Stakes Testing?" *Teacher Education Quarterly* 36(1):43–58.

Au, W., and B. Bigelow, eds. 2007. *Rethinking Our Classrooms*, Vol. 1: *Teaching for Equity and Justice*. Williston, Vt.: Rethinking Schools.

August, D., C. Goldenberg, and R. Rueda. 2006. "Native American Children and Youth: Culture, Language, and Literacy." *Journal of American Indian Education* 45(3):24–37.

Baker, Colin. 2011. *Foundations of Bilingual Education and Bilingualism*, 5th ed. Clevedon, UK: Multilingual Matters.

Baldwin, Daryl. 2013. Ken Hale Memorial Lecture. Presented June 17 at the Revisiting the State of Indigenous Languages National Conference, University of Arizona, Tucson.

Baptiste, H. P., and M. L. Baptiste, eds. 1979. *Developing the Multicultural Classroom Instruction: Competencies for Teachers*. Washington, D.C.: University Press of America.

Barnhardt, Ray. 2005. "Creating a Place for Indigenous Knowledge in Education: The Alaska Native Knowledge Network." In *Local Diversity: Place-based Education in the Global Age*, edited by G. Smith and D. Gruenewald, 125–62. Hillsdale, N.J.: Lawrence Erlbaum Associates.

Barnhardt, Ray, and Oscar Kawagley. 2005. "Indigenous Knowledge Systems and Alaska Native Ways of Knowing." *Anthropology and Education Quarterly* 36(1):8–23.

Barrington, John. 2008. *Separate but Equal? Māori Schools and the Crown 1867–1969*. Wellington, NZ: Victoria University Press.

Barton, K., and L. Levstik. 2004. *Teaching History for the Common Good*. Mahwah, N.J.: Lawrence Erlbaum Associates.

Basso, K. 1996. *Wisdom Sits in Places: Landscape and Language among the Western Apache*. Albuquerque: University of New Mexico Press.

Beatty, Willard. 1961. "A History of the Navajo," *America Indigena* 21:7–31.

Beaulieu, David. 2010. Statement of David Beaulieu, Professor of Education Policy and Director of the Electa Quinney Institute for American Indian Education, University of Wisconsin, at Senate Hearing 111-713, "Indian Education: Did the No Child Left Behind Act Leave Indian Students Behind?" before the Committee of Indian Affairs, United States Senate, June 17, 2010, accessed March 1, 2014, http://www.gpo.gov/fdsys/pkg/CHRG-111shrg62197/html/CHRG-111shrg62197.htm.

———. 2012. "The Obama Administration's Blaming of American Indians as Policy." *Indian Country Today,* July 9, accessed October 22, 2014, http://indiancountrytodaymedianetwork.com/2012/07/09/obamaadministrations-blaming-american-indians-policy.

Belich, James. 2001. "Foreword." In *A Civilising Mission: Perceptions and Representations of the New Zealand Native Schools System*, edited by Judith Simon and Linda Tuhiwai Smith. Auckland, NZ: Auckland University Press.

Benally, AnCita, and Denis Viri. 2005. "*Diné Bizaad* (Navajo Language) at a Crossroads: Extinction or Renewal?" *Bilingual Research Journal* 29(1):85–108.

Benham, Maenette K. P., and Ronald H. Heck. 1998. *Culture and Educational Policy in Hawai'i* Mahwah, N.J.: Lawrence Erlbaum Associates.

Benton, Richard. 2007. "*Mauri* or Mirage? The Status of the Māori Language in Aotearoa New Zealand in the Third Millennium." In *Language Policy, Culture, and Identity in Asian Contexts,* edited by Amy B. M. Tsui and James Tollefson, 163–81. New York: Lawrence Erlbaum Associates.

Berlo, Janet C., and Ruth B. Philips. 1998. *Native North American Art*. New York: Oxford University Press.

Between Sacred Mountains: Navajo Stories and Lessons from the Land. (1982) 1994. Rock Point, Ariz.: Rock Point Community School. Reprint, Tucson: University of Arizona Press.

Bigelow, B. 2008. *A People's History for the Classroom*. Milwaukee, Wis.: Rethinking Schools.

Bigelow, B., and B. Peterson, eds. 1998. *Rethinking Columbus: The Next 500 Years. Resources for Teaching about the Impact of the Arrival of Columbus in the Americas*. Milwaukee, Wis.: Rethinking Schools.

Bishop, Russell, James Ladwig, and Mere Berryman. 2014. "The Centrality of Relationships for Pedagogy: The *Whanaungatanga* Thesis." *American Educational Research Journal* 51:184–214.

Blackman, Jon S. 2013. *Oklahoma's Indian New Deal.* Norman: University of Oklahoma Press.

Blanchard, K. 1981. *The Mississippi Choctaws at Play.* Urbana: University of Illinois Press.

Bloom, Benjamin S. 1985. *Developing Talent in Young People.* New York: Ballantine Books.

Bowden, Henry Warner. 1981. *American Indians and Christian Missions: Studies in Cultural Conflict.* Chicago: University of Chicago Press.

Bowen, J. J. 2004. *The Ojibwe Language Program: Teaching Mille Lacs Band Youth the Ojibwe Language to Foster a Stronger Sense of Cultural Identity and Sovereignty.* Cambridge, Mass.: The Harvard Project of American Indian Economic Development, John F. Kennedy School of Government/Harvard University.

Brayboy, Bryan Mckinley Jones, and Angelina E. Castagno. 2009. "Self-determination through Self-Education: Culturally Responsive Schooling for Indigenous Students in the USA," *Teaching Education* 20(1):31–53.

Brayboy, Bryan Mckinley Jones, and E. Maughan. 2009. "Indigenous Knowledges and the Story of the Bean." *Harvard Educational Review* 79(1):1–21.

Brayboy, Bryan Mckinley Jones, H. R. Gough, R. Leonard, R. F. Roehl, and J. A. Solyom. 2012. "Reclaiming Scholarship: Critical Indigenous Research Methodologies." In *Qualitative Research: An Introduction to Methods and Designs,* edited by S. Lapan, M. L. Quarteroli, and F. Reimer, 423–50. San Francisco: John Wiley and Sons.

Bridgeland, J. M., J. J. DiIulio, Jr., and K. B. Morison. 2006. *The Silent Epidemic: Perspectives on High School Dropouts.* Washington, D.C.: Civic Enterprises (a report of the Bill & Melinda Gates Foundation).

Brown, D. 1970. *Bury My Heart at Wounded Knee.* New York: Holt, Rinehart and Winston.

Cajune, Julie. 2001. *Developing Culturally Integrated Content Lessons: Guidelines for American Indian Content.* Accessed February 20, 2014, http://www.ed .psu.edu/educ/dcec/ailp_guidlelines_for_american_indian_content.pdf.

Castagno, Angelina E., and Bryan McKinley Jones Brayboy. 2008. "Culturally Responsive Schooling for Indigenous Youth: A Review of the Literature." *Review of Educational Research* 78:941–93.

Castells, Manuel. 1996. *The Rise of the Network Society.* Malden, Mass: Blackwell.

Cenoz, Jasone, and F. Genese, eds. 1998. *Beyond Bilingualism: Multilingualism and Multilingual Education.* Clevedon, UK: Multilingual Matters.

Clark, Ann Nolan. 1969. *Journey to the People.* New York: Viking.

Cleary, Linda Miller. 2008. "The Imperative of Literacy Motivation When Native Children Are Being Left Behind." *Journal of American Indian Education* 47(1):96–117.

Cleary, Linda Miller, and Thomas D. Peacock. 1998. *Collected Wisdom: American Indian Education.* Boston: Allyn and Bacon.

Closs, M. 1986. *Native American Mathematics.* Austin: University of Texas Press.

Coles, G. 2000. *Misreading Reading: The Bad Science that Hurts Children.* Portsmouth, N.H.: Heinemann.

Contemporary Sioux Painting. 1970. Rapid City, S.Dak.: U.S. Department of Interior.

Costanino, M., and Denny S. Hurtado. 2006. "Northwest Native American Reading Curriculum." *Journal of American Indian Education* 45(2):45–49.

Crago, Martha. 1992. "Communicative Interaction and Second Language Acquisition: An Inuit Example." *TESOL Quarterly* 26(3):487–505.

Crawford, James. 2000. *At War with Diversity.* Clevedon, UK: Multilingual Matters.

———. 2004. *Educating English Language Learners: Language Diversity in the Classroom,* 5th ed. Los Angeles: Bilingual Educational Services.

———. 2007. "A Diminished Vision of Civil Rights," *Education Week* 26(39)31, 40.

Culin, Stewart. 1902. "American Indian Games." *American Anthropologist* 51:58–64.

———. (1907) 1992. *Games of the North American Indians.* Twenty-fourth Annual Report of the Bureau of American Ethnology. Washington, D.C.: U.S. Government Printing Office. Reprint, Lincoln: University of Nebraska Press.

Cummins, Jim. 1989. *Empowering Minority Students.* Sacramento: California Association for Bilingual Education.

———. 1992. "The Empowerment of Indian Students." In *Teaching American Indian Students,* edited by Jon Reyhner, 3–12. Norman: University of Oklahoma Press.

———. 2000. *Language, Power and Pedagogy: Bilingual Children in the Crossfire.* Clevedon, UK: Multilingual Matters.

Davidson, A. L. 1996. *Making and Molding Identity in Schools: Student Narratives on Race, Gender, and Academic Achievement.* Albany, N.Y.: SUNY Press.

Davis, B. 1996. *Teaching Mathematics: Toward a Sound Alternative.* New York, Garland.

Dawes Act. 1887. U.S. Statutes at Large 24:388. Accessed February 28, 2014, http://www.ourdocuments.gov/doc.php?flash=true&doc=50.

Decker. Peter R. 2004. *The Utes Must Go!* Golden, Colo: Fulcrum.

DeJong, David H. 1993. *Promises of the Past.* Golden, Colo.: North American Press.

Deloria, Jr., Vine. 1994. *God is Red: A Native View of Religion.* Golden, Colo.: Fulcrum.

Deloria, Jr., Vine, and Daniel R. Wildcat. 2001. *Power and Place: Indian Education in America.* Golden, Colo.: Fulcrum.

Demmert, Jr., William G. 2001. *Improving Academic Performance among Native American Students: A Review of the Research Literature.* Charleston, W.Va.: ERIC Clearinghouse on Rural Education and Small Schools.

Demmert, Jr., William G., and J. C. Towner. 2003. *A Review of the Research Literature on the Influences of Culturally Based Education on the Academic*

Performance of Native American Students. Portland, Oreg.: Northwest Regional Educational Laboratory. Contract #ED-01-0038/0002.

Derman-Sparks, L., and the ABC Task Force. 1989. *Anti-Bias Curriculum: Tools for Empowering Young Children.* Washington, D.C.: National Association for the Education of Young Children.

Deyhle, Donna. 1992. "Constructing Failure and Maintaining Cultural Identity: Navajo and Ute School Leavers," *Journal of American Indian Education* 31(2):24–47.

Diaz, Natalie. 2013. "The Next Generation of Native Language Speakers." Paper presented June 17 at the Revisiting the State of Indigenous Languages National Conference, University of Arizona, Tucson.

Dick, G. S., D. W. Estell, and T. L. McCarty. 1994. "Saad Naakih Bee'enootiilji Na'alkaa: Restructuring the Teaching of Language and Literacy in a Navajo Community School." *Journal of American Indian Education* 33(3):31–46. Accessed August 31, 2006, http://jaie.asu.edu/v33/V33S3res.htm.

Doran, H. C. 2003. "Adding Value to Accountability." *Educational Leadership* 61(3):55–59.

Dunbar-Ortiz, Roxanne (2014). An Indigenous Peoples' History of the United States. Boston: Beacon Press.

Duff, Alan. 1993. *Māori: The Crisis and the Challenge.* Auckland, New Zealand: Harper Collins.

Edwards, Betty. 1989. *Drawing on the Right Side of the Brain.* New York: Tarcher/Putnam.

Enos, Anya Dozier. 2002. "Deep Sovereignty: Education in Pueblo Indian Communities." Paper presented November 4 at the annual meeting of the National Indian Education Association, Albuquerque, N.Mex.

Evans, M. D. R., J. Kelley, J. Sikora, and D. Treiman. 2010. "Family Scholarly Culture and Educational Success: Books and Schooling in 27 Nations." *Research in Social Stratification and Mobility* 28:171–97.

Faircloth, Susan C., and John W. Tippeconnic III. 2010. *The Dropout/Graduation Rate Crisis among American Indian and Alaska Native Students.* Los Angeles: The Civil Rights Project at UCLA and The Pennsylvania State University Center for the Study of Leadership in American Indian Education.

Feddersen, Joe, and Elizabeth Woody. 1999. "The Story as Primary Source: Educating the Gaze." In *Native American Art in the 20th Century,* edited by W. Jackson Rushing III, 174–83. New York, Routledge.

Fedullo, Mick. 1992. *Light of the Feather.* New York: Morrow.

Felson, Richard B. 1991, "Blame Analysis: Accounting for the Behavior of Protected Groups," *American Sociologist* 22(1):5–23.

Feurer, Hanny. 1990. *Multicultural Education: An Experimental Project by the Cree Indians of Waskaganish in Quebec, Canada.* ERIC Document Reproduction Service No. ED 337 045.

Fillerup, Michael. 2005. "Keeping Up with the Yazzies: The Impact of High-Stakes Testing on Indigenous Language Programs." *Language Learner* (September/October):14–16.

———. 2011. "Building a 'Bridge of Beauty': A Preliminary Report on Promising Practices in Native Language and Culture Teaching at Puente de Hózhǫ́ Trilingual Magnet School." In *Indigenous Languages Across the Generations: Strengthening Families and Communities,* edited by Mary Eunice Romero-Little, Simon J. Ortiz, Teresa L. McCarty, and Ran Chen, 145–64. Tempe: Arizona State University Center for Indian Education.

Fleras, Augie. 1989. "Te Kōhanga Reo: A Māori Renewal Program in New Zealand." *Canadian Journal of Native Education* 16(2):78–88.

Fordham, S., and J. U. Ogbu. 1986. "Black Students' School Success: Coping with the 'Burden of "Acting White."'" *Urban Review* 18(3):176–206.

Forgeard, Marie, Ellen Winner, Andrea Norton, and Gottfried Schlaug. 2008. "Practicing a Musical Instrument in Childhood is Associated with Enhanced Verbal Ability and Nonverbal Reasoning." *Plos ONE* 3(10):1–8.

Fosnot, C. T. 2005. "Preface." In *Theory, Perspective, and Practice,* 2d ed., edited by C. T. Fosnot, ix–xii. New York: Teachers College Press.

Fosnot, C. T., and M. Dolk. 2005. "'Mathematics' or 'Mathematizing'?" In *Theory, Perspective, and Practice,* 2d ed., edited by C. T. Fosnot, 175–92. New York: Teachers College Press.

Fosnot, C. T., and R. S. Perry. 2005. "Constructivism: A Psychological Theory of Learning." In *Theory, Perspective, and Practice,* 2d ed., edited by C. T. Fosnot, 8–38. New York: Teachers College Press.

Foster, S. 1999. "The Struggle for American Identity: Treatment of Ethnic Groups in United States History Textbooks." *History of Education* 28(3):251–78.

Fox, Sandra. 2000. *Creating a Sacred Place to Support Young American Indian and Other Learners in Grades K–3,* 2 vols. Polson, Mont.: National Indian School Board Association.

———. 2001a. *Creating Sacred Places for Children in Grades 4–6.* Polson, Mont.: National Indian School Board Association.

———. 2001b. *Creating a Sacred place for Students in Grades 7 & 8.* Polson, Mont.: National Indian School Board Association.

———. 2001c. *Creating Sacred Places for Students in Grades 9–12.* Polson, Mont.: National Indian School Board Association.

———. 2003. *Creating Sacred Places for Students in Grades 9–12: Science.* Polson, Mont.: National Indian School Board Association.

———. 2006. *Indian Education for All: Connecting and Classrooms,* Helena: Montana Office of Public Instruction. Accessed February 20, 2014, http://www.opi.mt.gov/pub/pdf/IndianEd/ConnectingCultures.pdf.

Francis, Norbert, and Jon Reyhner. 2002. *Language and Literacy Teaching for Indigenous Education: A Bilingual* Approach. Clevedon, UK: Multilingual Matters.

Freeman, C., and M. A. Fox. 2005. *Status and Trends in the Education of American Indians and Alaska Natives.* Washington, D.C.: U.S. Department of Education, National Center for Educational Statistics.

Freire, P. (1970) 1993. *Pedagogy of the Oppressed.* Trans. Myra Bergman Ramos. New York: Continuum.

Freischlag, Jerry. 1978. "Ethnic Minorities in Physical Education: Assimilation or Cultural Pluralism?" *Physical Educator* 35:30–35.

Fuchs, Estelle, and Robert G. Havighurst. 1972. *To Live on This Earth: American Indian Education.* Garden City, N.Y.: Doubleday.

Garan, E. M. 2002. "Beyond the Smoke and Mirrors: A Critique of the National Reading Panel Report on Phonics." In R. L. Allington, *Big Brother and the National Reading Curriculum: How Ideology Trumped Evidence* (Allington 2002, 90–111).

García, Ofelia. 2009. *Bilingual Education in the 21st Century: A Global Perspective.* Malden, Mass.: Wiley-Blackwell.

García, Ofelia, and Colin Baker, eds. 2007. *Bilingual Education: An Introductory Reader.* Clevedon, UK: Multilingual Matters.

Gaser, C., and G. Schlaug. (2003). "Brain Structures Differ between Musicians and Non-Musicians." *Journal of Neuroscience* 23(27):9240.

Gates, Arthur. 1962. "The Word Recognition Ability and the Reading Vocabulary of Second- and Third-Grade Children." *Reading Teacher* 15:443–48.

Gay, Geneva. 1990. "Achieving Educational Equity through Curriculum Desegregation." *Phi Delta Kappan* 70:56–62.

———. 2010. *Culturally Responsive Teaching: Theory, Research, and Practice,* 2d ed. New York: Teachers College Press.

Gergen, K. J. 1995. "Social Construction and the Educational Process." In *Constructivism in Education,* edited by L. P. Stefe and J. Gale, 17–39. Hillsdale, N.J.: Lawrence Erlbaum Associates.

Gibson, M. A. 1984. "Approaches to Multicultural Education in the United States: Some Concepts and Assumptions." *Anthropology and Education Quarterly* 151:94–120.

Gilbert, Willard Sakiestewa. 1987. "Traditional Games of the Hopi People of Northeastern Arizona." Dissertation, University of New Mexico.

———. 2005. "Developing Culturally Responsive Science." *NABE News* 28(3):30.

———. 2007. "Testimony of Dr. Willard Sakiestewa Gilbert, President-elect, National Indian Education Association, before the U.S. House of Representatives Education and Labor Committee." *NIEA News* 38(1):28–33.

———. 2009. "Contemporary Native American Education Issues in the United States: A Year in Review" *Journal of American Studies of Turkey* 26:91–106.

Gilbert, Willard Sakiestewa, and R. Carrasco. 1999 (June). *Final Report of the Native Science Connections in Native American Communities.* Washington, D.C.: National Science Foundation.

Goodman, Kenneth S., Patrick Shannon, Yvonne S. Freeman, and Sharon Murphy. 1988. *Report Card on Basals*. Katonah, N.Y.: Richard C. Owen.

Greenberg, Henry, and Georgia Greenberg. 1996. *Power of a Navajo: Carl Gorman: The Man and His Life*. Santa Fe, N.Mex.: Clear Light.

Grimes, John Richard. 2005. "I.A.I.A and the New Frontier." In *Changing Hands: Art without Reservation*. Vol. 2, *Contemporary Native North American Art from the West, Northwest and Pacific*, edited by David Revere McFadden and Ellen Napiura Taubman, 180–81. New York: Museum of Arts and Design.

Grueninger, R. W. 1992. "Physical Education." In *Teaching American Indian Students*, edited by J. Reyhner, 251–64. Norman: University of Oklahoma Press.

Grunwald, M. 2006. "Billions for an Inside Game on Reading." *Washington Post*, October 1, B1. Accessed August 11, 2013, http://www.washingtonpost.com/wp-dyn/content/article/2006/09/29/AR2006092901333.html.

Hakuta, Kenji. 1986. *Mirror of Language: The Debate on Bilingualism*. New York: Basic Books.

Hakuta, Kenji, Yuko Goto Butler, and Daria Witt. 2000 (January). "How Long Does It Take English Learners to Attain Proficiency?" University of California Linguistic Minority Research Institute Policy Report 2000–2001. Accessed August 17, 2013, http://www.stanford.edu/%7Ehakuta/Publications/(2000)%20-%20HOW%20LONG%20DOES%20IT%20TAKE%20ENGLISH%20LEARNERS%20TO%20ATTAIN%20PR.pdf.

Hall, D. A., and D. W. McCurdy. 1990. "A Comparison of a Biological Science Curriculum Study (BSCS) Laboratory and a Traditional Laboratory on Student Achievement at Two Private Liberal Arts Colleges." *Journal of Research in Science Teaching* 27:625–36.

Hall, Edward. T. 1976. *Beyond Culture*. New York: Doubleday.

Hallett, D., M. J. Chandler, and C. E. Lalonde. 2007. "Aboriginal Language Knowledge and Youth Suicide." *Cognitive Development* 22:392–99.

Hankes, J. E. 1998. *Native American Pedagogy and Cognitive-based Mathematics Instruction*. New York: Garland.

Harper, Stephen. 2008. "Prime Minister Harper Offers Full Apology on Behalf of Canadians for the Indian Residential Schools System." *Prime Minister's Office*, June 11. Accessed June 18, 2014, http://pm.gc.ca/eng/news/2008/06/11/prime-minister-harper-offers-full-apology-behalf-canadians-indian-residential.

Havighurst, J. 1971. *The Education of Indian Children and Youth: Summary Report and Recommendations*. National Study of American Indian Education, series 4, no. 6. Minneapolis: Training Center for Community Programs, University of Minnesota.

Hawai'i Guidelines for Culturally Healthy and Responsive Learning Environments. 2002. Accessed January 20, 2009, http://www.olelo.hawaii.edu/olelo/nhmo.php.

Hazari, S., A. North, and D. Moreland. 2009. "Investigating Pedagogical Value of Wiki Technology." *Journal of Information Systems Education* 20:187–98.

Heal, N. A., G. P. Hanley, and S. A. Layer. 2009. "An Evaluation of the Relative Efficacy of and Children's Preferences for Teaching Strategies that Differ in Amount of Teacher Directedness." *Journal of Applied Behavior Analysis* 42:123–43.

Heidenreich, C. Adrian. 1985. "Background and Interpretation of Crow and Gros Ventre Ledger Art Done at Crow Agency, Montana between 1879 and 1897." In *Ledger Art of the Crow and Gros Ventre Indians: 1879–1897,* by C. Adrian Heidenreich and Christopher Warner. Billings, Mont.: Yellowstone Art Center.

Hernandez, D. J., and E. Charney, eds. 1998. *From Generation to Generation: The Health and Well-being of Children in Immigrant Families.* Committee on the Health and Adjustment of Immigrant Children and Families, Board on Children, Youth, and Families, National Research Council and Institute of Medicine. Washington, D.C.: National Academy Press.

Herrnestein, R. J., and C. Murray. 1994. *The Bell Curve: Intelligence and Class Structure in American Life.* New York: Free Press.

Hess, D. 2009. *Controversy in the Classroom: The Democratic Power of Discussion.* New York: Routledge.

Hill, Sr., Richard W. 2002. "Art of the Northeast Woodlands." In *Uncommon Legacies: Native American Art from the Peabody Essex Museum,* edited by John R. Grimes, Christian F. Feest, and Mary Lou Curran, 188–209. New York: American Federation of Arts in Association with University of Washington Press.

Hirschfelder, Arlene B., and Beverly R. Singer, eds. 1992. *Rising Voices: Writings of Young Native Americans.* New York: Charles Scribner's Sons.

Hogg, T. C., and M. R. McComb. 1969. "Cultural Pluralism: Its Implications for Education." *Educational Leadership* 27:235–38.

Holm, Agnes, and Wayne Holm. 1990. "Rock Point, A Navajo Way To Go to School: A Valediction." *Annals of the American Academy of Political and Social Science* 508:170–84.

———. 1995. "Navajo Language Education: Retrospect and Prospects." *Bilingual Research Journal* 19(1):141–67.

Holm, Wayne. 2006. "The 'Goodness' of Bilingual Education for Native American Children." In *One Voice, Many Voices: Recreating Indigenous Language Communities,* edited by T. L. McCarty and O. Zepeda, 1–46. Tempe: Arizona State University Center for Indian Education.

Holm, Wayne, Irene Silentman, and Laura Wallace. 2003. "Situational Navajo: A School-Based, Verb-Centered Way of Teaching Navajo." In *Nurturing Native Languages,* edited by J. Reyhner, O. Trujillo, R. L. Carrasco, and L. Lockard, 25–52. Flagstaff: Northern Arizona University.

Hornberger, Nancy H. 2002. "Multilingual Language Policies and the Continua of Biliteracy: An Ecological Approach." *Language Policy* 1(1):27–51.

——. 1997. "Language Policy, Language Education, and Language Rights: Indigenous, Immigrant, and International Perspectives." Keynote Address, American Association for Applied Linguistics Annual Conference, Orlando, Fla.

Hornberger, Nancy H., and Kendall A. King. 1996. "Bringing the Language Forward: School-based Initiatives for Quechua Language Revitalization in Ecuador and Bolivia." In *Indigenous Literacies in the Americas: Language Planning from the Bottom Up*, edited by Nancy H. Hornberger, 299–310. Berlin: Mouton de Gruyter.

House, Deborah. 2002. *Language Shift Among the Navajos.* Tucson: University of Arizona Press.

Hoyt-Goldschmidt, Diane. 1993. *Pueblo Storyteller.* New York: Houghton-Mifflin.

Huizinga, Johan. 1950. *Homo Ludens: A Study of Play of the Play Element in Culture.* Boston, Mass.: Beacon Press.

Illich, Ivan. 1971. *Deschooling Society.* New York: Harper & Row.

Ilutisk, E. A. 1994. "The Founding of Ciulistet: One Teacher's Journey." *Journal of American Indian Education* 33(3):6–13.

Indian Nations at Risk Task Force. 1991. *Indian Nations at Risk: An Educational Strategy for Action.* Washington, D.C.: U.S. Department of Education. Accessed January 20, 2009 http://www.tedna.org/pubs/nationsatrisk.pdf.

Iverson, Peter, ed. 2002. *"For Our Navajo People": Diné Letters, Speeches and Petitions 1900–1960.* Albuquerque: University of New Mexico Press.

James, George Wharton. 1908. *What the White Race May Learn from the Indian.* Chicago: Forbes.

Johnson, Florian Tom, and Jennifer Wilson. 2005. "Navajo Immersion in the Navajo Nation." *NABE News* 28(4):30–31.

Johnson, Florian Tom, and Jennifer Legatz. 2006. "Tséhootsooí Diné Bi'ólta'." *Journal of American Indian Education* 45(2):26–33.

Jordan, Cathy. 1984. "Cultural Compatibility and the Education of Hawaiian Children: Implications for Mainland Educators." *Educational Research Quarterly* 8(4):59–71.

Kabotie, Fred, with Bill Belknap. 1977. *Fred Kabotie.* Flagstaff: Museum of Northern Arizona.

Kagle, M. S. 2007. *Math in a Cultural Context: A Third Space between School and Indigenous Culture.* Dissertation, Harvard University.

King, Dorothy F. 1990. "Toward Excellence in Educating Navajo Students, One School's Journey: An Interview with Helen Zongolowicz. *Journal of Navajo Education* 7(2):22–27.

Kipp, D. 2009. "Encouragement, Guidance and Lessons Learned: 21 Years in the Trenches of Indigenous Language Revitalization." In *Indigenous Language*

Revitalization: Encouragement, Guidance and Lessons Learned, edited by J. Reyhner and L. Lockart, 1–9). Flagstaff: Northern Arizona University. Accessed January 20, 2009, http://jan.ucc.nau.edu/~jar/ILR/.

Kisker, E. E., J. Lipka, B. L. Adams, A. Rickard, D. Andrew-Ihrke, E. E. Yanez, and A. Millard. 2012. "The Potential of a Culturally Based Supplemental Mathematics Curriculum to Improve the Mathematics Performance of Alaska Native and Other Students." *Journal for Research in Mathematics Education* 43(1):75–113.

Kleinfeld, Judith S. 1979. *Eskimo School on the Adreafsky: A Study of Effective Bicultural Education.* New York: Praeger.

Kneale, Albert H. 1950. *Indian Agent.* Caldwell, Idaho: Caxton.

Krashen, Stephen D. 2004. *The Power of Reading: Insights from the Research,* 2d ed. Westport, Cont.: Libraries Unlimited.

Kroskrity, Paul V. 2012. *Telling Stories in the Face of Danger: Language Renewal in Native American Communities.* Norman: University of Oklahoma Press.

Kroskrity, Paul V., and Margaret C. Field, eds. 2009. *Native American Language Ideologies: Beliefs, Practices, and Struggles in Indian Country.* Tucson: University of Arizona Press.

Ladson-Billings, Gloria. 1994. *The Dreamkeepers: Successful Teachers of African American Children.* San Francisco: Jossey-Bass.

———. 2001. *Crossing Over to Canaan: The Journey of New Teachers in Diverse Classrooms.* San Francisco: Jossey-Bass.

Lawson, R. 1940. *They Were Strong and Good.* New York: Viking.

Lee, O. 2003. "Equity for Linguistically and Culturally Diverse Students in Science Education: A Research Agenda." *Teachers College Record* 105:465–89.

Lemkin, Raphaël. 1944. *Axis Rule in Occupied Europe.* Washington, D.C.: Carnegie Endowment for International Peace.

Leslie, Mike. 1998. "Native American Artists: Expressing Their Own Identity." In S. E. Boehme, Gerald E. Conaty, and David Warren, *Powerful Images, Portrayals of Native America,* 111–33. Seattle: Museums West/University of Washington Press.

LeVine, Robert A., and Donald T. Campbell. 1972. *Ethnocentrism.* New York: John Wiley.

Levinson, M. 2012. *No Citizen Left Behind.* Cambridge, Mass.: Harvard University Press.

Libhart, Myles, and Vincent Price. 1970. *Contemporary Sioux Painting.* Rapid City, S.Dak.: U.S. Department of the Interior, Indian Arts and Crafts Board.

Lindsay, Brendan C. 2012. *Murder State: California's Native American Genocide, 1846–1873.* Lincoln.: University of Nebraska Press.

Lipka, J. 1989. "A Cautionary Tale of Curriculum Development in Yup'ik Eskimo Communities." *Anthropology and Education Quarterly* 20(3):216–31.

———. 1991. "Toward a Culturally Based Pedagogy: A Case Study of One Yup'ik Eskimo Teacher. *Anthropology and Education Quarterly* 22(3):203–23.

———. 1994a. "Culturally Negotiated Schooling: Toward a Yup'ik Mathematics." *Journal of American Indian Education* 33(3):14–30.

———. 1994b. "Language, Power, and Pedagogy: Whose School Is It?" *Peabody Journal of Education* 69(20):71–93.

Lipka, J., and B. Adams. 2004. *Culturally Based Math Education as a Way to Improve Alaska Native Students' Math Performance.* Appalachian Collaborative Center for Learning, Assessment and Instruction in Mathematics. Working Paper no. 20. Athens: Ohio University.

Lipka, J., and T. L. McCarty. 1994. "Changing the Culture of Schooling: Navajo and Yup'ik Cases." *Anthropology and Education Quarterly* 25(3):266–84.

Lipka, J., G. V. Mohatt, and the Ciulistet Group. 1998. *Transforming the Culture of Schools: Yup'ik Eskimo Examples.* Mahwah, N.J.: Lawrence Erlbaum Associates.

Lipka, J., J. P. Webster, and E. Yanez. 2005a. "Factors That Affect Alaska Native Students' Mathematical Performance." *Journal of American Indian Education* 44(3):1–8.

Lipka, J., N. Sharp, B. Brener, E. Yanez, and F. Sharp. 2005b. "The Relevance of Culturally Based Curriculum and Instruction: The Case of Nancy Sharp." *Journal of American Indian Education* 44(3):31–54.

Lipka, J., M. P. Hogan, J. P. Webster, E. Yanez, B. Adams, S. Clark, and D. Lacy. 2005c. "Math in a Cultural Context: Two Case Studies of a Successful Culturally Based Math Project." *Anthropology and Education Quarterly* 36(4):367–85.

Lipka, J., N. Sharp, B. Adams, and F. Sharp. 2007. "Creating a Third Space for Authentic Biculturalism: Examples from Math in a Cultural Context." *Journal of American Indian Education* 46(3):94–115.

Lippard, Lucy R. 1990. *Mixed Blessings: New Art in a Multicultural America.* New York: Pantheon.

Littlebear, Richard. 1999. "Some Rare and Radical Ideas for Keeping Indigenous Languages Alive." In *Revitalizing Indigenous languages,* edited by J. Reyhner, G. Cantoni, R. N. St. Clair and E. P. Yazzie, 1–5. Flagstaff: Northern Arizona University. Accessed January 20, 2009, http://jan.ucc.nau.edu/~jar/RIL_1.html.

Loewen, J. 1995. *Lies My Teacher Told Me: Everything Your American History Textbook Got Wrong.* New York: Simon and Schuster.

Mankiller, Wilma. 2004. *Every Day Is a Good Day: Reflections by Contemporary Indigenous Women.* Golden, Colo.: Fulcrum.

Manzo, K. K. 2007. "Reading Curricula Don't Make Cut for Federal Review." *Education Week* online (August 15).

Matanovic, Milenko, ed. 1985. *Lightworks: Explorations in Art, Culture and Creativity.* Issaquah, Wash.: Lorain Press.

Matz, L. D. 1970. "Sports, Games and Physical Education of Ancient and Modern Indians." Master's thesis, University of California at Los Angeles.

May, Stephen. ed. 1999. *Indigenous Community-Based Education.* Clevedon, UK: Multilingual Matters.

McCardle, Peggy, and William Memmert, eds. Report of a National Colloquium, I: Programs and Practices and II: Research. 2006. "Improving Academic Performance among American Indian, Alaska Native, and Native Hawaiian Students: Assessment and Identification of Learning and Learning Disabilities." Workshop summary from March 16–18, 2005, conference in Santa Fe, New Mexico. *Journal of American Indian Education* 45(2–3).

McCarty, Teresa L. 2002. *A Place to Be Navajo: Rough Rock and the Struggle for Self-Determination in Indigenous Schooling.* Mahwah, N.J.: Lawrence Erlbaum Associates.

———. 2003. "Revitalising Indigenous Languages in Homogenising Times." *Comparative Education* 39(2):147–63.

———. 2012. "Indigenous Languages and Cultures in Native American Student Achievement: Promising Practices and Cautionary Findings." In *Standing Together: American Indian Education as Culturally Responsive Pedagogy,* edited by Beverly J. Klug, 97–119. Lanham, Md.: Rowman and Littlefield.

———. 2013. *Language Planning and Policy in Native America: History, Theory, Praxis.* Bristol, UK: Multilingual Matters.

McCarty, Teresa L., and Galena Sells Dick. 2003. "Telling The People's Stories: Literacy Practices and Processes in a Navajo Community School." In *Multicultural Issues in Literacy Research and Practice,* edited by Arlette I. Willis, Georgia E. García, Rosalinda B. Barrera, and Violet J. Harris, 101–22. Mahwah, N.J.: Lawrence Erlbaum Associates.

McCarty, Teresa L., Mary Eunice Romero, and Ofelia Zepeda. 2006. "Reclaiming the Gift: Indigenous Youth Counter-Narratives on Native Language Loss and Revitalization." *American Indian Quarterly* 30(1–2):28–48.

McCarty, Teresa L, and Ofelia Zepeda. 2010. "Native Americans." In *Handbook of Language and Ethnic Identity: Disciplinary and Regional Perspectives,* Vol. 1, 2d ed., edited by Joshua A. Fishman and Ofelia Garcia, 323–39. Oxford, UK: Oxford University Press.

McClinton, Rowena. 2007. "Epilogue." In *The Moravian Springplace Mission to the Cherokees,* Vol. 2, *1814–1821,* 439–43, edited by R. McClinton. Lincoln: University of Nebraska Press.

McDermott, Ray. 2005. "Commentary on Part I, '. . . An Entry into Further Language': Contra Mystification by Language Hierarchies." In *Language, Literacy, and Power in Schooling,* edited by Teresa L. McCarty, 111–24. Mahwah, N.J.: Lawrence Erlbaum Associates.

McDougall, Gay J. 2009. Foreword. In *State Of The World's Minorities And Indigenous Peoples,* edited by Preti Taneja. London: Minority Rights Group International.

McKay, Graham. 1996. *The Land Still Speaks: Review of Aboriginal and Torres Strait Islander Language Maintenance and Development Needs and Activities.* Commissioned Report no. 14. Canberra, Australia: Government Publishing Service, 1996).

McLaughlin, Daniel. 1992. *When Literacy Empowers: Navajo Language in Print.* Albuquerque: University of New Mexico Press.

McREL Research Staff. 2005. *Mathematics Lesson Interactions and Contexts for American Indian Students in Plains Region Schools: An Exploratory Study.* McREL Regional Education Laboratory. Contract #ED-01-CO-0006.

Meier, Deborah, and George Wood, eds. 2004. *Many Children Left Behind: How the No Child Left Behind Act is Damaging Our Children and Our Schools.* Boston: Beacon Press.

Meriam, Lewis, ed. 1928. *The Problem of Indian Administration.* Baltimore: John Hopkins University. Accessed August 31, 2007, http://www.alaskool.org /native_ed/research_reports/IndianAdmin/Indian_Admin_Problms.html.

Meyer, Richard J., and Kathryn F. Whitmore, eds. 2011. *Reclaiming Reading: Teachers, Students, and Researchers Regaining Spaces for Thinking and Action.* New York: Routledge.

———. 2014. *Reclaiming Writing: Composing Spaces for Identities, Relationships, and Actions.* New York: Routledge.

Midgette, S. 1977. "The Native Languages of North America: Structure and Survival." In *American Indian Studies: An Interdisciplinary Approach to Contemporary Issues,* edited by D. Morrison, 27–45. New York: Peter Lang.

Miller, James Roger. 1996. *Shingwauk's Vision: A History of Native Residential Schools.* Toronto: University of Toronto Press.

Milloy, John S. 1999. *A National Crime: The Canadian Government and the Residential School System, 1879 to 1986.* Winnipeg: University of Manitoba Press.

Montejo, Victor D. 1998. "Dreams of an *Ah Tz'ib* (Writer) in the Maya Land." In *Speaking for the Generations: Native Writers on Writing,* edited by Simon J. Ortiz, 196–216. Tucson: University of Arizona Press.

Montgomery, M., B. Manuelito, T. Chock, and D. Buchwald. 2012. "The Native Comic Book Project: Native Youth Making Comics and Healthy Decisions." *Journal of Cancer Education,* 27:S41-S46.

Moss, B. and T. S. Young. 2010. *Creating Lifelong Readers through Independent Reading.* Newark, Del.: International Reading Association.

Mullis, I. V. S., M. Martin, A. M. Kennedy, and P. Foy. 2007. *PIRLS 2006 International Report: IEA's Progress in International Reading Literacy Study in Primary Schools in 40 Countries.* Boston: International Association for the Evaluation of Educational Achievement.

Museum of Indian Arts and Culture. 2008. *Comic Art Indigène.* New Mexico Department of Cultural Affairs. Accessed February 8, 2014, http://www.indian artsandculture.org/ComicArt/?p=release.

National Academy of Sciences. 1996. *National Science Education Standards.* Washington, D.C.: National Academy Press.

National Geographic Society. 2014. "Disappearing Languages," accessed September 8, 2014 from http://www.nationalgeographic.com/mission/enduringvoices/.

"Native Americans: A Statistical Profile." 2013 (Dec. 4). *Education Week* 33(13):15.

NRP [National Reading Panel]. 2000. *Teaching Children to Read: An Evidence-based Assessment of the Scientific Research Literature on Reading and Its Implications for Reading Instruction: Reports of the Subgroups.* Rockville, Md. National Institute of Child Health and Human Development.

NRC [National Research Council], Commission on Behavioral and Social Science Education. 2005. *How Students Learn: History, Mathematics, and Science in the Classroom.* Washington, D.C.: National Academy Press.

———. 2000. *How People Learn: Brain, Mind, Experience, and School.* Washington, D.C.: National Academy Press.

Navalta, Wildred S. 1978. "The Sports and Games of the Makahiki Festival: A History and a Unit of Instruction." Dissertation, Brigham Young University.

———. 1981. "The Hawaiian Olympics." *Journal of Physical Education, Recreation and Dance* 52(9):26–28.

NCES [National Center for Educational Statistics]. 2012. *National Indian Education Study 2011: The Educational Experiences of American Indian and Alaska Native Students at Grades 4 and 8.* Washington, D.C.: U.S. Department of Education.

Nelson-Barber, S., and E. Estrin. 1995. "Bridging Native American Perspectives to Mathematics and Science Teaching." *Theory into Practice* 34(3) 174–85.

Nersessian, David. 2005. "Rethinking Cultural Genocide under International Law." *Human Rights Dialogue* 2(12). Accessed June 15, 2010, http://www.cceia.org/resources/publications/dialogue/2_12/section_1/5139.html.

Ness, J., and J. Huisken, J. 2002. *Expanding the Circle: Respecting the Past, Preparing the Future.* Minneapolis: University of Minnesota Institute on Community Integration.

New London Group. 1996. "A Pedagogy of Multiliteracies: Designing Social Futures." *Harvard Educational Review* 66(1):60–92.

Nicholas, Sheilah. 2008. "Becoming 'Fully' Hopi: The Role of the Hopi Language in the Contemporary Lives of Hopi Youth: A Hopi Case Study of Language Shift and Vitality." Dissertation, University of Arizona.

———. 2009. "'I Live Hopi, I Just Don't Speak It': The Critical Intersection of Language, Culture, and Identity in the Lives of Contemporary Hopi Youth." *Journal of Language, Identity, and Education* 8(5):321–34.

———. 2005. "Negotiating for the Hopi Way of Life Through Literacy and Schooling." In Language, Literacy, and Power in Schooling, edited by T. McCarty, 29–46. Mahwah, N.J.: Lawrence Erlbaum Associates.

Nichols, S. L., and D. C. Berliner. 2007. *Collateral Damage: How High–Stakes Testing Corrupts America's Schools.* Cambridge, Mass.: Harvard Education Press.

NIEA [National Indian Education Association]. 2005. *Preliminary Report on No Child Left Behind in Indian Country.* Washington, D.C.: NIEA.

———. 2012 (July 3). "Leading Advocate for Native Students Comments on NAEP American Indian/Alaska Native Report." NIEA Press Release. Accessed August 17, 2013, http://www.niea.org/News/?id=138.

Nixon, Richard M. 1971. "Special Message to the Congress on Indian Affairs." In *Public Papers of the Presidents of the United States, Richard Nixon, Containing the Public Messages, Speeches, and Statements of the President, 1970.* Washington, D.C.: U.S. Government Printing Office.

No Child Left Behind Act. 2001, Title I: Improving the Academic Achievement of the Disadvantaged. Washington, D.C.: National Clearinghouse for Bilingual Education, George Washington University.

Novak, J. R., and B. Fuller. 2003. *Penalizing Diverse Schools?* PACE Policy Brief 03–04. Accessed April 26, 2007, http://pace.berkeley.edu/policy_brief_03–4_Pen.Div.pdf.

Ochs, Eleanor. 1988. *Culture and Language Development: Language Acquisition and Language Socialization in a Samoan Village.* Cambridge, UK: Cambridge University Press.

Office of Diné Culture, Language and Community Service, Division of Diné Education. 2000. *T'áá Shá Bik'ehgo Diné Bí Ná nitin dóó Íhoo'aah* (Diné Cultural Content Standards). Window Rock, Ariz.: Office of Diné Culture. Accessed January 20, 2009, http://www.odclc.navajo.org/view_taa_yellow.htm.

Ogbu, John U. 1995. "Understanding Cultural Diversity and Learning," In *Handbook of Research on Multicultural Education,* edited by James A. Banks and C. A. M. Banks, 582–93. New York: Macmillan.

———. 2003. *Black American Students in an Affluent Suburb: A Study of Academic Disengagement.* Hillsdale, N.J.: Lawrence Erlbaum Associates.

Paley, A. R. 2007. "Key Initiative of 'No Child' under Federal Investigation." *Washington Post,* April 21, A1. Accessed August 11, 2013, http://www.washingtonpost.com/wp-dyn/content/article/2007/04/20/AR2007042002284_pf.html.

Parker, W. 2003. *Teaching Democracy: Unity and Diversity in Public Life.* New York: Teachers College Press.

Pease, J. 2004. "New Voices, Ancient Words." *Tribal College* 15(3):15–18.

Peshkin, Alan. 1997. *Places of Memory: Whiteman's Schools and Native American Communities.* Mahwah, N.J.: Lawrence Erlbaum Associates.

Philips, Susan U. 1993. *The Invisible Culture: Warm Springs Children in Community and Classroom.* Prospect Heights, Ill.: Waveland Press, Inc.

Piegan Institute. *Cuts Wood School.* Accessed August 4, 2010, http://www.piegan institute.org/cutswoodschool.html.

Pinxten, R., I. van Dooren, and E. Soberon. 1987. *Towards a Navajo Indian Geometry.* Ghent, Belgium: KKI Books.

Plank, David N. 1998. "Foreword." In Maenette K. P. Benham and Ronald H. Heck, *Culture and Educational Policy in Hawai'i.* Mahwah, N.J.: Lawrence Erlbaum Associates.

Platero, Dillon. 1975. "Bilingual Education in the Navajo Nation," In *Proceedings of the First Inter-American Conference on Bilingual Education,* edited by C. Troike and N. Modiano, 56–61. Washington, D.C.: Center for Applied Linguistics.

Platt, Rita. 2004. "Standardized Tests: Whose Standards Are We Talking About?" *Phi Delta Kappan* 85:381–87.

Pogrow, S. 2000. "Success for All Does Not Produce Success for Students." *Phi Delta Kappan* 82(1):67–80.

Powell, John Wesley. 1896. "The Need of Studying the Indian in Order to Teach Him." In *Annual Report of the Board of Indian Commissioners.* Washington, D.C.: Government Printing Office.

Prakash, Madhu Suri, and Gustavo Esteva. 1998. *Escaping Education: Living as Learning within Grassroots Cultures.* New York: Peter Lang.

Pressley, Michael, K. R. Hilden, and R. K. Shankland. 2006. *An Evaluation of End-grade-3 Dynamic Indicators of Basic Early Literacy Skills (DIBELS): Speed Reading Without Comprehension, Predicting Little.* East Lansing: Michigan State University, College of Education, Literacy Achievement Research Center (LARC).

Qöyawayma, Polingaysi (Elizabeth Q. White). 1964. *No Turning Back: A Hopi Indian Woman's Struggle to Live in Two Worlds,* as told to Vada F. Carlson. Albuquerque: University of New Mexico Press.

Renner, J. W., and E. Marek. 1988. *The Learning Cycle and Elementary School Science Teaching.* Portsmouth, N.H.: Heinemann.

Report on BIA Education: Excellence in Indian Education Through the Effective School Process, Final Review Draft. 1988. Washington, D.C.: Office of Indian Education Programs, Bureau of Indian Affairs, U.S. Department of the Interior.

Research Agenda Working Group: M. Pavel, J. Reyhner, C. Avison, C. Obester, and J. Sayer. 2003. *American Indian and Alaska Native Education Research Agenda Literature Review.* (Commissioned paper prepared for American Indian and Alaska Native Education Federal Interagency Task Force.) Rockville, Md.: Westat.

Returned Student Survey #24, Part 5. 1917. Ponca Agency Superintendent in Oklahoma, manuscript in the Ayer Collection of the Newberry Library, Chicago, p. 88.

Reyhner, Jon. 1990. "A Description of the Rock Point Community School Bilingual Education Program." In *Effective Language Education Practices and Native Language Survival,* edited by J. Reyhner, 95–106. Choctaw, Okla.:

Native American Language Issues. Accessed January 20, 2009, http://jan
.ucc.nau.edu/~jar/NALI7.html.

———. 1992a. *Plans for Dropout Prevention and Special School Support Services for American Indian and Alaska Native Students.* (Paper commissioned by the Indian Nations at Risk Task Force.) Accessed August 31, 2013, http://jan.ucc .nau.edu/~jar/INAR.html.

———. 1992b. "American Indians Out of School: A Review of School-Based Causes and Solutions." *Journal of American Indian Education* 31(3):37–56.

———. 2001a. "Cultural Survival *vs.* Forced Assimilation," *Cultural Survival Quarterly* 25(2):22–25.

———. 2001b. *Family, Community, and School Impacts on American Indian and Alaska Native Students' Success.* (Literature review prepared for American Indian/Alaska Native Education Research Initiative.) Accessed August 31, 2013, http://jan.ucc.nau.edu/~jar/AIE/Family.html.

———. 2005 (November/December). "Cultural Rights, Language Revival, and Individual Healing." *Language Learner* 22–24. Accessed August 31, 2007, http://jan.ucc.nau.edu/~jar/LLcultural.html.

———. 2006a. "Issues Facing New Native Teachers." In *The Power of Native Teachers,* edited by D. Beaulieu and A. M. Figueira, 63–92. Tempe: Center for Indian Education, Arizona State University.

———. 2006b, March. "Creating Sacred Places for Children." *Indian Education Today,* 19–20. Accessed January 20, 2009, http://jan.ucc.nau.edu/~jar/AIE /IETplaces.htm.

———. 2006c. *Education and Language Restoration.* Philadelphia: Chelsea House.

———. 2010. "Indigenous Language Immersion Schools for Strong Indigenous Identities." *Heritage Language Journal* 7(2):138–52.

———. 2014. "Improving American Indian Education through Best Practices." In *American Indians at Risk,* edited by J. I. Ross, 599–614. Santa Barbara, Calif.: ABC-CLIO.

———, ed. 1992. *Teaching American Indian Students.* Norman: University of Oklahoma Press.

Reyhner, Jon, and Jeanne Eder. 2004. *American Indian Education: A History.* Norman, Okla.: University of Oklahoma Press.

Reyhner, Jon, and Denny Hurtado. 2008. "Reading First, Literacy, and American Indian/Alaska Native Students." *Journal of American Indian Education* 47(1):82–95.

Reyhner, Jon, and Navin K. Singh. 2013. "Culturally Responsive Education for Indigenous Communities." In *Indigenous Peoples: Education and Equity,* edited by R. G. Craven, G. Bodkin-Andrews, and J. Mooney, 139–59. Charlotte, N.C.: Information Age.

Ricento, Thomas K., and Nancy H. Hornberger. 1996. "Unpeeling the Onion: Language Planning and Policy and the ELT Professional." *TESOL Quarterly* 30(3):401–27.

Richards, J. 1995. "Constructivism: Pick One of the Above." In *Constructivism in Education,* edited by L. P. Stefe and J. Gale, 57–64. Hillsdale, N.J.: Lawrence Erlbaum Associates.

Richardson, T. A. 2007. "Vine Deloria, Jr. as a Philosopher of Education: An Essay of Remembrance." *Anthropology and Education Quarterly* 38(3):221–30.

Rickard, A. 2005. "Constant Perimeter, Varying Area: A Case Study of Teaching Mathematics to Design a Fish Rack." *Journal of American Indian Education* 44(3):80–100.

Robinson, Shirleene, and Jessica Paten. 2008. "The Question of Genocide and Indigenous Child Removal: The Colonial Australian Context." *Journal of Genocide Research* 10(4):501–18.

Romero-Little, Mary Eunice. 2010. "Best Practices for Native American Language Learners." In *Best Practices in ELL Instruction,* edited by Guofang Li and Patricia A. Edwards, 273–98. New York: Guilford Press.

Rosaldo, Renato. 1989. *Culture and Truth: The Remaking of Social Analysis.* Boston. Beacon Press.

Rose, Mike. (1989) 2005. *Lives on the Boundary.* New York: Penguin.

Rosier, Paul, and Wayne Holm. 1980. *The Rock Point Experience: A Longitudinal Study of a Navajo School Program.* Bilingual Education Series: 8; Saad Naaki Bee Na'nitin. Washington, D.C.: Center for Applied Linguistics.

Rudd, Kevin. 2008 (February 13). *Apology to Australia's Indigenous Peoples, House of Representatives, Parliament House, Canberra.* Accessed August 28, 2009, http://www.pm.gov.au/node/5952.

St. Charles, J., and M. Costantino. 2000. *Reading and the Native American Learner: Research Report.* Olympia, Wash.: Office of the Superintendent of Public Instruction, Office of Indian Education.

Sanchez, T. 2007. "The Depiction of Native Americans in Recent (1991–2004) Secondary American History Textbooks: How Far Have We Come?" *Equity and Excellence in Education* 40:311–20.

Sandoz. Mari. 1961. *These Were the Sioux.* Lincoln: University of Nebraska Press.

Scarcella, Robin. 2003. "Academic English: A Conceptual Framework." University of California Linguistic Minority Research Institute Technical Report 2003–1. Accessed August 17, 2013, http://escholarship.org/uc/item/6pd082d4#page-2.

Schellenberg, E. Glenn. 2004. "Music Lessons Enhance IQ." *Psychological Science* 15(8):511–14.

Schifter, D. 2005. A Constructivist Perspective on Teaching and Learning Mathematics. In *Constructivism: Theory, Perspective and Practice,* 2d ed., edited by C. T. Fosnot, 80–98. New York: Teachers College Press.

Scott, Colin. 1908. *Social Education.* New York: Ginn.

Seixas, P. 1994. "Confronting the Moral Frames of Popular Film: Young People Respond to Historical Revisionism." *American Journal of Education* 102(3):261–85.

Senate Indian Affairs Committee Oversight Hearing on Indian Education. 2010 (June 17). "Did the No Child Left Behind Act leave Indian Students Behind?" Accessed July 9, 2010, http://www.indian.senate.gov/public/_files/BeaulieuTestimony.pdf.

Shirley, J., Jr. 2005 (March 30). "Another Viewpoint: Red Lake Tragedy Points to Loss of Traditional Ways." *Navajo-Hopi Observer* 25(13):5.

Siedentop, Daryl. 2000. *Developing Teaching Skills in Physical Education,* 4th ed. Mountain View, Calif.: Mayfield.

Simard, Jean-Jacques. 1990. "White Ghosts, Red Shadows: The Reduction of North American Indians." In *The Invented Indian: Cultural Fictions and Government Policies,* edited by J. A. Clifton, 333–69. New Brunswick, N.J.: Transaction Publishers.

Simon, Judith, and Linda Tuhiwai Smith, eds. 2001. *A Civilising Mission: Perceptions and Representations of the New Zealand Native Schools System.* Auckland, NZ: Auckland University Press.

Singer, Beverly R. *Wiping the War Paint Off the Lens: Native American Film and Video.* 2001. Minneapolis: University of Minnesota Press.

Skutnabb-Kangas, Tove, and Robert Dunbar. 2010. "Indigenous Children's Education as Linguistic Genocide and a Crime against Humanity? A Global View." *Gáldu Čála: Journal of Indigenous Peoples' Rights* 1(entire issue).

Smith, Donald. 1987. *Sacred Feathers.* Lincoln: University of Nebraska Press.

Smith, Frank. 1987. *Joining the Literacy Club: Further Essays into Education.* Portsmouth, N.H.: Heinemann.

Smithsonian Institution. National Museum of the American Indian. 2014. *Artist Leadership Program.* Accessed February 28, 2014, http://nmai.si.edu/connect/artist-leadership-program/.

Smithsonian Student Art Exhibition. 2009. *Tradition Is My Life, Education Is My Future.* Accessed February 29, 2014, http://www2.ed.gov/news/press releases/2009/07/07172009.html.

Special Subcommittee on Indian Education, Senate Committee on Labor and Public Welfare. 1969. *Indian Education: A National Tragedy, a National Challenge.* Senate Report 91–501 (Kennedy Report).

Stairs, A., Peters, M., and Perkins, E. 1999. "Beyond Language in Indigenous Language Immersion Schooling." *Practicing Anthropology* 20(2): 44–47.

Standing Bear, Luther. 1928. *My People the Sioux,* edited by E. A. Brininstool. Boston: Houghton Mifflin.

———. 1933. *Land of the Spotted Eagle.* Boston: Houghton Mifflin.

Stanton, C. 2012. "Hearing the Story: Critical Indigenous Curriculum Inquiry and Primary Source Representation in Social Studies Education." *Theory and Research in Social Education* 40(4), 339–70.

Sternberg, R., J. Lipka, T. Newman, S. Wildfeure, and E. L. Grigorenko. 2006. "Triarchically-Based Instruction and Assessment of Sixth-grade Mathematics in a Yup'ik Cultural Setting in Alaska." *Gifted and Talented International* 21(2):9–19.

Stiles, D. B. 1997. "Four Successful Indigenous Language Programs." In *Teaching Indigenous Languages,* edited by J. Reyhner, 148–262. Flagstaff: Northern Arizona University. Accessed February 8, 2013, http://jan.ucc.nau.edu/~jar/TIL_21.html,

Stocker, Karen. 2005. *I Won't Stay Indian, I'll Keep Studying.* Boulder: University Press of Colorado.

Street, Brian V. 2008. "New Literacies, New Times: Developments in Literacy Studies." In *Encyclopedia of Language and Education,* Vol. 2: *Literacy,* 2d ed., edited by Brian V. Street and Nancy H. Hornberger, 3–14. New York: Springer.

Sutherland, W. J. 2003. "Parallel Extinction Risk and Global Distribution of Languages and Species." *Nature* 423:276–79

Sweet, R. W., Jr. 2004. "The Big Picture: Where We Are Nationally on the Reading Front and How We Got Here." In *The Voice of Evidence in Reading Research,* edited by P. McCardle and V. Chhabra, 13–44. Baltimore, Md. Paul H. Brookes.

Swisher, Karen, and Donna Deyhle. 1992. "Adapting Instruction to Culture." In *Teaching American Indian Students,* edited by Jon Reyhner, 81–95. Norman: University of Oklahoma Press.

Swisher, Karen, and C. Swisher. 1986. "A Multicultural Physical Education Approach: An Attitude." *Journal of Physical Education, Recreation and Dance* 57(7):35–39.

Szasz, Margaret. 1994. *Between Indian and White Worlds.* Norman, Okla.: University of Oklahoma Press.

Te Kōhanga Reo o Ngaio web site, accessed September 11, 2014, http://www.ngaio kohanga.co.nz/about-us.

Tharp, Roland G. 1982. "The Effective Instruction of Comprehension: Results and Description of the Kamehameha Early Education Program." *Reading Research Quarterly* 17:503–27.

Tharp, Roland G., and Ronald Gallimore. 1988. *Rousing Minds to Life: Teaching, Learning, and Schooling in Social Context.* Cambridge, UK: Cambridge University Press.

Thompson, C. J. 2006. "Preparation, Practice, and Performance: An Empirical Examination of the Impact of Standards Based Instruction on Secondary Students' Math and Science Achievement." *Research in Education* 81(1):53–62.

Thompson, Paul. (1978) 1988. *The Voice of the Past: Oral History.* Oxford, UK: Oxford University Press.

Thompson, William N. 2005. *Native American Issues: A Reference Handbook.* Santa Barbara, Calif.: ABC-CLIO.

Thornton, S. 2004. *Teaching Social Studies that Matters: Curriculum for Active Learning.* New York: Teachers College Press.

———. 2008. "Continuity and Change in Social Studies Curriculum." In *Handbook of Research in Social Studies Education,* edited by L. Levstik and C. Tyson, 15–32. New York: Routledge.

Thornton, S., and K. Barton. 2010. "Can History Stand Alone? Drawbacks and Blind Spots of a 'Disciplinary' Curriculum." *Teachers College Record* 112:2471–95.

Townsend-Gualt, Charlotte. 1999. "Hot Dogs, A Ball Gown, Adobe, and Words." In *Native American Art in the Twentieth Century,* edited by W. Jackson Rushing III. New York: Routledge.

Twain, Mark [Samuel L. Clemens]. (1876) 1958. *The Adventures of Tom Sawyer.* New York: Dodd, Mead.

UNESCO (United Nations Educational, Scientific and Cultural Organization). 1953. *The Use of Vernacular Languages in Education.* Monographs on Fundamental Education VIII. Paris: United Nations Educational, Scientific and Cultural Organization.

United Nations. 1948. Universal Declaration of Human Rights, accessed September 12, 2014, http://www.un.org/en/documents/udhr/.

United Nations, Office of the United Nations High Commissioner for Human Rights. 1992. Declaration on the Rights of Persons Belonging to National or Ethnic, Religious and Linguistic Minorities, accessed September 12, 2014, http://www.ohchr.org/Documents/Publications/GuideMinorities Declarationen.pdf.

United Nations. 2007. Declaration on the Rights of Indigenous Peoples, G.A. Res. 61/295, September 13, accessed January 20, 2009, http://www.un.org/esa /socdev/unpfii/en/declaration.html.

USCCR (United States Commission on Civil Rights). 2003 (July). *A Quiet Crisis: Federal Funding and Unmet Needs in Indian Country.* Washington, D.C.: USCCR. Accessed August 11, 2013, http://www.usccr.gov/pubs/na0703/nao 731.pdf.

United States Department of Education, Office of Inspector General. 2006. *The Reading First Program's Grant Application Process: Final Inspection Report.* Washington, D.C.: USDE.

Valenzuela, A. 1999. *Subtractive Schooling: U.S.–Mexican American Youth and the Border.* Albany: State University of New York Press.

Vercoe, Eruera. 1998. *Educating Jake: Pathways to Empowerment.* Auckland, NZ: Harper Collins.

Vick-Westgate, Anne. 2002. *Nunavik: Inuit-Controlled Education in Arctic Quebec.* Calgary, Alta.: University of Calgary Press.

Vizenor, Gerald. 1990. "Socioacupuncture: Mythic Reversals and the Striptease in Four Scenes." In *Out There: Marginalization and Contemporary Cultures,* edited by Russell Ferguson, et al. New York and Cambridge, Mass: New Museum of Contemporary Art and MIT Press.

Von Glasersfeld, E. 1995. "A Constructivist Approach to Teaching." In *Construc-tivism in Education,* edited by L. P. Stefe and J. Gale, 17–39. Hillsdale, N.J.: Lawrence Erlbaum Associates.

Wade, Edwin L. 1981. "The Ethnic Art Market and the Dilemma of Innovative Indian Artists." In *Magic Images,* edited by Edwin L. Wade and Rennard Strickland, 11–14. Norman: Oklahoma University Press.

Walkingstick, Kay, and Ann Marshall. 2001. *So Fine!: Masterworks of Fine Art from the Heard Museu*m. Phoenix, Ariz: Heard Museum.

Warschauer, Mark. 2001 (October). "Language, Identity, and the Internet." *Mots Pluriels* 19. Accessed August 17, 2013, http://motspluriels.arts.uwa.edu.au /MP1901mw.html.

Watahomigie, Lucille J., and Teresa L. McCarty. 1996. "Literacy for What? Hual-apai Literacy and Language Maintenance." In *Indigenous Literacies in the Americas: Language Planning from the Bottom Up,* edited by Nancy H. Hornberger, 95–113. Berlin, Germany: Mouton de Gruyter.

Webster, J. P., P. Wiles, M. Civil, and S. Clark. 2005. "Finding a Good Fit: Using MCC in a 'Third Space.'" *Journal of American Indian Education* 44(3):9–30.

What Works Clearinghouse. 2007 (August 13). *WWC Topic Report: Beginning Read-ing.* Washington, D.C.: Institute for Education Sciences, U.S. Department of Education. Accessed September 9, 2014, http://ies.ed.gov/ncee/wwc/.

White, Louellyn. 2009. *Free to be Kanien'kehaka: A Case Study of Educational Self-determination at the Akwesasne Freedom School.* Dissertation. University of Arizona. Ann Arbor, Mich.: ProQuest.

Wilder, Laura Ingalls. (1935) 1971. *Little House on the Prairie.* New York: Harper and Row.

Wilkins, L. 2008. "Nine Virtues of the Yakima Nation." *Democracy and Education* 17(2):29–32.

Willeto, Angela A. 1999. "Navajo Culture and Family Influences on Academic Suc-cess: Traditionalism Is Not a Significant Predictor of Achievement among Young Navajos." *Journal of American Indian Education* 38(2):1–21.

Willgoose, Carl E. 1979. *The Curriculum in Physical Education,* 3rd ed. Englewood Cliffs, N.J.: Prentice-Hall.

Wilson, Bruce. 2014a. *Review of Indigenous Education in the Northern Territory: Draft Report.* Accessed March 23, 2014, http://www.education.nt.gov.au/__ data/assets/pdf_file/0016/36205/Indigenous-Education-Review_DRAFT .pdf.

———. 2014b. *A Share in the Future: The Review of Indigenous Education in the Northern Territory.* Report submitted to the Hon. Peter Chandler MLA, Minister of Education, Parliament House, Mitchell Street, Darwin, NT, Australia. Accessed September 12, 2014, http://www.education.nt.gov.au/__ data/assets/pdf_file/0007/37294/A-Share-in-the-Future-The-Review-of -Indigenous-Education-in-the-Northern-Territory.pdf.

Wilson, Ronald, and Mick Dodson. 1997. *Bringing Them Home: National Inquiry into the Separation of Aboriginal and Torres Strait Islander Children from Their Families.* Sydney: Commonwealth of Australia.

Wilson, William H. 1991. "American Indian Bilingual Education: Hawaiian Parallels." *NABE News* 15(3):9–10.

———. 2011. "Insights from Indigenous Language Immersion in Hawai'i. In *Immersion Education: Practices, Policies, Possibilities,* edited by Diane J. Tedick, Donna Christian, and Tara Williams Fortune, 36–57. Bristol, UK: Multilingual Matters.

Wilson, William H., and Kauanoe Kamanā. 2008 (February). "Ke Kula 'O Nawahiokalani'opu'u: An Indigenous Language Revitalization Laboratory School." *ACIE Newsletter* 10(2):entire issue. Retrieved August 17, 2013 from http://www.carla.umn.edu/immersion/acie/vo111/No2/febo8_school profile.html.

Wilson, William H., and Keiki Kawai'ae'a. 2007. "I Kumu; I Lālā: 'Let There Be Sources; Let There Be Branches': Teacher Education in the College of Hawaiian Language." *Journal of American Indian Education* 46(3):37–53.

Winograd, Peter N. 1989. "Introduction: Understanding Reading Instruction." In *Improving Basal Reading Instruction,* edited by Peter N. Winograd, Karen K. Wison, and Marjorie Y. Lipson, 1–20. New York: Teachers College Press.

Wong Fillmore, Lily, and Catherine Snow. 2000 (August 23). "What Teachers Need to Know About Language." Clearinghouse on Languages and Linguistics Special Report. Washington, D.C.: U.S. Department of Education, Office of Educational Research and Improvement.

Wyman, Leisy T., Teresa L. McCarty, and Sheilah E. Nicholas, eds. 2014. *Indigenous Youth and Multilingualism: Language Identity, Ideology, and Practice in Dynamic Cultural Worlds.* New York: Routledge.

Yatvin, L. 2000. "Minority View." In National Reading Panel, *Teaching Children to Read: An Evidence-based Assessment of the Scientific Research Literature on Reading and Its Implications for Reading Instruction, Reports of the Subgroups.* Rockville, Md. National Institute of Child Health and Human Development. Accessed August 31, 2007, http://www.nichd.nih.gov /publications/nrp/report.cfm.

Yazzie, Evangeline Parsons. 1995. *A Study of Reasons for Navajo Language Attrition as Perceived by Navajo Speaking Parents.* Dissertation. Northern Arizona University.

———. 2003. "Missionaries and American Indian Languages." In *Nurturing Native languages,* edited by J. Reyhner, O. Trujillo, R. L. Carrasco, and L. Lockard, 165–78. Flagstaff: Northern Arizona University. Accessed January 20, 2009, http://jan.ucc.nau.edu/~jar/NNL/NNL_14.pdf.

Years: Resources for Teaching about the Impact of the Arrival of Columbus in the Americas. Milwaukee, Wis.: Rethinking Schools.

Zah, Peterson. 1985. "Preface." In *Navajo Nation Educational Policies*. Window Rock, Ariz.: Navajo Division of Education.

Zepeda, Ofelia. 1992. "Foreword." In *Literacy Events in a Community of Young Writers,* edited by Yetta M. Goodman and Sandra Wilde, ix–xi. New York: Teachers College Press.

———. 1995. "The Continuum of Literacy in American Indian Communities." *Bilingual Research Journal* 19(1):5–15.

Zinn, Howard. *The Zinn Education Project,* accessed October 1, 2014, https://zinnedproject.org/.

DISCOGRAPHY

Secola, Keith. "NDN Kars." *Circle*. AKINA Records. ©1992 by Keith Secola.

Trudell, John. "Tribal Voice." *Tribal Voice*. Peace Company. ©1983 by John Trudell.

———. "See the Woman." *Child's Voice: Children of the Earth*. Peace Company. ©1992 by John Trudell.

———. and Bad Dog. *Crazier Than Hell*. Sobeit Recordings/Asitis Productions. ©2010 by John Trudell.

Contributors

Ward Cockrum holds a B.A. in Elementary Education and M.Ed. in Reading Education from the University of Arizona and a Ph.D. in Curriculum and Instruction from Arizona State University. With more than thirty years of involvement in literacy education, Cockrum's teaching experience includes being a reading specialist in a K–4 school, a middle school reading and science teacher, a fifth-grade teacher, and a pre–first- grade teacher. He is a Professor of Education at Northern Arizona University and has coauthored two reading methods textbooks, *Locating and Correcting Reading Difficulties* and the *Ekwall/Shanker Reading Inventory.*

Willard Sakiestewa Gilbert is an enrolled member of the Hopi Tribe, and a Professor of Bilingual/Multicultural Education in the College of Education at Northern Arizona University, where he has served as a faculty member, researcher, and administrator since 1988. He served as the 2007–2008 President of the National Association for Indian Education (NIEA) and vice-president of the National Association for Bilingual Education. Dr. Gilbert is author or coeditor of several books, including *"Honoring Our Children: Culturally Appropriate Approaches for Teaching Indigenous Students,"* and many book chapters.

Chad Hamill (Spokane Tribe) is an Assistant Professor in Applied Indigenous Studies at Northern Arizona University, where he also serves as faculty advisor for Native Americans United and co-chair of the Commission for Native Americans. His book *Songs of Power and Prayer in the Columbia Plateau: The Jesuit, the Medicine Man, and the Indian Hymn Singer* explores song as a vehicle for spiritual power among tribes of the Pacific Northwest. His current book project, "American Indian Jazz: Mildred Bailey and the Undiscovered Origins of America's Art Music," focuses on the untold story of American Indian musicians in the development of jazz.

Michael Holloman (Confederated Tribes of the Colville Indian Reservation) is Associate Professor of Art History at Washington State University, where he is also Coordinator of the American Indian Studies program. He previously served as Director of American Indian programs, exhibitions, and collections at the Northwest Museum of Arts and Culture in Spokane and Associate Professor of Fine Arts at Seattle University.

Loren Hudson (Diné/Navajo) is Todich'iinii (Bitterwater clan) born for Kinyaa'aanii (Towering House clan). Dr. Hudson serves as administrator for the Puente de Hozho Language Institute at Coconino High School in Flagstaff, Arizona, and teaches Diné/Navajo Language and Diné/Navajo History and Government. He works closely with the Northern Arizona community to improve Native American student achievement in the Flagstaff Unified School District.

Florian (Tom) Johnson (Diné/Navajo) was raised on Navajo land in Rock Point, Arizona, and attended a bilingual school, speaking only Navajo—English was learned later. Building on these experiences and some graduate training in Language Literacy and Sociocultural Studies from the University of New Mexico, Johnson became a Navajo educator, working as a teacher, academic counselor, principal, and now as Director of Navajo Studies at Rough Rock Community School, where he focuses on perpetuating the Navajo language and Navajo ways of knowing and doing through schooling.

Christine K. Lemley is Associate Professor in the Bilingual/Multicultural Education Department and affiliated faculty in the Sustainable Communities Program at Northern Arizona University. She taught French and English for four years and served as a Peace Corps volunteer in the Philippines. Her research, teaching, and service focus on social justice issues and preparing education students for twenty-first-century classrooms. Celebrating Indigenous voices and addressing issues of power and privilege, her recent publications include *Redirecting Our Gaze: Seeing Things as They Are* and *Your Stories Will Feed You: An Oral History Unit.*

Teresa L. McCarty is on the faculty of the Graduate School of Education at the University of California, Los Angeles. She has been a faculty member and codirector of the Center for Indian Education at Arizona State University, codirector of the American Indian Language Development Institute at the University of Arizona, and a curriculum developer at the Rough Rock Community School within the Navajo Nation. Her books include *A Place To Be Navajo: Rough Rock and the Struggle for Self-determination in Indigenous Schooling, One Voice, Many Voices: Recreating Indigenous Language Communities* (with Ofelia Zepeda), *"To Remain an Indian": Lessons in Democracy from a Century of Native American Education* (with K. T. Lomawaima), and *Language Planning and Policy in Native America: History, Theory, Praxis.*

Sheilah E. Nicholas (Hopi), an Associate Professor of Language, Reading and Culture at the University of Arizona, teaches classes in language and culture in education, teacher research, and Indigenous oral traditions. Her scholarly work focuses on Indigenous/Hopi language maintenance, revitalization, ideologies, and epistemologies, and on cultural and linguistic issues in American Indian education. Nicholas is coeditor of *Indigenous Youth and Bi/ Multilingualism: Language, Identity, Ideology, and Practice in Dynamic Cultural Worlds.*

Jon Reyhner, Professor of Bilingual Multicultural Education at Northern Arizona University, taught and was an administrator in schools serving American Indians for more than a decade. Reyhner's books include *Language and Literacy Teaching for Indigenous Education: A Bilingual Approach, Indigenous Language Revitalization, Honoring Our Heritage, American Indian Education: A History,* and *Teaching American Indian Students,* and he has written more than fifty book chapters and articles and given over a hundred workshops, presentations, and speeches at regional, national, and international conferences. Reyhner maintains the *American Indian/Indigenous Education* web site at http://nau.edu/aie and *Teaching Indigenous Languages* web site at http:// nau.edu/til.

David Sanders (Oglala Sioux) was born in Pine Ridge, South Dakota. He earned a bachelor's degree in Mathematics and a master's and Ph.D. in Curriculum and Instruction in Mathematics Education from the University of Colorado, and taught mathematics for four years at Chinle High School in Chinle, Arizona. Sanders also served as Director of the University of Colorado Upward Bound Program. He is Research Director at the American Indian College Fund.

Navin Kumar Singh earned his Ph.D. in Curriculum and Instruction from Northern Arizona University. He holds a B.A. in English language and literature and a Master's in Education from Tribhuvan University, Nepal. His research includes globalization, bilingual and multicultural education, higher education, multiethnic diversity, social justice and equity, human rights, indigenous peoples and communities, and contemporary educational issues. Singh is the author of *Multilingual Trends in a Globalized World: Prospects and Challenges.*

Jeremy D. Stoddard is the Spears Distinguished Associate Professor of Education at The College of William and Mary and an affiliated faculty member in the Film and Media Studies Program. His research focuses on authentic pedagogy and curriculum in social studies, the role of media in democratic education, and how teachers and young people engage with media in learning and teaching history and politics. Stoddard is coauthor of *Teaching History with Film: Strategies for Secondary Social Studies* and *Teaching History with Museums: Strategies for K–12 Social Studies.*

Index